Heroin

DRUGS AND ALCOHOL — *Contested Histories*

Heroin

The Treatment of Addiction in Twentieth-century Britain

Alex Mold

NORTHERN ILLINOIS UNIVERSITY PRESS DEKALB

© 2008 by Northern Illinois University Press

Published by the Northern Illinois University Press, DeKalb, Illinois 60115

Manufactured in the United States using acid-free paper

All Rights Reserved

Design by Julia Fauci

Library of Congress Cataloging-in-Publication Data

Mold, Alex.

Heroin : the treatment of addiction in twentieth-century Britain / Alex Mold.

   p. cm. (Drugs and alcohol)

Includes bibliographical references and index.

ISBN 978-0-87580-386-9 (clothbound : alk. paper)

1. Heroin abuse—Great Britain—20th century. 2. Heroin abuse—Great Britain—
Prevention. 3. Heroin abuse—Treatment—Great Britain. 4. Drug control—
Great Britain. I. Title.

HV5840.G7M66 2008

616.89'060941--dc22

2007045010

FOR MY FAMILY

Contents

Acknowledgments

In the years I have spent working on this book, I have accumulated many debts that I can never repay. First amongst my creditors is Matthew Hilton, who supervised the PhD thesis on which this book is based. His support, guidance and encouragement went far beyond what one could reasonably expect of a doctoral supervisor. Through our discussions he has become both a source of intellectual inspiration and a good friend. Thanks must also go to Pat Thane from the Centre for Contemporary British History at the Institute of Historical Research (University of London) and Katherine Watson from the University of Birmingham, who examined my thesis and made many helpful suggestions for improvements. I am also grateful for the counsel and friendship of other colleagues from the University of Birmingham (where this project began) including Jonathan Reinarz, Leonard Schwartz, Francesca Carnevali, Elaine Fulton, Antje Pieper and James McKay. Since moving to the London School of Hygiene and Tropical Medicine (LSHTM) in 2004, my list of creditors has grown yet longer. It has been a privilege to work with Virginia Berridge, whose knowledge of the field is unsurpassed. Her advice has been invaluable, as has her patience, allowing me the time to develop my dissertation into this book. Other members of the Centre for History in Public Health at the LSHTM, especially Susanne MacGregor, Martin Gorsky, Ornella Moscucci, Stuart Anderson, Sue Taylor, Rachel Herring, Virginia Smith and Ingrid James have also provided essential academic and practical support.

The research for this book was carried out at a number of archives and libraries. I am much obliged to the staff of The National Archives, Kew; the Contemporary Medical Archives Centre at the Wellcome Library; the Modern Records Centre at the University of Warwick; the London Metropolitan Archives; the Wellcome Library for the History and Understanding of Medicine, the Radcliffe Science Library, Oxford and the libraries of the University of Birmingham, the University of Warwick and the London School of Hygiene and Tropical Medicine. Working on a topic of contemporary history has also allowed me to speak with many of the individuals involved, and I appreciate their time and the insight that this has provided. I am particularly grateful to Ann Dally, who allowed me access to her private papers (held by the Contemporary Medical Archives Centre) before they were catalogued. She was a significant presence in the field of heroin addiction treatment, and her work figures largely in this book. It is, therefore, with sadness that I note her recent death, in March 2007.

Turning a doctoral thesis into a book is not always an easy process, but it has been greatly facilitated by comments from two anonymous reviewers on the draft manuscript, the editorial board of the 'Drugs and Alcohol: Contested Histories' series and staff at Northern Illinois University Press, especially Melody Herr. Some sections of material in this book have been published elsewhere in academic journal articles. Chapter Two is based on "The 'British System' of Heroin Addiction Treatment and the Opening of Drug Dependence Units", *Social History of Medicine* 17:1 (2006): 501–17, used here courtesy of Oxford University Press; Chapter Five draws on "'Grave Cause for Concern?' Private Practice, Professional Disputes and the Treatment of Heroin Addiction in Britain during the 1980s", *Contemporary British History,* work to be published by Taylor and Francis; and the Introduction contains excerpts from the review essay "'Consuming Habits': Histories of Drugs in Modern Societies", *Cultural and Social History* 4:2 (2007): 261–70 (copyright Social History Society). These are reproduced with permission, and I am grateful to the anonymous reviewers and editorial staff of these journals for their input. Thanks must also go to conference and seminar audiences who helped me develop this work at the University of Lancaster, the University of Birmingham, the London School of Hygiene and Tropical Medicine and the European Association for the History of Medicine and Health conference in Paris, 2005.

Unusually, perhaps, most of my debts are figurative and not financial. For that, I must thank the Arts and Humanities Research Board (as it then was) who provided a PhD studentship from 2000 to 2003, the Departments of Medieval and Modern History at the University of Birmingham for a teaching fellowship during 2003/4 and employment as a Research Fellow in the Centre for History in Public Health at the LSHTM on an Economic and Social Research Council funded project from 2004 to 2007.

Last, but by no means least, I must thank my family, friends and partner. I could never have started this project, much less finished it, without the love and support of my parents, Richard and Lindsay Mold, my sister, Becky Mold, and my two grandmothers, Elsie Mold and Doreen Tanswell. That my grandfather, Peter Mold, did not live to see the fruits of my apparently endless time as a student will always be a source of sorrow, but I know he would be as proud of me as I was of him. Perhaps the largest debt of all is owed to my partner, Noelle Plack. She has read drafts, listened to papers, participated in lengthy discussions and has come to know far more about the history of heroin addiction treatment in Britain than she could ever have wanted to know. She has helped me climb at times what seemed an unassailable mountain: I hope that we are long able to enjoy the view together.

Heroin

Introduction

In February 1923, Dr E.W. Adams produced a memorandum on the subject of drug addiction for his employers at the Ministry of Health. Adams stated that 'the mere satisfaction of the craving of the drug addict, whether this is attained by the provision of the drugs by the addict himself or through an intermediary, comes under the head of illicit dealing'. But, 'On the other hand, drug addiction can only be regarded as a disease—as a pathological state calling urgently for treatment and relief'. Adams concluded that 'The whole problem of the drug addict needs careful consideration'.[1] This book is concerned with the 'careful consideration' of heroin addiction that followed Adams's memorandum throughout the twentieth century and into the twenty-first. During this period, the essential dilemma posed by Adams about how to deal with addiction persisted. Was drug addiction a disease that required treatment or a 'vicious indulgence' that demanded strict control?

Experts of all kinds were (and still are) divided about what drug addiction was, what it meant to be addicted, what caused this condition and, therefore, how to deal with it. Competing understandings of addiction developed and led to competing responses. In the 1910s and 1920s the idea that drug addiction was a 'vice' and strongly connected to criminal behaviour helped facilitate the creation of a criminal or penal response to drug use. Laws to control the distribution, sale and possession of 'dangerous drugs', including heroin, morphine and cocaine, were introduced during and just after the First World War, partly in tandem with international controls and also as a reaction to a 'moral panic' about drug use. But, at around the same time, a disease-based notion of addiction gained official support. In 1926, the Departmental Committee on Morphine and Heroin

Addiction (known after its chairman as the Rolleston Committee) accepted the view that drug addiction was a disease that required treatment, not a criminal act that required punishment. A medical response to addiction therefore existed alongside legal controls. But by the 1960s, yet another view of addiction began to gain ground: that of heroin addiction as a social problem. This resulted in a dual approach, one that saw medical, treatment-oriented measures combining with aspects of social control. Moreover, these different responses—penal, medical and social—were themselves rarely homogeneous. For instance, there was no one 'medical' response to heroin addiction. This can instead be separated into at least three categories: the psychiatric view, the public health response and that offered by community-based practice. Even within these categories there were differences; some psychiatrists, for example, disagreed with each other about the treatment of addiction.

This book attempts to make sense of these varying responses and will show how the relationship between different understandings of addiction created a dynamic situation that impacted the treatment of heroin addiction in a multitude of ways. The British approach to dealing with heroin addiction during the twentieth century, although bound by legal controls, was largely directed by the medical profession and took the form of varying kinds of treatment. However, under the rubric of 'treatment,' other non-medical goals were often pursued. Treating heroin addiction also became a way of controlling it. Clearly the different approaches to heroin addiction could combine and work together as well as in opposition. But at the same time, differing goals could lead to conflict and uncertainty. The treatment of heroin addiction became a strongly politicised field. Key disputes revolved around what methods should be used in the treatment of addiction and what kind of expertise was required to administer this. These disputes did much to shape the response to heroin addiction over the last eighty years, but other factors were important too. Also significant were who was using heroin and why. Middle-aged, middle-class addicts who had become addicted as a result of medical treatment during the 1920s were dealt with differently than the young, recreational heroin addicts of the 1960s and 1970s. This parallels the findings of other historians in other places and at other times: as American historian David Courtwright put it, 'what we think about addiction very much depends on who is addicted'.[2] But broader factors were also relevant. Changing conceptions of disease, deviance and the nature of social problems also affected the treatment response. This book will, therefore, place the treatment of heroin addiction within its wider socio-political context: heroin was not an isolated problem but was influenced by developments in other areas.

Despite this, heroin seemed to loom large in the popular consciousness. Heroin was often thought of as the 'hardest' drug, as the most dangerous of the illegal psychoactive substances: 'It's so good, don't even try it once'.[3] Heroin, though it was never the most widely used illicit drug in

Britain (since the 1950s that place has overwhelmingly been held by cannabis), is the one that has caused the most consternation. This might be explained, in part, by the mode of drug delivery. Intravenous injection provokes a certain kind of horror and brings with it a series of complications such as blood-borne infections and collapsed veins. A further explanation lies also in the apparent 'addictiveness' of heroin. Other drugs, such as cannabis, cocaine, LSD and amphetamines have often been regarded as being merely 'habit forming' or 'dependence producing' rather than addictive.[4] This is partly because long-term heroin users exhibit two signs that have been integral to the notion of addiction: tolerance (increasing doses of the drug are required to achieve the same effect) and withdrawal (symptoms are displayed when the drug is removed). These are not found, or found to a lesser extent, with other drugs. Yet these characteristics are just some of many attributed to addiction over the centuries. To better understand the implications of defining a substance as addictive, it is necessary to appreciate where this concept comes from and how this meaning has changed over time.

LOCATING ADDICTION

Psychoactive substances have been used throughout human history and across the entire planet.[5] Opium was known in ancient Greece, Rome and Arabia. Viticulture, the cultivation of grapes for wine, probably began in the Black Sea region between 6000 and 4000BC.[6] For as long as these substances have been taken, individuals have pointed to problems associated with their use. There are numerous comments on the effects of alcohol in the Bible. Isaiah states that 'the priest and the prophet have erred through strong drink, they are swallowed up of wine' (Isaiah 28:7). Classic Chinese poets also spoke of the dangers of alcohol. Tu Fu, in the eighth century of the Common Era wrote 'I give way to drink; I have long ceased to care that all men ignore me'.[7] There is, however, some debate as to when the concept of addiction was first applied to the persistent problematic use of substances like alcohol and opium. For historian Jessica Warner 'the modern conception of alcohol addiction' began in the seventeenth century. Contemporaries were aware that the regular consumption of alcoholic beverages could result in habitual drunkenness, a state, Warner argues, that Stuart clergymen often described in terms of addiction. She found that early modern preachers referred to parishioners 'addicted to drunkennese' whose drinking had turned from 'delight into necessitie'.[8] A disease concept of alcoholism, according to Roy Porter, first originated in the writings of eighteenth-century commentators such as Bernard Mandeville and George Cheyne.[9] But it was the work of Benjamin Rush in America and Thomas Trotter in England at the very end of the eighteenth century that helped solidify a disease-based notion of addiction.[10] Harry Gene

Levine has, therefore, located the 'discovery' of addiction in America in the late 1700s. He asserted that doctors associated with the temperance movement created the addiction paradigm in order to explain the overwhelming desire for drink among their patients. Crucially, these doctors thought that addiction was a disease derived from the consumption of alcoholic drinks, that alcohol itself was inherently addictive. After the prohibition era, however, Levine notes a change in the addiction paradigm. He argues that the disease of addiction was no longer located in alcohol but in the alcoholic.[11]

Disease was also an essential element in the emergence of the concept of addiction in Britain. Most historians date the 'birth' of addiction, and its application to opiate drugs, to the nineteenth century. A number of reasons have been put forward for this. Firstly, new, more potent drugs were developed. The isolation of the alkaloid morphine from opium first took place in the early 1800s; commercial production began in the 1820s.[12] Diacetylmorphine, which was twice as potent gram for gram as morphine, was developed in London in 1874. In 1898 German pharmaceutical firm Bayer began commercial production of diacetylmorphine, marketed as 'Heroin' from the word 'herosich' or 'heroic'.[13] Secondly, a more effective way of delivering these drugs became available. The hypodermic syringe, invented by Alexander Wood in 1856, allowed for the injection of large quantities of opiate drugs, resulting in the intensification of the physiological complaints associated with opiate use.[14] Hypodermic use also involved doctors in addiction to a greater extent than previously, and once doctors intervened, as Virginia Berridge points out, 'medical involvement itself helped to define the problem and its contribution to disease views'.[15] This brings us to the third factor in the development of addiction in the nineteenth century: the role played by professional groups. As will be discussed in greater detail below, doctors took hold of the disease concept of addiction as they encountered more opiate use among their patients. Addiction became a way of explaining continued drug use and also a way of removing the blame from doctors for causing this disease as a result of their incautious administration of opiate drugs.[16] Finally, the development of the concept of addiction could also be connected to the emergence of the temperance movement. The idea that drinking resulted in a loss of control over behaviour, that drinking became compulsive and that the only way to avoid this was to abstain from alcohol all together became strongly tied to temperance ideology. Addiction was regarded as a 'disease of the will'.[17]

This conception of addiction points to a combination of medical and moral influences within the disease paradigm. Indeed, deciphering precisely what various commentators meant by 'addiction' or 'alcoholism' is complex. William L. White has shown that numerous terms were used to describe the excessive and problematic use of alcohol and other drugs in the United States during the nineteenth century. Words such as 'ine-briety', 'dipsomania' and 'narcomania' were used as well as 'alcoholism' and 'addiction'.[18] Even when addiction was used, the meaning of this term was unstable. Moral and medical elements were both frequently present, bound together through the notion of disease. Geoffrey Harding argues that addiction was initially constructed as a moral failing by or-ganisations such as the Society for the Suppression of the Opium Trade (SSOT). However, morality was connected to disease through the idea that the addict suffered from a 'pathologically impaired moral faculty'—that the use of opium resulted in physical damage to the will. Yet the SSOT were not the only body to describe compulsive opium use in terms of pathology and morality; this view also gained credence within the medical profession during the nineteenth century. Doctors too began to refer to addiction as a 'moral pathological phenomenon', such that 'by the late nineteenth century the effects of opium could be commonly un-derstood, either directly or by implication, in terms of a pathologically debilitated moral faculty'.[19] This combination of medical and moral ap-proaches to addiction expressed through 'disease' has been emphasised by other commentators on the period. Terry Parssinen and Karen Kerner maintain that there was a broad consensus on the disease theory of ad-diction during the nineteenth century, encompassing a range of voices and authorities. Some referred to addiction as a 'moral insanity', others to a 'disease of the will', yet, 'these definitions did not reflect fundamen-tal disagreements . . . but rather differing emphases on parts of the same problem'.[20] Berridge reaches a similar conclusion. She asserts that 'med-ical as well as moral perceptions defined disease theory', that 'addiction was disease and vice'.[21]

Despite disparities dating the emergence of the term 'addiction,' most accounts hint at a surprising degree of continuity surrounding the conceptualisation of addiction as a medico-moral disease. The work of Michel Foucault has done much to illuminate the relationship between these two seemingly different authorities. His histories of sexuality and of madness indicate that during the nineteenth century an inseparable bond was formed between morality and medicine.[22] As the extensive lit-erature on the history of sexuality has indicated, the medical profession was central to Victorian attacks on 'deviant' sexual practices.[23] Health and moral purity became entwined in campaigns against the sexual be-haviour of subjects created by a medico-moral discourse. There are obvi-ous parallels here between the history of sexuality and the history of drugs. As Janet Farrell Brodie and Marc Redfield argue 'Like the homo-sexual . . . the addict emerged with development, a little more than a century ago, of a medico-legal discourse capable of preconceiving hu-man identity in the language of pathology'.[24] The 'moral-pathological' view of 'addiction' was thus part of a wider trend in which the medical and moral were often inseparable.

However, as Mariana Valverde has demonstrated in her work on alcohol in the late-nineteenth and early-twentieth centuries, tensions did exist between medical and moral approaches to addiction. Valverde argues that the medicalisation of addiction was damaged by its conception as a disease of the will, that the discourse of medical experts on alcoholism was constantly being undermined by references to vice and habit.[25] As a result, the medical profession could not agree on a universally accepted definition of alcoholism or approved treatment method. This confusion about the nature of addiction and its proper treatment continued well into the mid-twentieth century. Like Valverde, sociologist Carol Smart has criticised the medicalisation thesis as a way to explain ideas about addiction.[26] She argues that scientific, legal and moral discourses have intermingled in responses to addiction since the nineteenth century, that no one force was solely responsible for the making of drug policy. It would be wrong, she states, to see attempts to regulate drug use in the early twentieth century as the outcome of conflict between, on the one hand, doctors who saw addiction as a disease and, therefore, a medical problem and, on the other, the Home Office which saw it as a moral issue and, therefore, a social problem. She asserts that the medical understanding of addiction was imbued with a sense of morality and that doctors did not work in opposition to the Home Office but in conjunction with it.[27]

Conflicting views on addiction were still present by the 1920s, but the famous conclusion of the Rolleston Committee that addiction 'must be regarded as a manifestation of disease and not as a mere form of vicious indulgence' added official weight to the disease concept.[28] The coexistence of the disease-based notion of addiction with a system of legal regulation and control will be discussed in greater detail in Chapter One, but it is important to note that even as the disease-based notion of addiction received official recognition, it was not the only view of this condition. A further element was added to understandings of addiction during the mid-1960s. In 1965 the second Interdepartmental Committee on Heroin Addiction (the Brain Committee) defined addiction as a 'socially infectious condition', a development that had a number of practical implications, which will be explored in Chapter Two.[29] Addiction began to be seen as a threat to public health and society, but at the same time, the Brain Committee was also convinced that addiction was 'an expression of mental disorder rather than a form of criminal behaviour'.[30] During the 1970s, this psychiatric view of addiction as a mental illness began to gain ground. The 'psychiatrisation' of addiction (the focus of Chapter Three) was in some ways represented by the introduction of a new word to describe this state: 'dependence'. Dependence was thought to more accurately convey the psychological rather than physical aspects of continued drug use.[31] As will be seen in later chapters, by the 1980s and 1990s, the concepts of addiction or dependence were joined by other ideas about drug use. Emphasis was placed on the 'problem drug taker' and 'drug related harm', especially following the emergence of HIV/AIDS. However, the notion of addiction was still important within both of these categories: dependence was consistently identified as a 'problem' arising from drug use, one that could cause considerable 'harm' to the user and to society. Indeed even in contemporary definitions of addiction, moral elements appear to remain. In the American Psychiatric Association's (APA) *Diagnostic and Statistical Manual* (fourth edition) and the World Health Organisation's (WHO) *International Classification of Diseases* (tenth edition) traces of moral judgments about drug addiction can be found. Both texts refer to the 'abuse' of psychoactive substances as a symptom of 'dependence', powerfully suggesting that there is a 'right' and 'wrong' way to use drugs.[32]

THE 'BRITISH SYSTEM' OF HEROIN ADDICTION TREATMENT

The current widespread use of the APA and WHO definitions of drug dependence represent the internationalisation of the concept of addiction, a development partly facilitated by the introduction of international laws and codes over the course of the twentieth century to govern the trade in narcotic drugs.[33] Yet despite these systems of international control, domestic drug policies differed sharply. There is much that is peculiar, and significant, about the British case. The British approach to the treatment of heroin addiction, known as the 'British System', has been seen as particularly important by international observers, especially those from the USA. Indeed, the views of these commentators helped create what has been described as the 'myth' of the British System. The British System is usually understood to have been based on the idea that addiction was a disease to be treated, not a crime to be punished, and that treatment could involve long-term prescription of an opiate drug to the addict, a practice known as maintenance. This British System was based on the findings of the Rolleston Committee, and it is thought that the term British System might have been coined by one of the secretaries to the Rolleston Committee in the 1920s.[34] What is significant, however, is that it was an American sociologist, Alfred Lindesmith, who first highlighted this term in the late 1950s.[35] Lindesmith was one of a number of American commentators such as Edwin Schur, Horace Freeland Judson and, later on, Arnold Trebach, who contrasted the British System favourably with the response to heroin addiction in the USA.[36] They believed that the British System of prescribing opiate drugs to heroin addicts was a liberal alternative to what they saw as the 'prohibitionist' stance of American drug policy in the 1960s and 1970s. In the US, the Harrison Narcotics Act of 1914 had effectively outlawed long-term prescription.[37] The British System was put forward as evidence pointing to the need for a change in American drug policy in general and in support of maintenance in particular.[38] This political context undoubtedly helped create the image of the British System.

Yet, for many observers of heroin addiction treatment in Britain, such as the addiction specialist John Strang and the psychologist Michael Gossop, the British System was largely a 'mythical creature'.[39] Other individuals involved with the British System, such as Professor Griffith Edwards, former Director of the Addiction Research Unit, and H.B. 'Bing' Spear, former Chief Inspector of the Home Office Drugs Branch, deny that the British System ever existed, or at least not in the way many commentators have portrayed it. Both argue that concentration on Rolleston's justification for the prescription of drugs to addicts has obscured the strong elements of control within the British System.[40] Indeed, other protagonists, including Strang, have argued that the British System was based on a medical approach within a penal framework.[41]

The 'myth' of the British System has also been partially demolished by historians and other policy analysts. Berridge argues that there were actually three 'British Systems': a lay/commercial system of control that operated until the mid-nineteenth century; a system of pharmaceutical control that began with the Pharmacy Act in 1868; and the medico-penal system that was legitimated by Rolleston.[42] Other commentators have questioned how far the British System was a system at all. The criminologist Trevor Bennett argues that 'the word "system" is perhaps too strong, as it connotes organisation, planning, and directives. In contrast, British drugs policy has actually evolved out of practice rather than planning'.[43] This view was supported by David Downes, who famously branded the British System as one of 'masterly inactivity in the face of a non-existent problem'.[44] Most commentators now accept that it was the nature of the drug problem in this period—its small scale and the fact that most addicts were middle-aged, middle-class and had begun taking drugs as part of treatment for another condition—that accounted for the British System and not the other way round. As Berridge notes 'Rolleston was the *result* rather than the *cause* of the low number of addicts in Britain and their middle-class profile'.[45]

Despite this critical onslaught, the 'myth' of the British System persists. The British System is consistently referred to by almost every recent book on drug policy in Britain and in many other countries too, if only to reject the idea that such a thing was ever present.[46] This is partly because the British System retains its symbolic importance for those who seek to change the drug laws and end the 'war on drugs'. The example of the British System is consistently employed to support the arguments of groups and individuals who seek to reform international drug legislation and domestic drug policy. For example, the British voluntary agency Transform, in their 2006 report *After the War on Drugs: Options for Control*, assert that 'Evidence [for heroin prescription to addicts] also comes from the UK which pioneered heroin prescription in the 1920s'.[47] The Rolleston report and the British System have often been mentioned in interviews with contemporary drug user activists as important examples of a legitimate approach to drug control and by others who seek to legalise drugs.[48] The British System may be largely misunderstood and misrepresented, but it refuses to go away.

Unpacking the myth of the British System is also important because it has done much to shape accounts of heroin addiction treatment during the twentieth century. This book is the first to expose the treatment of heroin addiction in Britain following the Rolleston report through detailed historical analysis. While there is relatively little historical work on drug policy between 1960 and the present, there are a plethora of other texts published during the period in question—and from a range of different perspectives—that deal with this subject. The boundary between primary and secondary sources, between active participant and historical commentator, is often indistinct. A key example of this is Bing Spear's book *Heroin Addiction Care and Control*. Spear was the Chief Inspector of the Home Office Drugs Branch from 1977 until his retirement in 1986. His book presents an invaluable insider's account of heroin addiction treatment in the period under consideration based primarily, but not exclusively, on his own observations and experiences as an actor in the shaping of policy. This is the book's great asset but also its great flaw: it is not a balanced work of history but a personal account, and Spear's own view (which is nonetheless important) dominates throughout. By drawing on a range of sources—including archival collections of government records and private papers, articles, letters and comment pieces in medical journals and newspapers, Parliamentary debates, committee reports and published and unpublished oral history sources—this book will expose the political debates and conflicts that ran through the treatment of heroin addiction in the twentieth century but will also set these in their wider historical context.

BOOK OVERVIEW

This book begins by further debunking the myth of the British System by demonstrating that the earliest legislative and regulatory approaches to heroin were about the treatment of addiction *and* its control. Chapter One demonstrates that control elements (interpreted as a penal or criminal response) existed alongside, and interacted with, medical, treatment-oriented approaches. This chapter examines the establishment of the first legal controls on narcotic drugs as well as attempts by the Rolleston Committee in 1926 and the Brain Committee in 1961 to produce a definitive statement on the treatment of addiction. Not only does this 'set the scene' for the developments discussed in the rest of the book, but such a discussion also points to the existence of a fundamental uncertainty about what addiction was and how best to deal with it. This uncertainty about addiction also occurs in Chapter Two, which examines the redefinition of addiction as a socially infectious condition by the second incarnation of the Brain Committee in 1965. I argue that this understanding of addiction resulted in an approach that combined medical treatment with social control. This response was articulated through the establishment of specialised Drug Dependence Units (DDUs). The DDUs were also important because they became a site around which the development of the treatment of addiction as a psychiatric specialty could coalesce. Chapter Three examines the creation of expertise and expert bodies around heroin addiction in the 1960s and 1970s, both in the form of clinical practice and in the form of academic research. Yet during the 1970s the actual treatment offered by the DDUs also began to change. There was a move away from the prescription of heroin to addicts on a maintenance basis and towards the prescription of orally administered methadone on a short-term or withdrawal basis.

This shift in treatment policy coincided with a significant growth in heroin use. The number of known heroin addicts rose from just over 2,000 in 1977 to more than 10,000 by 1987.[49] Chapter Four explores the consequences of this expansion for the treatment of addiction. In the 1980s heroin became a political and media 'issue' in a way that it had not been previously. This helped expand what Berridge has called the 'policy community' around drugs, as new groups and individuals became involved in dealing with the drug problem.[50] At the same time, general practitioners (GPs), who had largely been excluded from the treatment of addiction after the second Brain report, began to become more involved. This chapter will examine the reasons behind the re-intervention of the generalist and will show how this caused considerable tension within the treatment of addiction. This tension spilled over into a public dispute between doctors treating addicts in the DDUs and those treating addicts in the community. Chapter Five shows how this clash underpinned a further debate about the treatment of addiction in private practice. Critics of private addiction treatment saw this as little short of legalised drug dealing, but private practitioners argued that they provided a valuable service to addicts in place of the failing DDUs. In this chapter the example of one private practitioner, Dr Ann Dally, will be explored in detail. Dally faced disciplinary action by the General Medical Council (GMC) in 1983, but this case was as much about defending a threat to the expert status of the DDU psychiatrist as it was about the actions of one doctor.

However, the challenge that doctors like Dally posed was also about the methods they used to treat addicts and the way they viewed addiction. Chapter Six analyses a further debate between those who supported maintenance and those who advocated short-term, abstinence orientated withdrawal. Some argue that this dispute was driven by a difference of opinion over the very nature of addiction and disease. This conflict was fought out once more in a GMC hearing, as Dally faced a second case in 1986/7. Despite the power and position of those who advocated withdrawal (the DDU psychiatrists), maintenance could not entirely be discredited as a legitimate form of treatment for addiction. Indeed, the role of long-term prescription in the treatment of addiction was reappraised in the latter half of the 1980s in the wake of HIV/AIDS. Chapter Seven examines the impact of HIV/AIDS on heroin addiction treatment. AIDS was considered to represent a greater threat to public health than drug use, and as a result, attention focused on reducing the harm associated with heroin use. This 'harm reduction' approach did lead to some new developments, such as needle exchanges, but treatment services changed rather less. Maintenance prescription remained contentious, suggesting that the fundamental debates about the treatment of addiction persisted. In fact, these tensions are still present. In the final chapter, recent developments in the treatment of addiction are considered. A key change has been the focus on a supposed link between drug use and crime. This could be interpreted as indicative of the 'criminalising' of drug policy, but medical treatment retains a key role. Treatment and criminal justice have actually become more closely entwined, as the reduction of crime is now recognised as a key outcome of drug addiction treatment. Within this, the role of maintenance has once more been reassessed. Methadone maintenance is thought to reduce crime, but this form of treatment still provokes controversy and heated debate. The recent return to criminal justice and the continued disagreement over maintenance might suggest that little has changed within the treatment of addiction over last eighty years. This book is, therefore, about continuities as well as changes. A deep-seated uncertainty about addiction can be detected throughout this period, and this has ensured that the treatment of addiction remains a contentious, but fascinating, topic.

CHAPTER ONE

Treatment and Control

The 'British System', 1916–1961

O n 10 February 1916, Horace Dennis Kingsley and Rose Edwards were each sentenced to six months imprisonment with hard labour for selling cocaine to Canadian soldiers on leave in the port of Folkestone.[1] The fact that Kingsley, a petty thief, and Edwards, a prostitute, had actually acquired their supply of the drug legitimately, from a chemist's, caused much consternation. Indeed, the illegality of their actions was questionable: both were convicted on charges of 'selling a powder to members of His Majesty's Forces, with intent to make them less capable of performing their duties', and no specific law against the sale of cocaine, or other drugs later to be defined as 'dangerous', existed.[2] This situation was quickly altered. In July 1916 the Defence of the Realm Act, which had restricted the sale of alcoholic beverages since 1915, was extended to cover cocaine and opium. It became an offence for anyone other than a licensed medical practitioner or pharmacist to buy, sell or be in possession of such drugs without a prescription.[3] This was Britain's first domestic attempt to control the use of specific drugs.

Yet the law was not the only interested authority involved in the drug issue. A rather different fate from that of Kingsley and Edwards befell Thomas Henderson. Henderson was a fifty-eight-year-old miniature painter and self-confessed 'morphia addict'. In a statement to the Home Office, written in 1922, Henderson asserted that he had begun taking morphine to alleviate the pain of neuralgia and gastritis, but 'As the gastritis was indeed chronic, I had to resort to it many times.' This repeated use of morphine was, he argued, 'never as a vice, but only always as a painkiller and medical aid'. Henderson concluded that 'Morphia has not corrupted me Sir, it has never tempted me to do wrong in any respect . . . I only ask to be left in the hands of my doctor.'[4] Henderson's request was granted. In 1926, the Rolleston Committee, a group of medical men appointed by the Ministry of Health to investigate morphine and heroin use, acknowledged that addiction was to be regarded as 'a manifestation of disease and not as a mere form of vicious indulgence'.[5] Drug addiction was thus confirmed as a medical matter.

These two stories would seem to encapsulate two very different approaches to drug use. The Kingsley and Edwards case exemplified a penal or legal model within which drugs, and those who used them, were controlled and punished by the state. The Henderson case was indicative of a medical model in which drug users were regarded as sick individuals who required treatment by doctors. Yet both systems existed alongside one another: the medical did not replace the penal or vice versa. The origins of these different systems will be discussed in this chapter and this will expose a number of themes that run through more recent attempts to deal with drugs. A key issue was not so much the nature of the drug itself but of who was using it and why. The contrasting experiences of Kingsley, Edwards and Henderson demonstrated that separate systems emerged to cope with the working-class dealers of drugs and their middle-class users. At the same time, the broader historical context in which drugs were being taken was clearly crucial. Concern about cocaine use among troops during the Great War rapidly escalated into a full-scale 'drug panic'. This panic was fuelled, as Marek Kohn has demonstrated, as much by fear of the immigrant 'other' and the sexual danger he posed to white women as by the real threat that cocaine posed to society.[6]

Domestic legislation to control drugs was introduced in this climate of panic, but international controls on drugs had been in place for a number of years. International regulations helped model domestic drug policy, as Britain signed agreements first under the League of Nations and later the United Nations to control the supply of 'narcotic' drugs such as opium, heroin and cocaine.[7] International commitments, however, did not mean that all countries had identical domestic drug agendas. Indeed, this period saw the emergence of the so-called British System of heroin addiction treatment. Under the British System an opiate addict could be prescribed opiate drugs on a long-term, or maintenance, basis if he or she could not stop taking these. This policy differed sharply from that of many other countries, most notably the USA, where maintenance had been effectively outlawed under the Harrison Narcotic Act of 1914.[8]

Yet the British System was never quite what it appeared to be. Firstly, an extensive debate existed over the treatment of addiction, and while maintenance was accepted as a legitimate treatment method, there was also strong support for the idea that addicts should be forced off drugs as quickly as possible. This debate about treatment methods between those who supported long-term prescription or maintenance and those who advocated short-term withdrawal has characterised the treatment of addiction in Britain ever since. Secondly, the British System was never just about treatment but also about the control of addiction, addicts and the drugs they used. The British System actually brought medical and penal approaches together, despite this system's largely medical appearance. How this system came into being and why it acquired the reputation it did is one consideration of this chapter. This not only 'sets the scene' for the analysis of heroin addiction treatment policy since the 1960s (which is considered in the main body of this book) but also demonstrates the extent to which fundamental uncertainty about the nature of addiction shaped more recent attempts to treat this condition.

DRUG CONTROL IN LATE NINETEENTH- AND EARLY TWENTIETH-CENTURY BRITAIN

The earliest measures to control drugs in Britain were shaped by both domestic and international agendas. As discussed in the Introduction, drug use, and the use of opiate drugs in particular, only began to appear to be problematic during the mid to late nineteenth century. Prior to this, opium was widely used at all levels of Victorian society.[9] The boundaries between medical and non-medical, or recreational, use were often ill-defined, yet the belief that the working classes were taking opium for its 'stimulant' properties in a 'non-medical' context resulted in the construction of the 'opium problem'.[10] Opium use among the working class was thought to be damaging to morality and detrimental to production, echoing elements of the temperance movement's attack on alcohol. This combination of public health concerns and fears about working-class 'stimulant' use prompted the inclusion of opium on the list of poisons regulated by the 1868 Pharmacy Act.[11] But as Berridge points out, upper-class social controllers largely misunderstood or misinterpreted working-class use of opium, and therefore a distinction was made between 'use' (medical) and 'abuse' (non-medical) that persisted into the twentieth century and beyond.

A separation between medical and non-medical use of drugs was also crucial to the emergence of international systems to control what became known as 'narcotic' drugs. According to Berridge and Bewley-Taylor, American concern about the use of opiates in the Far East prompted a series of international meetings that began in Shanghai in 1909 and ended at The Hague in 1914. These meetings resulted in the Hague Convention, 1912, which restricted the international trade not just in opium but of other 'narcotic' drugs such as morphine and cocaine.[12] While 'narcotic' technically referred only to those drugs that had a sleep-inducing effect, such as the opiates, the term was used to mean drugs governed by these systems of international control.[13] Signatories to the Hague Convention agreed to confine the import and export of narcotic drugs to 'legitimate medical purposes'. Yet many countries did not immediately ratify the convention, and there was no central body to ensure that it was upheld. This situation changed after the First World War. The Versailles Treaty included a provision that countries agree to control the international trade in narcotics and entrusted the League of Nations with overseeing this system.[14] Further international meetings in the mid-1920s resulted in cannabis being added to the list of proscribed substances.[15]

This system of international control increased pressure on the British government to introduce domestic legislation to limit the use of drugs. The Defence of the Realm Act was essentially a war-time measure, created to protect the nation from the potentially damaging effect that cocaine might have on soldiers and, therefore, the war effort. The extension of war-time controls to the post-war period was achieved under the Dangerous Drugs Act in 1920. It became an offence for any individual to buy, sell or possess opiates, like heroin and morphine, and other drugs such as cocaine, unless that person was a licensed medical practitioner or pharmacist or in possession of a valid prescription. Yet the Dangerous Drugs Act was not just the consequence of international commitments but also the result of a further 'panic' about drug use. The death of actress Billie Carleton from an overdose of cocaine at a victory ball in 1918 and the subsequent trial of her supplier, Reggie de Veulle, exposed recreational drug use among a group of upper-class 'Bohemians' in London's West End. The press seized upon the Carleton case, depicting a debauched 'drug scene' in which drug taking was imbued with sexual and racial danger. Women were seen as being particularly vulnerable, especially at parties where drugs were taken. *The Times* reported that at one of these gatherings: 'disgusting orgies took place extending from the Saturday night until early in the Sunday afternoon.'[16]

For Kohn, these kinds of stories illustrated not just concern about drug use but about the changing position of women in society and other contemporary anxieties. 'Drugs', he argued, 'permit the terrors of the social subconscious to be voiced.'[17] Another element that can clearly be detected in the drug panic following the First World War is that of demonisation of the racial 'other'. In the 1920s this focussed on two groups: the Chinese 'yellow peril' and the black West Indian 'dope king'. These 'folk devils' were blamed for the 'flood' of drugs in London and accused of using drugs to ensnare innocent women and young people.[18] Real figures involved in the drug trade, such as the restaurant owner Brilliant Chang and the Jamaican jazz musician Edgar Manning, became mixed up with fictional characters in popular films such as D.W. Griffiths' *Broken Blossoms* and Sax Rohmer's *Dope*.[19] The lines between fact and fiction in the drug panic became increasingly blurred, converging to produce a heightened sense of immorality and criminality around drug taking. A letter to *The Times* in 1922 from 'M.D.' opined that 'The cocaine traffic is not, as so many people think, merely a matter of the supply of a "drug of addiction". Its immense danger lies in the fact it is purveyed by and to men and women leading grossly immoral lives for purposes connected with immorality.'[20] To guard against such a danger, legal controls, like the Dangerous Drugs Act, were thought to be required.

THE ROLLESTON COMMITTEE, 1923–1926

While these legal controls regulated the sale and distribution of opiate drugs such as morphine and heroin as well as cocaine, a rather different response was offered to individuals regarded as being addicted to these. To explain why, it is necessary to consider the deliberations of the Departmental Committee on Morphine and Heroin Addiction (the Rolleston Committee) in some detail. The Rolleston Committee and their report, published in 1926, were important for drug addiction treatment policy in this and subsequent periods as their recommendations acquired symbolic significance. As discussed in the Introduction, the Rolleston Committee was credited with the creation of the British System of drug addiction treatment. This was seen as a medical response to drug addiction in contrast to the penal approach characterised by the Dangerous Drugs Act. However, the distinction between these two agendas can be too starkly drawn. Collaboration between medical and penal approaches can be found in both the discussions that led to the establishment of the Rolleston Committee and in the deliberations of the committee itself.

The Rolleston Committee emerged when the Home Office realized that medical advice on aspects of the drug problem was required. The particular issue concerning Sir Malcolm Delevingne, the Under-Secretary at the Home Office dealing with drugs, was the amount of morphine and heroin being prescribed by a handful of doctors. The Home Office suspected that in many such cases drugs were being prescribed to individuals addicted to opiates and wished to know if such a practice was medically justifiable.[21] The Dangerous Drugs Act allowed 'any duly qualified medical practitioner or registered dentist' to possess, supply and prescribe opiate drugs 'so far as is necessary for the practice of his profession'.[22] Although the Home Office conceded that 'It is not expressly provided in the [Dangerous Drug] Regulations that prescriptions for the drugs must be for bona fide medical purposes . . . this is of course the intention of the Regulations.'[23] Delevingne wanted clarification as to what 'bona fide' medical purposes were in the case of prescription of opiate drugs to addicts as well as 'an authoritative statement which we could use when dealing with practitioners, and to which we could refer the Courts'.[24] The 'penal' approach was thus drawing on the 'medical'.

The precise form that this medical advice should take was, however, the subject of some debate. In 1924, Minister of Health John Wheatley appointed a committee, chaired by Sir Humphrey Rolleston, to 'consider and advise as to the circumstances, if any, in which the supply of morphine and heroin (including preparations containing morphine and heroin) to persons suffering from addiction to these drugs may be regarded as medically advisable'.[25] Rolleston chaired a committee composed entirely of medical men, but not all were of the same view of addiction and its treatment, and neither were the witnesses called to give evidence.

Broadly speaking, there were two schools of thought. The first was represented by the views of Sir William Wilcox, a medical advisor to the Home Office. Wilcox believed that addiction began as vice and only became a medical condition after some time. To treat this condition, the rapid withdrawal of the drug from the addict was required. He argued that such treatment should be compulsory and take place in an institution.[26] This opinion was largely supported by the evidence of prison doctors who spoke to the Rolleston Committee. Dr W.R.K. Watson, Senior Medical Officer at Brixton Prison, 'summed up his experience of the method of abrupt withdrawal by saying that after two or three days of moderate distress the patients were all right, and that when discharged . . . they appeared normal and had lost all craving for drugs'. Watson, however, was clear that such a method 'was not practicable outside an institution', a view endorsed by other practitioners of the rapid withdrawal method.[27] This experience also tallied with what Dr Adams, a staff medical officer at the Ministry of Health, had heard about treatment in the USA. While rapid withdrawal was the norm in America, it was also thought to be 'impracticable except in institutions'.[28]

Other doctors, such as Dr F.S.D. Hogg, Medical Superintendent of the Dalrymple House Retreat (a private treatment facility for 'inebriates') were completely opposed to rapid withdrawal in whatever setting. Hogg considered it 'barbarous and inhumane to expose a person unnecessarily to dangerous and severe shock and acute suffering' by suddenly removing a drug to which the patient was addicted.[29] Instead, Hogg felt that 'in some of the cases in which long continued addiction leads neither to increase of the dose nor any apparent harmful effect and in which a fixed dose of opiate seems necessary for normal conduct, the medical practitioner would be justified in advising the continuance of the drug.'[30] This practice of prescribing drugs to addicts over a long period, known as maintenance, was obviously at odds with the views of men like Wilcox and Watson, nor did it meet with universal approval among other witnesses. Dr Ivy Mackenzie, a hospital doctor and consulting physician, stated, 'I do not believe it to be necessary for any young and otherwise healthy person to be addicted to narcotics in order to enable them to continue as useful and decent members of society. I do not believe', she continued, 'that anyone can be addicted to drugs without incurring the risk of physical and moral harm.'[31]

Despite these concerns, in their final report published in 1926, the Rolleston Committee endorsed maintenance as an acceptable method of treatment for heroin addiction. Rolleston recommended that 'every effort' should be made to cure an individual of addiction by withdrawing the drug (either gradually or rapidly) but if this failed 'prolonged administration of morphine or heroin may be necessary'. The committee envisaged two types of patient who might be suitable for maintenance treatment. These were 'Those in whom a complete withdrawal of morphine or heroin produces serious symptoms which cannot be treated satisfactorily' and 'Those who are capable of leading a fairly normal and useful life so long as they take a certain quantity, usually small, of their drug of addiction'.[32]

This support for maintenance, despite the strong arguments made against it, can be explained by the broader characteristics of the 'problem' the committee investigated. Firstly, addiction to morphine and heroin was rare and actually appeared to be declining.[33] No figures on the prevalence of addiction exist for this period—data on the number of known addicts was only collected from 1934 onwards when the Home Office established the Addicts Index—but it seems likely that during the 1920s addicts could be counted in the hundreds, not thousands.[34] In 1935, the first full year for which figures exist, there were thought to be 700 addicts.[35] Secondly, addicts were mostly middle-aged, middle-class and had become addicted, like Thomas Henderson, as the result of taking opiate drugs for another condition.[36] Moreover, a disproportionate number of these addicts were doctors or other medical professionals who came into contact with opiate drugs as a result of their work.[37]

This 'class' of patient clearly invited a more sympathetic response than that offered to the recreational cocaine addicts of the West End. This response was framed around medical treatment rather than penal control. The Rolleston Committee were unequivocal that the particular problem they were describing was a medical one, and this was reflected in their definition of addiction. According to the Rolleston Committee an addict was 'a person who, not requiring the continued use of a drug for the relief of symptoms of organic disease, had acquired, as a result of repeated administration, an overpowering desire for its continuance, and in whom withdrawal of the drug leads to definite symptoms of mental or physical distress'.[38] Yet medical treatment was not presented as a binary alternative to penal control. Rolleston accepted that legal restrictions on the export, manufacture, sale and possession of opiate drugs were required and did not seek to challenge the law in any way. Treatment could even be seen as offering another form of control: drugs could only be given to addicts in certain conditions and under the watchful gaze of his or her general practitioner. Establishing that doctors should be responsible for supplying drugs to addicts legally actually gave the medical profession a clear role in the control mechanisms that surrounded narcotic drugs. This form of 'control through treatment' became increasingly important during the late 1960s but was clearly present in the Rolleston era.

THE CALM BEFORE THE STORM? DRUG CONTROL, 1930–1955

The British System put in place by Rolleston (such as it was) remained unchanged for nearly forty years. This was because the situation highlighted by the committee's report also stayed the same. Addicts were still small in number, of a therapeutic origin and largely middle-aged and middle class.[39] As a result, the most significant developments in British drug policy from the 1930s to the 1950s took place on the international stage. The system introduced by the League of Nations to control the trade in narcotic drugs was strengthened in 1931 with an international convention limiting narcotic production to amounts that were needed for medical treatment and scientific research only. This was intended to limit the diversion of drugs to the illicit market, but as Alan Block argues, this simply led criminal entrepreneurs to produce their own supplies of drugs, rather than eliminating the trade altogether.[40] Following the Second World War, the United Nations took over the international control of narcotics. In 1946, the Commission on Narcotic Drugs was established to implement the international conventions on drugs and keep these systems under continuous review.[41]

The health-related aspects of drug use were largely dealt with by the World Health Organisation (WHO).[42] The WHO became the scene for an international dispute when, in 1954, it attempted to introduce a complete ban on the use of heroin in medical practice. The proposed ban (suggested by the Americans) was met with a storm of professional protest in Britain.[43] This was partly because British doctors regarded the drug as a peerless analgesic (pain-killer), but also because a ban would conflict with professional autonomy. *The Times* posed the question that 'If a body of medical opinion, neither small nor cranky, is convinced that heroin is necessary for treatment, and if no evil may be shown to spring from its prescription in Britain, what right has a ministry or a Government to stand between a doctor and his patient on the subject?'[44] In 1956 the British government withdrew from the proposed ban on a technicality, and medical freedom was preserved.

THE FIRST INTERDEPARTMENTAL COMMITTEE ON HEROIN ADDICTION (THE BRAIN COMMITTEE), 1956–1961

Professional independence with specific regard to the treatment of addiction was reconsidered in that same year, although there is nothing to suggest the disputed heroin ban led directly to a review of addiction treatment policy. Rather, the Ministry of Health were of the opinion that 'it was most undesirable that medical advice given thirty years ago should still be circulated to doctors as if it fully represented present views on such matters.'[45] A re-examination of heroin addiction treatment was prompted, as it had been in the 1920s, by the Home Office's need for advice.[46] There were three main areas of concern. The first was how to control the growing number of new analgesics that were becoming available to doctors. The Home Office wished to know if these were addictive, and if they were, whether they should be regulated in the same way as opiate drugs like morphine and heroin. The second issue was how to deal with troublesome doctors. These fell into two categories: doctors who were addicted to drugs themselves and those who prescribed drugs to addicts without any attempt to reduce the dose in order to make money. The final, and most significant, of the Home Office's concerns was over the appropriateness of long-term prescription in the treatment of heroin addiction.[47] Rolleston had established two conditions where maintenance might be permissible: when withdrawal could result in serious side-effects and when an addict could live a normal life while still taking the drug. The Home Office questioned whether 'in the light of medical progress since the Committee reported either of [these] the conditions can be completely justified on medical grounds nowadays'. Officials at the Home Office noted that the notion that opiate drugs should be administered solely on account of the severity of withdrawal symptoms had long fallen out of favour in the United States and Canada and that the idea that an individual could work while under the influence of opiate drugs had also come in for some criticism. It was, the Home Office argued, 'undeniable that a narcotic drug usually impairs a person's faculties, so that if he can work while receiving a drug, he ought to be able to work better if he can be helped to do without it.'[48]

In order to examine these issues, an advisory committee was convened. They were tasked with reviewing the advice given by Rolleston on the treatment of addiction and to 'consider whether any revised advice should also cover other drugs liable to produce addiction or be habit-forming'. The committee also considered whether specialist treatment facilities for persons addicted to drugs were required and made recommendations for any changes as they saw fit.[49] Once more the committee was comprised entirely of medical men, an issue that did not escape the notice of the National Council of Women of Great Britain.[50] The Ministry of Health insisted that members of the committee were picked for their connections to professional bodies and supposedly relevant expertise.[51] The committee was chaired by Sir (later Lord) Russell Brain, a neurologist and former president of the Royal College of Physicians. Other members included A. Lawrence Abel, who was nominated by the Royal College of Surgeons; D.M. Dunlop of the Royal College of Physicians; Donald Hudson, representing the Pharmaceutical Society; A.D. MacDonald, a pharmacologist and member of the WHO's Expert Advisory Panel on the Drugs that Produce Addiction; A.H. Macklin and S. Noy Scott from the British Medical Association and M.A. Partridge, who was nominated by the Royal Medico-Psychological Association, a predecessor to the Royal College of Psychiatrists.[52] The composition of the committee thus helped confirm the treatment of addiction as a medical matter. Indeed, the Chief Medical Officer was insistent that the committee be chaired by a general physician rather than a psychiatrist, rejecting Professor Aubrey Lewis in favour of Sir Russell Brain.[53] It is unclear why this was the case, but as will be discussed in greater detail in Chapter Three, the 'psychiatrisation' of addiction was not yet complete. The treatment of addiction was not yet regarded as a specialist area of either medicine or psychiatry.

While the Brain Committee were undoubtedly illustrious, few of their members actually had any experience of treating addiction. This was partly because, as the evidence submitted by the Home Office demonstrated, heroin addiction was still thought to be a relatively rare condition. There were 616 known addicts in 1936, 620 in 1937, 519 in 1938, 534 in 1939, 199 in 1947, 226 in 1950, 260 in 1954, 347 in 1958, and 442 in 1959.[54] Most of the witnesses who gave evidence to the Brain Committee were also sure that heroin addiction was not increasing.[55] The small rise in numbers detected was attributed to better policing rather than an increase in drug-taking.[56] This allowed the committee to conclude that 'we are of the opinion that in Great Britain the incidence of addiction to dangerous drugs . . . is very small'.[57] At the same time, there was no evidence to suggest that a market in illicit drugs had developed; most addicts received their drugs on prescription from a doctor.[58] Case histories presented to the committee and summarised in their final report also suggested that addicts themselves had changed little since the Rolleston era. Mrs 'A' was thought to be typical. A late middle-aged housewife, Mrs A had begun taking the opiate drug pethidine by prescription from her general practitioner for pain following surgery to remove carcinoma in the breast. She had been taking three to four tablets a day for ten years, and on 'this dosage she is relatively free from symptoms and is able to undertake her own housework'. There were no signs that the dose needed to be increased, but numerous attempts at withdrawal or substitution with another drug had been met with 'pain and incapacity'.[59]

As was the case with Rolleston, the nature of this addict population seems to have shaped the Brain Committee's view of addiction and its treatment. Drawing on the WHO's definition of addiction, the first Brain Committee defined addiction as 'a state of periodic or chronic intoxication produced by repeated consumption of a drug'.[60] The committee went on to outline five key characteristics of addiction: firstly, 'an overpowering desire or need (compulsion) to continue taking the drug'; secondly, 'a tendency to increase the dose'; thirdly, a 'psychological and physical dependence on the effects of the drug'; fourthly, 'characteristic abstinence syndrome in a subject from whom the drug is withdrawn'; and finally, 'an effect detrimental to the individual and society'. The precise nature of this final characteristic was not elaborated on by the Brain report. No additional measures were proposed to combat the potentially detrimental effect heroin addiction might have on society. Brain remained sure that 'addiction should be regarded as an expression of mental disorder rather than as a form of criminal behaviour . . . every addict should be treated energetically as a medical and psychiatric problem'.[61] This led the committee to reject some of the stricter control mechanisms available to it. The idea that addiction should be a notifiable disease (like other diseases thought to pose a threat to public health such as smallpox, typhoid and diphtheria) was set aside on the grounds that notification might prevent a patient from consulting his or her doctor. The fear was that the addict would then turn to the black market for their supply of drugs.[62] Compulsory treatment was thought unlikely to produce good results, and though the committee believed an institution was the best place for the treatment of addiction, they did not recommend the establishment of new facilities. In the committee's view, the low numbers of addicts did not justify their introduction, and compulsion went against the more general move away from enforced treatment of the mentally ill in this period.[63]

As had been the case with the Rolleston committee, the issue that caused the most debate centered on treatment methods. Some witnesses expressed scepticism about the concept of the 'stabilised addict', an individual who could live a normal life while taking drugs. The Royal Faculty of Physicians and Surgeons commented, 'If a person claimed he was a stabilised addict, he would be expected of concealing the true nature of his addiction.'[64] Other bodies, such as the British Medical Association (BMA) thought it a valid notion.[65] Yet others, such as the Royal Medico-Psychological Association (RMPA), asserted that while 'true' addicts could not be stabilised, their drug of addiction may be substituted with another. This, they claimed, was 'not a cure but may allow the patient to carry out his work effectively without the loss of moral or other standards'.[66] Opinion about the validity of the concept of the stabilised addict was split about evenly, but the committee decided to endorse the notion of the stabilised addict after considering case histories like that of Mrs A. The committee argued in their final report that many addicts had been 'taking small and regular doses for years' and many 'are often leading reasonably satisfactory lives'.[67] The long-term prescription of drugs to addicts was thus justified. The first Brain Committee clearly upheld Rolleston's advice on this key point.

The committee also dealt with the Home Office's other two concerns: the prescription of a growing range of analgesic drugs and the possibility that some doctors were prescribing these drugs to addicts without any attempt to treat them for their condition, often for personal gain. The Brain Committee believed that no new statutory powers were required to control new analgesic drugs, although it was recognised that these substances may have addictive properties. If this was found to be the case, the committee recommended that these drugs should be controlled in the same way as the opiates. The committee heard evidence indicating that there were doctors prepared to prescribe drugs to addicts 'without adequate medical supervision', but the committee reported that just one or two cases over the last twenty years had come to their attention. As a result, special tribunals to try cases in which irresponsible prescription was suspected were not required.[68] No additional controls on doctors or their addict-patients were needed.

THE FIRST BRAIN REPORT: REACTION AND IMPLICATIONS

In all the key areas, the first Brain report's conclusions could best be described as a reaffirmation of those reached by Rolleston. Yet before the report was even published, its findings were brought into question. Brain himself gave a preview of his committee's report to a meeting of the Society for the Study of Addiction in April 1961. At the meeting, a pharmacist from London's West End, Irving 'Benny' Benjamin, asserted that the number of opiate drugs users was much larger than the committee supposed and, furthermore, that addicts were receiving their drugs from doctors who routinely overprescribed to addict-patients. Brain responded that the committee had come to their conclusions based on the evidence they received, but their failure to take evidence from people like Benjamin would seem to have resulted in the committee forming a less than complete picture of the current state of the drug problem.[69] Just three years later, the Brain Committee were reconvened to re-examine their findings.

Spear, in his account of the response to heroin addiction in this period, was particularly critical of the first Brain report. He argued that the Home Office had presented the committee with evidence of at least four doctors who had routinely overprescribed to addicts, but the committee did not ask 'penetrating questions' and took no more than 'a perfunctory interest in the proceedings'.[70] Spear also suggested that there was evidence available to the committee to indicate that the number of known addicts was starting to rise during the late 1950s and early 1960s, and more significantly, 'therapeutic' addicts like Mrs 'A' were being replaced by those whose addiction was of a 'non-therapeutic' origin. Spear claimed in his 1955 report on the scale of drug addiction that of the forty-six new heroin addicts reported that year, forty-five were of 'non-therapeutic' origin.[71] If this finding did reach the Brain Committee, it did not make any impact. Spear accepted that 'most of the blame for the failure to bring the emergence of this new [addict] group to the attention of the Committee must rest with the Home Office' but he was also sure that 'the Committee cannot entirely escape responsibility. It simply will not do to claim "we were never told"'.[72]

Spear clearly had an interest in trying to defend the Home Office's role in the production of the first Brain report, but it is worthwhile considering who the committee took evidence from, and who they did not, in more detail. The committee heard from a long list of professional bodies, encompassing every potentially interested group from the Association of Anaesthetists to the Society for the Medical Officers of Health.[73] Yet they heard little testimony from individuals who had any experience treating addicts and refused point-blank to hear from addicts themselves. Michael Cullen, an addict imprisoned in Wormwood Scrubs, had written to the committee offering to 'give any information that you may require' about his condition, but his offer was dismissed.[74] The committee asserted that 'witnesses who are themselves addicts are notoriously unreliable'.[75] It would seem that the Brain Committee looked to professional status and authority rather than real experience of addiction and its treatment to make their recommendations.

The limited nature of the evidence the committee took therefore goes some way to explain their conclusion that heroin addiction was not a problem just as the number of known addicts started to increase. In 1960, there were 437 known cases of addiction; in 1961, 470; in 1962, 532; in 1963, 635; in 1964, 753.[76] With the benefit of hindsight, the first Brain Committee clearly got it wrong. But the total number of know heroin addicts was still small at this time, and the committee could hardly have been expected to realise that this was the beginning of an upward trend. The fact that they either did not receive or did not take sufficiently into consideration the Home Office statistics pointing to a rise in addiction and its move from being of therapeutic to non-therapeutic origin was also a reflection of the committee's medical composition and standing. The Brain Committee clearly felt that drug addiction was a medical matter and therefore took evidence and responded accordingly. While it would be too crude an analysis to suggest that the Brain Committee disregarded evidence pointing to overprescription by doctors in order to defend professional privilege, they did want to indicate that addiction could be adequately handled by the medical profession. However this should not be taken to mean that the medical view of addiction was gaining in strength at the expense of a more control-oriented approach. As the deliberations of the first Brain Committee indicated, there was no one 'medical' view of addiction and its treatment; doctors were divided on this topic just as they had been in the time of Rolleston. Furthermore, many of the control measures considered and rejected by the Brain Committee, such as notification and compulsory treatment, were accepted by the committee the second time it met. The issue was not so much that these methods were thought to be inappropriate in dealing with addiction but that they were unsuitable for the type of addiction and addict that the Brain Committee initially believed they were dealing with. As will be seen in Chapter Two, additional controls were thought necessary for the 'new' type of addicts brought to the attention of the Brain Committee in 1964. The symbiotic relationship between the medical and penal approaches to heroin addiction that began in the 1920s was clearly still present, albeit in a slightly different form, in the 1960s.

The New Addicts and the Establishment of the Drug Dependence Units, 1962–1968

Dr Lady Isabella Frankau was a London-based private practitioner. She was also a psychiatrist who specialised in the treatment of alcoholics. From the late 1950s onwards Frankau began treating heroin addicts. Frankau's method, outlined in an article in *The Lancet* published in 1960, was to prescribe 'adequate supplies' of heroin or cocaine to addicts to prevent them from obtaining drugs from 'pedlars', and once stable, to gradually withdraw the drug.[1] While those concerned with the treatment of heroin addiction in this period could find little wrong with Frankau's approach, concern was expressed at the amount of heroin she prescribed. In 1962 Frankau prescribed a total of six kilograms (600,000 tablets) of heroin. On one occasion she prescribed nine grams (900 tablets) of heroin to an addict and gave the same patient a further six grams (600 tablets) three days later to 'replace pills lost in an accident'.[2] Frankau's prescribing was on such a scale that Russell Brain is said to have remarked to his re-assembled Interdepartmental Committee on Heroin Addiction, 'Well Gentlemen, I think your problem can be summed up in two words, Lady Frankau'.[3]

Frankau and a handful of other doctors, largely working in National Health Service (NHS) general practice, were thought to be 'over-prescribing' heroin and other drugs to heroin addicts. Sir George Godber, the Chief Medical Officer, noted in 1964 that 'new evidence . . . has been accumulating since 1961 on the prevalence of excessive prescription for addicts'. Furthermore, Godber pointed out, there had also been 'an increase in heroin addiction, which is believed to be a consequence of this [over-prescription]'.[4] These two factors, overprescription and an apparent increase in heroin addiction, resulted in the reconvention of the Brain Committee in 1964. The committee were tasked with assessing whether their previous advice needed revising 'in the light of recent experience' and 'if so, to make recommendations'.[5] The second Brain Committee went on to propose a number of changes to the way heroin addiction was treated in Britain, the most important of which was the introduction of specialised Drug Dependence Units (DDUs); however, these practical measures were underpinned not just by an increase in drug use and the prescription of heroin but also by a more fundamental shift in the way in which heroin addiction was defined. Although the second Brain Committee still believed that 'the addict should be regarded as a sick person' and 'should be treated as such', addiction was 'a disease which (if allowed to spread unchecked) would become a menace to the community'. Heroin addiction, the committee argued, was a 'socially infectious condition'.[6]

Brain's redefinition of addiction as a socially infectious condition was motivated by two factors. Firstly, there was a change in the addict population. Not only were the numbers of addicts rising, but they also appeared to be getting younger. In 1959 11 per cent of reported addicts were under 35 years of age, but by 1964 40 per cent were in this group.[7] Furthermore, the younger addicts were more likely to have come to drug addiction by 'recreational' means. In 1964 94 per cent of newly reported addicts were of non-therapeutic origin.[8] These new addicts seemed to require new measures. The 'British medical leadership', according to commentator on heroin policy Arnold Trebach, could not countenance 'the prospect of treating defiant young heroin addicts the same as the deserving aged and infirm'.[9] Secondly, there was a broader shift in ideas about the location of disease. As medicine's 'gaze' widened from the individual body to the social body, and the pattern of sickness within a population could be traced more accurately through the growing use of epidemiology, disease became more 'social'. Disease came to be understood as something that could exist within, and spread throughout, society. Conditions such as heroin addiction came to be understood as 'social diseases' requiring not only medical treatment but also social control.

This supposed increased need for control has led some commentators to see the period following the second Interdepartmental Committee report and the introduction of the DDUs as the end of the British System. Arnold Trebach, Gerry Stimson and Edna Oppenheimer have all emphasised the elements of control inherent within the treatment of addiction after 1968.[10] However, others such as Griffith Edwards and David Whynes have seen the creation and running of specialised DDUs as an inherently medical response to a medical problem.[11] Presented in this chapter is a different interpretation, which shows that *both* elements were present: though tensions between medical and social approaches to addiction can be observed, these worked together as well as in opposition. The intricacies of this dynamic dialogue can be observed in four areas examined in this chapter. The first concerns the deliberations of the second incarnation of the Brain Committee and the production of their report in 1965. The second surrounds the reaction of the medical profession to the Brain report and the Ministry of Health's attempt to introduce new measures to deal with heroin addiction. The third area where the interaction between social and medical approaches can be discerned is in some of the problems encountered in putting Brain's recommendations into practice, particularly with the opening of the DDUs. Finally, one needs to step outside the confines of the NHS treatment system put in place by the Brain Committee to look at some of the other responses offered to the 'social disease' of heroin addiction, particularly in the voluntary sector. Just as was the case with the British System of the 1920s, heroin addiction in the 1960s presented a multi-faceted problem that was responded to in a variety of complex, and sometimes contradictory, ways.

THE SECOND INTERDEPARTMENTAL COMMITTEE ON HEROIN ADDICTION (THE BRAIN COMMITTEE), 1964–1965

The number of heroin addicts listed on the Home Office Addicts Index had begun to rise steadily since 1960 so that by 1964 there were 753 individuals known to be addicted to the drug.[12] Other kinds of evidence also pointed to an increase in heroin addiction. According to Spear, the Home Office Drugs Inspectorate tracked supplies of heroin from manufacturers to retail chemists and on to a growing number of individual patients. Inspectors also visited pharmacies and other places where addicts congregated in an attempt to paint a picture of the emerging 'drug scene'.[13] The Home Office's view was that this increase in addiction was being fuelled by the overprescription of heroin. A memorandum submitted by the Home Office to the second Brain Committee stated that 'many addicts have been receiving on prescription more heroin (and cocaine) than they need for the immediate satisfaction of their own addiction, and that they have been disposing of the surplus to acquaintances who have in this way become addicts'.[14] Lady Frankau's inflated heroin prescriptions were an extreme, but not isolated, case. The Home Office knew of other doctors who routinely overprescribed heroin to addicts and felt there was a need for additional measures to control the prescription of heroin. Spear argued that such controls could not be introduced 'until there was some idea of what measures would be acceptable to the medical profession, who should be made to take at least some responsibility for controlling wayward members'.[15] As a result, the Brain Committee was reconvened in July 1964.

The Second Interdepartmental Committee was initially seen as being primarily concerned with the problem of overprescribing. Godber, in a 1964 letter, referred to the 'Brain Committee on the control of prescribing', but the committee's remit quickly expanded.[16] At their first meeting, the Brain Committee decided to reconsider the treatment, registration and detention of addicts as well as overprescription and the appropriate controls required to curb this.[17] The committee met a further seven times, hearing evidence from the Home Office, the Ministry of Health and the Scottish Home and Health Department. The Home Office confirmed that the number of addicts was rising and that these individuals were obtaining their supplies from doctors, not from an illicit market in drugs.[18] The Brain Committee also took written and oral evidence from those with 'special experience in the field', including doctors thought to be overprescribing, such as Frankau.[19] After speaking with Frankau and other 'over-prescribers' (all of whom were in NHS general practice), the committee concluded that 'the doctors in question, although meaning well, had under-estimated the complexity of the problem of drug addiction.'[20] Other doctors treating addicts, especially those working in NHS hospitals such as Dr Bewley and Dr Chapple, 'felt that it was far too easy for an addict to get drugs from a doctor'. One witness 'urged a ban on the prescription of heroin by doctors and its supply only by a limited number of central clinics'.[21]

The Brain Committee clearly took this suggestion seriously, as the creation of specialised treatment centres was thought to be 'essential', and it was noted, 'if the addict were prevented from getting addictive drugs on prescription outside treatment centres there was no need to establish a closed centre or take compulsory powers [to treat addicts]'.[22] The establishment of treatment centres was to form a key part of the advice contained in the Brain Committee's report published in 1965. Central to their recommendations was a different interpretation of addiction. While the committee accepted that 'the addict should be regarded as a sick person and treated as such' their proposals reveal concerns that ran beyond the treatment of the individual addict.[23] The committee recommended that incidences of addiction be notified to a central authority, as with infectious diseases. This analogy was felt to be particularly apt 'for addiction is a socially infectious condition and its notification may offer a means for epidemiological assessment and control'.[24] Epidemiological information had already proved crucial in highlighting the potential dangers to health of smoking tobacco.[25] Brain's report must, therefore, be read within a context of greater authority being given to epidemiology in this period, as this became an important way of describing and responding to disease.[26] The 'infectiousness' of addiction was further reflected in the key recommendation made by the committee: that treatment for heroin addiction should be located in specialised institutions, or treatment centres. Furthermore, as the source of most of the heroin and cocaine being used was found to come from overprescription by GPs and private practitioners, the committee suggested that the ability to prescribe these drugs be confined to doctors working at the treatment centres.[27] Doctors outside DDUs would still be able to prescribe heroin for pain relief but not for those patients addicted to the drug, a proposal that would restrict doctors' freedom to prescribe drugs for the first time.

Analysis of the second Brain report suggests that these recommendations were the result of a shift in the definition of, and response to, drug addiction. As sociologists Gerry Stimson and Edna Oppenheimer argue: 'Hitherto most discussions had focused on the medical treatment of addicted individuals. The new element introduced in the 1960s was the emphasis on the social control of addiction.'[28] This change was attributed to a transformation in the population of addicts. Addicts were younger and had become addicted not as a consequence of medical treatment but as a result of recreational drug use. Heroin addiction was now a greater social problem. This did not, however, herald an era of enhanced social control over a population of addicts to the exclusion of medical treatment of the individual. Drug addiction treatment and control policy after 1968 was about just that: treatment and control. This combination slotted neatly into the existing British System as it aimed to both limit the drug problem and care for the addict. What was new after Brain reported was a greater conflation of these goals.

The emergence of this concept of addiction as a social disease was not based solely on the changed addict but was also the result of shifting perceptions about the location of disease within society. David Armstrong, in *The Political Anatomy of the Body*, maintains that the spread of contagious diseases like tuberculosis prompted doctors to examine the relationships between people, not just the environment, as a cause of disease.[29] This encouraged the extension of the medical 'gaze' (a concept developed by Michel Foucault in *The Birth of the Clinic*) from the individual to the whole community.[30] Disease was thus located not just in the individual body but also in the social body. Such a conceptualisation has been utilised by Rachel Lart to explain the comparable shifts in the location of addiction.[31] She argues that the collation of records of prescriptions to addicts from 1934 onwards made the addict more visible through increasing surveillance, which enabled the observation of not just the individual addict but also the pattern of disease within society.[32] Locating disease in society allowed for the intervention of government to protect society and prevent disease from spreading. This idea was central to long-standing notions of public health, but here too there was a shift in focus away from the environment to society, as campaigns began to target the health of the individual.[33]

It is clear that the Brain report was drawing on these concepts of public health when it argued that drug addiction, if allowed to spread, could become a 'menace to the community'.[34] This menace, however, was not merely the risk of contracting a physiological disease but, as Carol Smart indicates, the threat that the behaviour of drug addicts represented to the fabric of society.[35] The social threat that addicts posed was not just that they might spread their disease to others but also a more general concern that underlies public health—that it was a waste of human resources. Addiction was a disease that was wasteful and unproductive, thus posing a threat to the economic as well as social and physical health of the community. The combination of medical and social 'danger' expressed in public health rhetoric necessitated both the treatment and control of drug addiction. It is often difficult to separate these as two distinct strands of drug addiction policy. As Stimson has pointed out, staff at clinics fulfilled both treatment and control roles.[36] Although both treatment and control had always been the concern of drug policy, the DDUs represented a closer union of what had been characterised as 'medical' and 'social' responses. This development was facilitated by broader changes in the perception and location of disease, enabling Brain and his colleagues to describe addiction as a 'social' disease.

THE REACTION OF THE MEDICAL PROFESSION TO THE BRAIN REPORT

There is little evidence to suggest that the wider medical profession were profoundly moved by this view of addiction. Doctors were more concerned about the potential threat to their autonomy posed by the increased regulation of the treatment of addiction than deeper conceptual changes. An editorial in the *British Medical Journal* found notification of addiction to the Home Office to be a 'sound and acceptable' idea but was concerned about the proposed restrictions to the right to prescribe freely. Their main objection was that 'Because of the weakness—or worse—of a handful of doctors' prescription was to be restricted and this would be 'a grave step'.[37] It seems the *British Medical Journal*'s objection was based more on the defence of a principle than a specific complaint about the recommendations, as the article conceded that treatment centres were 'acceptable' and, 'Any practitioner with a case of addiction to heroin or cocaine will feel relieved if he knows he can send such a patient for treatment elsewhere.'[38] This was supported by the observation that few practitioners were actually willing to see addicts. An investigation by *The Times* found there were only two dozen doctors in London prepared to treat addicts because of the trouble they caused, and as Stimson and Oppenheimer note, protests about the restriction of prescription were 'muted' because 'the proposals would remove from the majority of doctors any need to do the medical "dirty work" of treating addicts'.[39] *The Lancet* raised even fewer objections to the Brain report than the *British Medical Journal*. While commenting that 'It certainly seems very hard that the whole profession should suffer this limitation on its professional judgement', it argued that doctors 'might be wise to accept the limitation, which is likely to save much frustration in an area where therapy by non-specialists is virtually impossible'.[40] The process that led the medical profession to accept restrictions on their powers of prescription was thus a dual one: on the one hand, addiction was seen as a social problem and not, therefore, the responsibility of the doctor, but on the other, the treatment of addiction was being portrayed as an increasingly specialised area of medicine beyond the capacities of the generalist.

This complex interplay between the social and medical can also be observed in the reaction to one of Brain's other central recommendations—notification. Despite both the *British Medical Journal* and *The Lancet* accepting the need to notify incidences and addiction to a central authority, Ministry of Health files reveal that not all sections of the medical community were happy with this proposal. The Scottish branch of the British Medical Association (BMA) were particularly displeased with notification, commenting, 'it is very difficult for a doctor to accept that he can, and indeed must, notify his patient without that patient's consent'.[41] Doctors, however, offered no organised resistance to notification. Indeed many were already informing the Home Office when they came into contact with an addict, so regulations introduced in 1968 making it a legal requirement for doctors to notify the Chief Medical Officer aroused little comment.[42] This lack of dissent over the issue of notification at first appears surprising given that it would seem to threaten the confidentiality of the doctor-patient relationship, yet this can be explained by the new way addiction was portrayed. By emphasising the social infectiousness of the disease of addiction, the Brain Committee encouraged doctors to see it in the same way as other dangerous communicable diseases, like tuberculosis. Viewed in this light, noting incidences of addiction was an acceptable loss of a few patients' rights for the good of society. As a Home Office official remarked to Trebach, 'Addicts have no rights simply because they are addicts.'[43]

Harmony on notification did not, however, mean that there was a broad consensus on how to approach heroin addiction more generally. The Brain report placed the treatment centre at the centre of the response to drug addiction, but achieving agreement on exactly what this should be was difficult. A Ministry of Health spokesman neatly summed up the situation in 1967 when he commented '"there is an experimental feel about this whole policy"'.[44] The Ministry were groping in the dark; they had little idea how to implement a policy that would control the spread of addiction and at the same time provide for the treatment of individual addicts. Officials questioned whether Brain had actually envisaged that clinics should have this dual function. A secretary of the committee confirmed that Brain had 'intended that treatment centres have two roles—treatment of addicts who desired cure (withdrawal of the drug, rehabilitation etc.) and the regular supply of heroin or other drugs to addicts who were not willing to accept treatment'.[45] Brain clearly thought clinics could both control the spread of addiction in the wider population and treat the individual addict.

When the Ministry of Health consulted a number of experts on drug addiction, they found that this dual function appeared to be somewhat contradictory. Although there were relatively few psychiatrists who had much experience treating addiction in the mid 1960s, those who did could roughly be divided into two camps. Some of the doctors consulted by officials recognised the social 'danger' of the spread of addiction and realised that not all addicts would be willing to come off drugs. Such addicts needed drugs to avoid the development of withdrawal symptoms, and it was thought that providing them with drugs prevented them from seeking supplies on the black market.[46] Doctors like Dale Beckett, who operated the Salter Unit for the treatment of drug addicts at Cane Hill Hospital, favoured a policy that would allow addicts who could not, or would not, give up heroin to be 'maintained' on the drug.[47] This, it was hoped, would prevent the development of an illicit market and the worsening of social problems associated with addiction.

Dr Thomas Bewley represented a second school of thought. He dismissed the prescription of heroin to addicts, arguing instead for transferring them to methadone, a synthetic opiate substitute.[48] He placed a greater emphasis on 'curing' the individual addict rather than allowing an addict to remain hooked on drugs. The Ministry were unconvinced by this argument, feeling that they were 'faced not with a bad and a good solution but with in fact a choice of evils. The great need was for containment in order to prevent the development of an international black market.'[49] For this reason they decided that clinics would be permitted to prescribe heroin on a maintenance basis. This was translated into policy through a Ministry of Health memorandum to doctors in 1967 that stated, 'The aim is to contain the spread of heroin addiction by continuing to supply this drug in minimum quantities where this is necessary in the opinion of the doctor, and where possible to get the addict to accept withdrawal treatment.'[50]

The central purpose of clinic policy having been established, the Ministry of Health began negotiations with those who would be asked to implement it. Brain had reported that most of the new drug addicts were to be found in London, so it seemed logical that attention be focused on the capital.[51] The Ministry proposed that treatment of addiction should be offered in outpatient units set up in the London undergraduate teaching hospitals.[52] This emphasis on outpatient treatment reflects a general trend towards non-residential care for psychiatric conditions and mirrors similar changes in the treatment of alcoholism. As Betsy Thom has shown, alcohol treatment units established in 1962 initially offered treatment for alcoholism primarily on an inpatient basis, but by the latter half of the decade, alcoholics were increasingly being seen as outpatients.[53] Although there were clear parallels with treatment of alcoholism, the creation of hospital-based treatment centres for heroin addiction contrasted with a more general reduction in the role of the institution in the provision of mental health services. In the late 1960s and early 1970s a community-based approach became more common.[54] Yet heroin addiction seemed to require a centrally controlled, institutional response, as had earlier 'social diseases' such as tuberculosis and venereal disease.[55]

Despite this apparent social imperative, officials found 'little enthusiasm' among staff at London teaching hospitals for the creation of outpatient addiction treatment centres.[56] Throughout the spring of 1967, representatives of the Ministry of Health visited London teaching hospitals to assess their individual reactions to setting up outpatient clinics for addicts.[57] These varied, but it is clear that there were three main concerns. Firstly, many were sceptical about the Ministry's suggestion that addicts be maintained on heroin if necessary. Doctors at Guy's Hospital did not want to 'become a dispensing service on demand to addicts'.[58] The board of St Mary's Hospital were 'dubious about the merits of "maintenance treatment"' but were happy to co-operate if there were extra funds available.[59] This highlights the second issue: cost. Those hospitals that agreed to take on the outpatient treatment of addicts were unanimous that they would require an increase in funds to do so. An official noted hospitals were 'hardly likely to give this priority over other cherished projects, and if they were to do anything it would have to be on the basis of some additional money for the purpose'.[60] Although the Ministry had previously anticipated that the running costs of the clinics would be 'inconsiderable', investigation proved this assumption incorrect.[61] An initial estimate of annual costs was in the region of £15,000 per clinic, approximately 20 per cent of the extra revenue allocation given to hospitals for projects in 1967/8.[62] The Ministry's initial tactic was to assure hospital boards that funding would be available if they began to run short towards the end of the financial year (this was in line with more general limitations to public spending), but by September 1967 grants covering full costs were being made to hospitals to set up clinics.[63] The third problem raised by the teaching hospitals was that the new centres would need staff, yet few doctors were prepared to treat addicts. Furthermore, those who did were concerned about the effect this could have on their careers. The House Governor of the Westminster Hospital warned, 'for the sake of his future no psychiatrist should be restricted to the subject of heroin addiction'.[64] This sentiment was echoed by doctors from St Thomas' Hospital, who, in a letter to the Ministry, argued that the treatment of addicts was 'a demanding but limiting sphere of work and no doctor should be encouraged to do this work and nothing else'.[65] The Ministry of Health appeared reluctant to approve rises in staffing levels at a number of hospitals, maintaining that the clinics could be manned by existing employees. This resulted in a dispute between officials and staff at Guy's, resolved only when the existence of the unit was in 'jeopardy'.[66] What these negotiations reveal is that a fundamental scepticism about the Ministry's proposals existed among doctors working at the London teaching hospitals. Doctors were unsure about the merits of the service they were to offer as 'treatment' and were reluctant to become involved in a project that was more concerned with the social control of addiction. This was recognised by Beckett, who observed in an article in *New Society* in 1967 that the development of DDUs was being held up by 'the doubts of the hospital boards and the doctors who will run them', and these doubts were the result of fundamental differences in approach. Beckett argued that psychiatrists are 'orientated medically, not sociologically, as in line with their training'.[67] Doctors, he implied, were more interested in curing the addict than attempting to control the social problem of addiction.

PUTTING RECOMMENDATIONS INTO PRACTICE—
THE ESTABLISHMENT OF THE DDUS

The prolonged negotiations between the Ministry of Health and the teaching hospitals meant that the Government appeared slow to act upon the advice of the Brain Committee, stimulating party-political interest in heroin addiction. Before 1966, there had been a cross-party consensus over the drugs issue, with members from both sides stressing the need for action.[68] As time went on, however, members of the Conservative Opposition began to express their frustration at the lack of progress. The Conservative MP for Ashford, William Deedes (speaking as much from his own interest in the drugs problem as a representative of any organised Tory policy on the issue), did not believe 'that the Government have measured up to the situation' branding the absence of action as 'inexcusable tardiness'.[69] The Health Minister, Kenneth Robinson, denied this, maintaining that time had been well spent.[70] Yet there was little transparency outside Whitehall about what the Ministry of Health were actually planning to do about the drug 'problem'. *The Sunday Times* quoted Lawrence Abel, a doctor who had sat on the first Brain Committee and now represented the National Association on Drug Addiction, as remarking '"Anyone who finds out what the Ministry is planning is a miracle worker."'[71] *The Guardian* were no clearer about the provision of facilities for addicts several months later, citing a doctor 'closely associated' with the new system as saying that when this came into force '"there will be nothing but bloody chaos."'[72] This lack of clarity is hardly surprising given that the Ministry of Health itself was unsure about the policy it was to implement.

The issue came to a head when a letter from a London GP complaining about the absence of facilities for drug addicts was published in *The Times* in July 1967.[73] Dr A.J. Hawes was struggling to cope with a flood of addict-patients, but his chief concern was that he did not know where he could refer these patients when he was no longer able to treat them. Hawes also sent a copy of his letter to the Ministry of Health, where it caused much consternation.[74] The hospitals that were in the process of setting up clinics had told the Ministry they did not want the existence of these to become widely known before they were completed for fear of being 'swamped' by addicts.[75] When officials replied to Hawes, they gave him a list of hospitals providing 'facilities' for the treatment of addiction and warned him that until these were available, 'it would be premature, and unhelpful to addicts as a whole, to give any publicity to the units concerned'.[76] Hawes ignored this advice, and after checking with the hospitals on the list about the 'facilities' they were said to have, wrote to *The Times* alleging that the Ministry had deliberately misled him. This made front-page news when it emerged that of the nine hospitals listed as offering treatment for drug addiction, only six of these provided outpatient treatment, and not all of these were available on a regular basis. The situation was confused still further by the government's Spokesman on Health in the House of Lords, Baroness Philips, who stated in a speech to the House that there were eleven outpatient clinics in London and plans for four more. A Ministry spokesman tried to excuse the gaffe by explaining that 'facilities' were different from 'units', that these were not the same as 'centres' or 'clinics' and that the letter sent to Hawes was simply meant to give an idea of the hospitals where addicts could be treated by doctors 'knowledgeable in their problems'.[77] This prompted a spate of negative articles in the press.[78] Hawes continued to be a thorn in the Ministry's side, arguing in *The Lancet* that 'I see not the slightest reason why addict clinics should not be set up in every hospital in London and all large cities— and that within a week.'[79]

The confusion over the location of the clinics was indicative of a wider confusion as to their purpose. An editorial in the *British Medical Journal* in 1967 asked, 'What are the realistic aims of treatment—cure or containment?' a question they were still unable to answer in March 1968, just a month before the clinics opened.[80] The Ministry of Health seemed to recognise there were contradictions in their policy. In a report used for the basis of the memorandum *Treatment and Supervision*, an official noted that the clinics were expected to 'try and contain heroin addiction and at the same time bring as many patients as possible under treatment'.[81] In this sense, the policy the Ministry were trying to implement encompassed both medical treatment and social control. This was to have a number of implications for the practical 'treatment' of drug addiction in clinics, as what was good for the health of the individual addict was not necessarily good for society. These apparent tensions between social control and medical treatment can be observed in the opening of the DDUs. On the one hand, the memorandum that dictated how drug addiction was to be treated prioritised social control, emphasising the need to control addiction through control of prescription.[82] For this reason doctors working at clinics would be allowed to prescribe heroin on a maintenance basis to stop the development of a black market and the spread of addiction. On the other hand, clinics were established at key London hospitals run by psychiatrists and support staff. The involvement of psychiatrists would indicate that there was a desire to 'cure' addicts of their addiction rather than just maintain them.

This dual policy was put into action in April 1968 when the Dangerous Drugs (Prescription to Addicts) Regulations were imposed. Only those doctors in possession of a licence to prescribe dangerous drugs could prescribe heroin to addicts. Approximately 600 of these licenses were granted by the Home Secretary, almost universally to doctors working in clinics. A total of 15 clinics opened in London, and by October there were 1,139 addict-patients attending treatment centres, 80 per cent of these in the capital.[83] The centres were all funded by the Ministry of Health, but facilities varied enormously. What is more, the location and even the description of these indicate that drug addiction occupied an ambiguous space. Some clinics were incorporated into the main body of the hospital, often as part of the psychiatric department and were clearly labelled 'Drug Dependency Clinic'. Others were hidden away in the bowels of the hospital, sometimes reached by a separate entrance, and were more euphemistically entitled 'Psychiatric Unit Annexe' or 'Special Psychiatric Clinic'.[84] A county medical officer in Cambridgeshire described the drug addiction facilities in his region as the 'containment unit'.[85] Many hospitals had made it a condition of their accepting the establishment of a clinic that it would be in separate facilities or held at different times from other outpatient surgeries to avoid the 'spread' of addiction to other patients. Dr Randall at Charing Cross Hospital, for example, insisted on holding the addiction clinic in the evenings to prevent mixing with 'ordinary' patients, and addicts were asked to enter the hospital through the back door.[86] Some psychiatrists working with addicts even claimed they were ostracised by other staff.[87] Addiction, it seemed, really was the 'socially infectious condition' depicted by Brain. Martin Mitcheson, a psychiatrist at the drug clinic at University College Hospital, commented that 'addiction has succeeded tuberculosis as a social disease and you hide addicts at the back of hospitals'.[88]

VOLUNTARY ORGANISATIONS AND THE 'REHABILITATION' OF HEROIN ADDICTS

The redefinition of heroin addiction as a social disease had the potential to bring in a wider range of non-medical actors to deal with heroin use and the problems it posed. Concern about heroin addiction led to the establishment of a number of different voluntary organisations performing a variety of roles.[89] Release, established in 1967, offered legal advice to individuals arrested for drug offences. They also campaigned on drug issues such as the legalisation of cannabis and the provision of treatment facilities for heroin addicts.[90] Other street-based organisations offered general advice, counselling and social support to heroin addicts. Many of these so-called 'street agencies', such as the Blenheim Project and the Community Drug Project, also allowed addicts to inject on the premises.[91] Some groups, such as New Horizon, even provided clean injecting equipment.[92]

Another area that saw significant voluntary action was the 'rehabilitation' of heroin addicts. In 1967 the standing committee tasked by Brain with monitoring drug addiction, the Advisory Committee on Drug Dependence (ACDD), met to consider what they termed the 'rehabilitation' of addicts. They argued that while successful medical treatment would result in physical withdrawal from heroin, 'The aim of rehabilitation must be to re-educate the individual to live without drugs and to assume or resume a normal life.' If treatment in the DDUs was able to get addicts off drugs, 'rehabilitation' was supposed to result in them staying off. Although the ACDD asserted that 'rehabilitation begins with the first contact of the addict with the out-patient clinic' they believed inpatient facilities were best equipped to rehabilitate the addict. The committee offered no particular view as to what these facilities should comprise, noting that, 'there is room for much experimentation and it would be unrealistic to advocate any particular method or methods.'[93] Moreover, the ACDD were clear that rehabilitation could be offered in both the statutory and the non-statutory sectors but that these should be funded by local authorities rather than central government.

In practice, most of the rehabilitation facilities that were established in the late 1960s were run by voluntary organisations, albeit with statutory financial support. Many of these rehabilitation centres were therapeutic communities of one sort or another. Therapeutic communities had been in existence in Britain since the 1940s, when psychiatrists like Bion, Foulkes and Main created groups on inpatient psychiatric wards where the community was 'both patient and the instrument of treatment'.[94] But the idea that therapeutic communities could be used in the treatment of drug addiction came principally from the USA. Rooted in the self-help traditions of Alcoholics Anonymous and Narcotics Anonymous, during the late 1950s and early 1960s a number of therapeutic communities began to appear across America. Groups such as Synanon in California, Daytop Village and Phoenix House in New York were established to confront and then address the reasons behind an individual's drug use.[95] According to Mitchell Rosenthal, a psychiatrist involved with Phoenix House in New York, 'Treatment is directed towards the integration of clients into society as productive individuals.' For Rosenthal, rehabilitation from drug addiction extended 'beyond sustained abstinence to include changes in negative attitudes, values and behaviour (which are as much a part of the drug abuse syndrome as chemical dependency) and to the acquisition of social and vocational skills necessary to support a rewarding drug free lifestyle'.[96]

The American therapeutic communities had a significant impact on the development of facilities for the rehabilitation of addicts in Britain. Therapeutic communities drawing on American models were established, such as Phoenix House in Forest Hill, southeast London, in 1969. Phoenix House, London, was established by psychiatrist and addiction researcher Griffith Edwards, following a visit to the American therapeutic communities in 1966.[97] According to David Warren Holland, director of Phoenix House during the 1970s, the community was designed to 'provide total rehabilitation for an individual in an existential context by challenging all that which is positive and normal in him so that he can eventually overcome that which is distorted and sick in his own personality'. 'Addiction', he maintained, 'as a way of life is merely a symptom.'[98] For that reason, all addicts entering Phoenix House had to be drug-free.[99] That is, they were expected to have already achieved abstinence from drugs before commencing 'rehabilitation'.

Phoenix House was not the only therapeutic community established in this period; there was also Alpha House in Portsmouth, the Ley Community in Oxford, Suffolk House in Uxbridge, and Culverlands in Wickham, as well as a number of Christian-based therapeutic communities, like the Coke Hole Trust in Hampshire. Furthermore, the Phoenix philosophy and methods were by no means universally accepted; different communities had different approaches to achieving rehabilitation. But, taken together, the establishment of therapeutic communities was an important development. The collective presence of these organisations raised the implication that dealing thoroughly with addiction ran beyond the treatment offered in the DDUs. The therapeutic communities offered a two-fold critique of the accepted view of addiction and the treatment response offered to this through the DDUs. Firstly, by being totally abstinence oriented, the therapeutic communities undermined the notion that maintenance could be seen as treatment. Continued prescription, in their eyes, was perpetuating addiction. Secondly, by asserting that abstinence from drugs was itself just the beginning of a process of 'rehabilitation' and not the end state of addiction 'treatment', the therapeutic communities diluted the authority of the DDUs as effective sources of treatment for addiction. This could have resulted in tension between the therapeutic communities and psychiatrists involved in the treatment of addiction in the DDUs, but the two institutions actually came to perform complementary roles. The DDUs came to see their role as primarily withdrawing from drugs, while the therapeutic communities were designed to help addicts address underlying problems and remain drug-free. Yet the presence of the therapeutic communities highlighted the continued instability of ideas about addiction as well as further uncertainty about what the proper response to this condition should be.

CONCLUSION

The involvement of voluntary organisations and other non-medical actors in the treatment of addiction did not mean that the social had superseded the medical in understandings of addiction. Though addiction was described as a social disease, the central response to this was articulated through a medical framework. Addicts were to be given what was described as 'treatment', and this was administered by medical professionals working in a hospital. But treatment also offered a way of controlling the spread of drug addiction: the two aims were tightly bound together as control of the drug problem was exercised *through* treatment. Tasked with this dual role, the DDUs were at the heart of a response to the 'social infection' of heroin addiction. However the DDUs also came to be a site around which the establishment of the treatment of addiction as a specialist area of medicine (or more accurately, psychiatry) could develop. This was facilitated by two practical factors. Firstly, few other doctors were interested in treating addicts, and secondly, after 1968, the prescription of heroin to addicts was largely restricted to doctors working in the DDUs. Yet there were also a number of other, much broader, forces at work. The treatment of addiction became 'psychiatrised' —an area of psychiatric specialisation—as psychiatry itself expanded. Alongside a public health understanding of addiction as a social disease, a psychiatric notion of addiction as mental illness gained authority. The numerous, multifaceted ways in which these two approaches to addiction interacted are the subject of the next chapter.

CHAPTER THREE

Psychiatry and the Treatment of Heroin Addiction, 1969–1979

In a paper given to the Co-ordinating Committee for Symposia on Drug Action, Dr Philip Connell, a consultant psychiatrist at the Bethlem Royal and Maudsley Hospital, asserted that drug dependence presented a 'challenge to the practice of medicine'. Connell's lecture, published in an edited collection in 1969, outlined a series of problems posed by the growing number of heroin addicts and some of the difficulties likely to be encountered by those doctors who were engaged in their treatment. Firstly, Connell stated, there was a diagnostic problem. How could a doctor establish that the patient was indeed addicted to heroin? Secondly, even if the patient was addicted to heroin, what was the appropriate dose of drug to prescribe? How could overprescription be prevented? This was particularly worrying, as thirdly, the addict was 'a skilled manipulator who plays on the kindness and weakness of doctors'. Moreover, all of these difficulties were exacerbated by the final problem Connell presented: the lack of research on drug addiction. 'The physician', Connell noted, 'who is supposed to be an expert, has no immediate expertise to help him.'[1]

Examined in this chapter are the medical profession's response to these and other challenges by looking at the development of heroin addiction treatment over the course of the 1970s. There are two key areas of analysis. The first is the emergence of heroin addiction treatment as a specialist area of medicine, or, more accurately, psychiatry. This process, which H.B. 'Bing' Spear (former Chief Inspector of the Home Office Drugs Branch) referred to as the 'psychiatrising' of addiction treatment policy, was reflected not just in the establishment of the DDUs in the psychiatric departments of the London teaching hospitals but also in the growing role played by psychiatrists in advising the government on drug policy and in the growth of addiction research.[2] Psychiatrists became the leading experts on drug addiction, offering their advice through bodies such as the Medical Research Council (MRC) working group on the evaluation of different methods of treatment for drug dependence, the Advisory Committee on Drug Dependence (ACDD) and later the Advisory Council on the Misuse of Drugs (ACMD). The emergence of the addiction psychiatrist as a specialist and as an expert took place at the same time as psychiatry itself began to expand and grow in status. Organisational changes, such as the incorporation of psychiatric hospitals within mainstream hospital services, coupled with the development of new, seemingly successful, pharmacological treatments for various mental illnesses, helped elevate what had long been seen as a low status medical speciality.[3] Psychiatry was an increasingly confident force.

At the same time, a body of academic research on drugs and addiction began to develop, partly through the efforts of the Addiction Research Unit (ARU). This further helped confirm the treatment of addiction as a specialist area. However not all of the research being conducted into drug addiction at places like the ARU automatically added weight to the psychiatrists' claims to expert status in addiction. Other kinds of knowledge were being produced about drugs as social scientists (sociologists, epidemiologists, social psychologists and others) became interested in heroin addiction and the problems it posed. Yet the 'psychiatrisation' of addiction treatment in this period was largely uncontested. This was partly due to the intense stigmatisation experienced by addict-patients. And, as a more detailed exploration of how addiction treatment was viewed (both by the doctors administering it and by the addicts receiving it) will reveal, addicts were a particularly problematic type of patient, and this clearly had implications for the doctor-patient relationship.

The dealings between addicts and doctors bring us to the second major area of analysis in this chapter: the nature of clinical practice in the treatment of addiction during the late 1960s and early 1970s. This section will look at some of the measures put in place to deal with the practical challenges highlighted by Connell, such as determining the appropriate dose to prescribe addict-patients. It is argued that these decisions were informed not so much by research as by clinical experience and the desire to achieve other goals, such as preventing diversion of drugs to the black market. This can also be seen in the way in which a fundamental change in addiction treatment in this period was introduced. When the DDUs were first established, between 60 and 80 per cent of patients received prescriptions for heroin, but by the end of the 1970s this practice had almost entirely disappeared as heroin was replaced by the opiate substitute methadone.[4] Although those instigating this change employed research to support it, the actual evidence for the value of methadone over heroin as a form of treatment was more equivocal.[5] Practitioners drew instead on American experience with methadone, which helped create the notion that methadone was a more 'medicinal' or 'therapeutic' drug than heroin. This did not mean, however, that the medical view of addiction had finally succeeded. Even within this new treatment modality, ideas about using treatment to control heroin addiction and heroin addicts persisted. The treatment of heroin addiction, therefore, remained an amalgamation of social and medical approaches.

THE 'PSYCHIATRISING' OF ADDICTION

Spear's description of the 'psychiatrising' of addiction during the late 1960s and early 1970s is a useful one, even if his discussion of how and why such a process took place is less adequate. Spear argued that in the period between the second Brain report and the opening of the DDUs, the Ministry of Health had turned to psychiatrists like Thomas Bewley and Philip Connell instead of appealing to the GPs who were thought to be responsible for the overprescription of heroin but who had nonetheless dealt with the majority of addicts.[6] Spear argued that the experience of the addict-friendly GPs was ignored in favour of the 'London psychiatric establishment', but he was unable to offer any explanation for how addiction became the 'fiefdom of the consultant psychiatrist' beyond thinly veiled attacks on the influence of 'medical politicians'.[7] This is plainly insufficient. A range of other aspects during this period needs to be considered, including the development of psychiatry as an area of medical practice.

The Development of Psychiatry, 1950s–1970s

It has long been accepted that a clear hierarchy of specialties exists within medicine, that 'high technology medicine such as cardiology and transplant surgery takes priority over mental health or geriatrics'.[8] As Charles Webster has demonstrated, mental health services were in a weak position in the early NHS, affecting the standing of psychiatry as a whole.[9] In the late 1950s and early 1960s, this situation gradually began to change. A number of factors were involved in this process, many of which were similar to those that had proved crucial to the establishment of other fields of medical speciality. George Weisz has pointed to the importance of the growth of medical research and education, the recognition by government of the specialty, the development of specialist administrative bodies and the increasing faith of the lay public in the notion of expertise as vital to the establishment of medical specialisation.[10] Many of these same developments can be seen in psychiatry during this period. Although psychiatry had been developing as a specialty since at least the eighteenth century, it had often existed outside and away from other medical services.[11] But during the mid-twentieth century, treatment for mental illness was increasingly provided in the same way as for other diseases: psychiatric hospitals were brought within the remit of the NHS in 1948, and mental health services were re-organised in the context of general medical services in the Hospital Plan of 1962.[12] The Hospital Plan also consolidated a drift towards community as opposed to hospital-based treatment for the mentally ill, as large public asylums closed and their patients were transferred to care in the community. This represented an internal reform of psychiatry, as psychiatrists went some way towards addressing concerns about the incarceration of the mentally ill and the critiques of madness offered by the anti-psychiatrists.[13]

The change of focus from the institution to the community was accompanied by a shift in ideas about, and definitions of, mental illness. As Roy Porter remarked, the decline of the psychiatric institution 'did not entail any withering away of psychiatry itself. Far from it: there was to be marked and continued growth in the numbers receiving psychiatric treatment.'[14] Attention switched from the most severe mental illnesses to more 'borderline' and supposedly widespread conditions such as depression, phobias, alcoholism and drug addiction. For Porter, this was representative of the 'psychiatrisation of everything', a process Nikolas Rose saw as part of the emergence of a 'therapeutic society' in which a whole range of 'psy' practices based on psychotherapeutic techniques offered counsel to individuals for an equally large array of problems.[15] As psychiatric conditions proliferated, so the expert status of the psychiatrist grew. Indeed, 'psychiatrisation' was not a term coined by Spear but describes a much wider process that took place during the twentieth century. Foucault described the 'psychiatrisation' of perverse behaviour in The History of Sexuality. He argued that a medico-moral discourse around certain kinds of behaviour produced specific subjects such as the perverse adult. Medical knowledge and expertise accumulated around these subjects so that an authority on the particular subject was created.[16] Rose developed this line of analysis by arguing that regulation based on these 'psy' disciplines and practices created governable subjects by claiming to 'know' the individual.[17] The power and authority of psychiatrists increased as they accumulated knowledge and expertise around certain kinds of subjects, like the addict.

This was further enhanced by the so-called 'pharmacological revolution' in psychiatry. According to Shorter, during the 1950s and 1960s, 'a veritable cornucopia of antipsychotic, antimanic, and antidepressant drugs poured forth, changing psychiatry from a branch of social work to a field that called for the most precise knowledge of pharmacology'.[18] Anti-psychotic drugs like chlorpromazine (Thorazine) were used in the treatment of schizophrenia during the 1950s, and these were followed by yet more new drugs such as cholordiazepoxide (Librium) and diazepam (Valium), which seemed to offer effective treatments for the new conditions identified by psychiatry, like anxiety and depression.[19] This therapeutic optimism helped further increase the confidence of psychiatrists, a mood epitomised by the foundation of the Royal College of Psychiatrists in 1971.[20] Psychiatry was thus well placed conceptually and organisationally during this period to take on the treatment of drug addiction.

The Making of Psychiatric Expertise around Addiction— Advising the Government on 'Drug Dependence'

Though it was Rolleston who had first suggested that addiction was more likely to be found in those with a history of 'mental or nervous instability', Brain was later unequivocal that addiction was 'an expression of mental disorder', and the best place for the treatment of the addict was the psychiatric ward of a general hospital.[21] By the late 1960s addiction was increasingly being seen as a disease without a clear biological cause. The Chairman of the Biological Council's Coordinating Committee for Symposia on Drug Action suggested in his introduction to a session on the social and clinical aspects of drug abuse in 1968 that 'there is little evidence to suggest that addiction is a disease in the biological sense.' Instead, 'social and psychological factors may have determined the onset of drug use.'[22]

It appeared to officials that psychiatrists, long tasked with dealing with the seemingly similar disease of alcoholism, knew more about this kind of problem than any other medical specialty.[23] Many of the doctors the Ministry of Health turned to for advice on the creation of the DDUs, such as Max Glatt, were psychiatrists with experience treating alcoholics.[24] Few, however, of these doctors had actually seen many drug addicts. Bewley told an interviewer from the journal *Addiction* that he became an 'expert' on addiction in 1964 when he had seen only 20 addict-patients, but this was far more than any other doctor had seen. He commented, 'This was how I became an "expert." I knew little, but everyone else knew less.'[25] Spear has been critical of the nature of this early expertise. He argued that psychiatrists credited with expert status in this area by the Ministry of Health were a 'Who's Who of the London psychiatric establishment', and doctors with any real experience of dealing with addicts, including the overprescribing GPs and a handful of unconventional psychiatrists, were not consulted.[26]

To explain this, the processes that led to the creation of an area of expertise need to be considered. For addiction to be thoroughly 'psychiatrised', psychiatry had to exclude generalists and those who did not adhere to the standard interpretation of addiction and its treatment in order to construct a unified body of expert knowledge. The exclusivity of addiction was reinforced by a change in the way the condition was described, as 'addiction' became 'drug dependence'. At the MRC Conference on Research into Drug Dependence in 1968, the Deputy Chairman, Sir Harold Himsworth, proposed that 'for the sake of semantic clarity the term "drug dependence" be used in place of all similar terms'.[27] It is likely that the MRC were taking their lead from the World Health Organisation's (WHO) Expert Committee on Addiction-Producing Drugs, who proposed in 1965 that the term 'drug dependence' be used instead of 'drug addiction', as this would eliminate the confusion of existing terminology.[28] This linguistic shift was, however, more than simple clarification; it confirmed the 'psychiatrisation' of addiction by creating a psychiatric term for the condition. Berridge has argued that 'addiction' seemed to place too much emphasis on the physical consequences of drug taking, whereas 'dependence' was intended to convey the psychological aspects of this condition.[29] Both terms were used seemingly interchangeably during the 1960s and 1970s, but 'drug dependence' was the more 'official' description—as exemplified by the use of 'Drug Dependence Unit', 'Advisory Committee on Drug Dependence' and the MRC 'Working Parties on Drug Dependence'.

The use of this term strongly suggests that the psychiatrisation of addiction was closely entwined with the formation of drug policy. Further evidence for the increasingly powerful role played by psychiatrists can be found by examining their position in the establishment and running of a number of bodies tasked with investigating addiction and advising on appropriate methods of dealing with this. Psychiatrists dominated the MRC working group set up in 1968 to evaluate different methods of treatment for drug dependence.[30] Although Anthony Dornhorst, a physiologist, chaired the group, the rest of the party were nearly all psychiatrists: Connell, Bewley, Owens and Willis all ran DDUs, and Gelder and Cawley worked at the Maudsley, the foremost psychiatric hospital in Britain. The remaining members were Spicer, a medical statistician, and D'Obran, a prison medical officer.[31]

Psychiatrists were also heavily represented on the Advisory Committee on Drug Dependence (ACDD). The ACDD was convened in 1966 as a result of the Brain Committee's recommendation that a standing advisory committee be established to monitor the 'whole problem of drug addiction'.[32] The ACDD was tasked with keeping 'under review the misuse of narcotic and other drugs which are likely to produce dependence and to advise on remedial measures that might be taken'.[33] The committee were initially appointed for three years and continued to operate until 1971 when the Advisory Council on the Misuse of Drugs (ACMD) was created through the Misuse of Drugs Act to replace them.[34] It had been agreed that the committee be chaired by Lord Brain, but when he died later that year, he was replaced by Sir Edward Wayne, Professor of Medicine at Glasgow University and former Professor of Pharmacology and Therapeutics at Sheffield University. Though the committee clearly contained the 'broadly-based representation' envisaged by Brain—including two MPs, two journalists, one magistrate, one senior police officer, one retail pharmacist, one pharmacologist, one prison governor, one probation officer, one researcher into student problems, one sociologist, one headmaster, the general manager of the Glaxo Group and Baroness Wootton of Abinger—the fact that of the six doctors on the group half were psychiatrists was deeply significant.[35] The initial membership of the ACDD thus reflected the diversity of groups and individuals becoming interested in drug addiction and at the same time reiterated the central importance being accorded to the psychiatrist in dealing with this condition.

Researching Addiction

The establishment of the Addiction Research Unit (ARU) at the Institute of Psychiatry in 1967 also appeared to enhance the role of the psychiatrist. The Institute was based at the Maudsley (which itself had an excellent reputation for psychiatric teaching and research) and under the leadership of Aubrey Lewis was credited with some of the key developments in British psychiatry in this period.[36] The creation of the ARU at such an important centre for psychiatry was indicative of the extent to which addiction was regarded as a psychiatric condition. The Ministry of Health had also received a 'reassuring response' from Guy's Hospital and University College Hospital about the possibility of setting up a unit, but the Chief Medical Officer was in no doubt 'that the Maudsley is the right place for our main effort'.[37] Headed by a psychiatrist (Griffith Edwards) and supported by a number of other consultant and academic psychiatrists, the ARU was, on one level, another example of the increasing power and authority of the psychiatrist in dealing with addiction.[38] However, a closer examination of the early research conducted by the unit points to the importance of the social sciences in assessing addiction. This occurrence fostered tensions between clinical psychiatry and the social sciences and between treatment and research, which could be read as a resurgence of the conflict between the medical and the social.

In addition to its psychiatrically trained personnel, the ARU also employed a team of social scientists so that by 1969 they had 21 research staff.[39] The inclusion of these individuals in the work of the ARU indicates that there were non-psychiatric approaches to addiction in this period. Smart argues that the ARU was a 'manifestation of the optimism that flourished during the 1960s, which was based on a belief that (social) scientific work could discover the cause, and hence provide the remedy, to complex social problems'.[40] The existence of an alternative locus of expertise on addiction, accompanied by a view of the condition that stressed its social rather than medical elements, could have posed a threat to the exclusive authority of the psychiatrist, and there were tensions between those who conducted research into addiction and those who offered treatment for this condition.

This tension between treatment and research can be observed in the discrepancy between the kind of research projects proposed by the ARU and the MRC working groups and the actual studies conducted. Initial research to be carried out at the ARU was intended to provide 'basic data which can be expected to provide the answers needed for effective action to reverse the present upward trend in incidence [of addiction]'. Studies were to 'evaluate, as soon as possible, the best methods for treating addicts and preventing further spread of addiction'.[41] It was therefore proposed that not only should there be socio-psychological and epidemiological studies of addiction but also some research into treatment, including a study comparing the rapid withdrawal of drugs from addicts with continued prescription (maintenance).[42] However, a report on the ARU's first year suggests that the research being carried out at the unit was primarily concerned with the social context of heroin use rather than investigating treatment methods. Projects begun or contemplated included: an investigation into heroin use in a provincial town, a study on the effects of injected methedrine, a survey of drug taking among inner city London schoolchildren, a follow-up study of persons known to use heroin, a study of heroin users and their siblings, an examination of the lifestyles of heroin addicts and a study on the social functioning of heroin users.[43] There were no studies assessing the relative benefits of different forms of treatment.

Nor was this research conducted under the auspices of the MRC, despite the council's working group on treatment methods also identifying the evaluation of these as a high priority. The group had pointed to two main areas requiring investigation. The first concerned the role of the DDUs. Members of the working group pointed out 'that it was an article of faith that the treatment centre was a useful institution, serving a valuable purpose in the treatment and "cure" (however defined) of heroin addicts', but 'the role and value' of these 'had never been objectively assessed, and that in view of the money and manpower being invested in them, it was of crucial importance to make some attempt to do this'.[44] The second area they believed required investigation was the relative merits of prescribing methadone as opposed to heroin in the maintenance treatment of addicts. The working group 'hoped that regular methadone is less harmful than heroin in its physical and psychological effects, and may allow more opportunity for eventual withdrawal'. They noted that 'These propositions require to be proved [sic], but the intention is therapeutic.'[45] This connection with methadone with a more 'therapeutic' approach to the treatment of heroin addiction will be discussed at greater length below, but it would appear that the

Working Party had noted a shift in the prescription policies of clinics towards methadone as a replacement for heroin and felt that this should be investigated.[46]

A combined Home Office and MRC survey of research in progress on drug dependence presented to the Council in 1972 indicates that the work on the evaluation of treatment methods had still not been carried out. The report listed 108 projects, of which only twelve dealt with heroin or drug dependence more generally.[47] These twelve studies, with just one exception, were not concerned directly with treatment practices.[48] There were descriptive studies, such as Bewley's survey of heroin users attending three treatment centres. There was a study on the effect of addiction on the addicts' general health conducted by Professor Marks and an examination of the effects of drug addiction on pregnancy by Elizabeth Tylden. There was even a study comparing British and American treatment methods, but very little of this research was directed towards the practical treatment of addiction.[49]

This absence did not go unnoticed. A review of British heroin addiction treatment policy ten years after the establishment of the clinics by Griffith Edwards (the director of the ARU) presented a dismal picture of the state of research into the treatment response to heroin addiction. He asserted that 'Discussion of the future of treatment policies is much handicapped by a lack of current information on what is actually being done and what is actually effective.'[50] There was no clinical trial either of maintenance versus withdrawal or the relative values of prescribing methadone rather than heroin until Richard Hartnoll and Martin Mitcheson's study on heroin maintenance was published in 1980.[51] The implications of this highly contentious study will be discussed in detail below, but it is worth noting at this point that it was not until the National Treatment Outcome Research Study (NTORS) was initiated in 1995 that a thorough survey of the relative benefits of treatment methods was conducted.[52] According to Edwards, important questions remained unanswered about the effectiveness of the strategies employed by the DDUs throughout the 1970s and into the 1980s.[53] An assessment of the clinics and the services they offered was not conducted until 1982. In her national survey of the DDUs, sociologist Carol Smart noted, 'it is perhaps surprising that relatively little is known about how DDUs, especially those outside London, are staffed and organised and that even less is known about the broad treatment policy that individual DDUs might adopt'. Smart further contended that 'What studies we have of DDUs have tended to concentrate on London and have also tended to say more about the people using treatment centres than about DDUs themselves.' Smart asserted that her own study would provide the kind of 'empirical research' so far lacking in the drug dependence field and on which policy decisions should, she claimed, be made.[54]

Smart was not the sole proponent of such an argument. Gerry Stimson, in his assessment of drug policy and research in the 1980s, noted that 'there has been a marked lack of research on treatment, then and now' and that 'treatment policies proceed largely without empirical investigation'.[55] Jayne Love and Michael Gossop, in their examination of the processes of referral and disposal within a London DDU in 1983, asserted that there was 'surprisingly little detailed information about the operation of the drug clinics' and not much was known about 'what actually happens to the addict within a drug dependence clinic,' that 'few studies have looked at this issue on an empirical basis'.[56] Dr David Owen, MP, in a lecture to the Society of Clinical Psychiatrists Research Fund in 1985 also bemoaned the 'paucity of research' and the way policy decisions were taken 'ad hoc without a sustained medical strategy that was deeply rooted in medical and scientific evidence.'[57]

An explanation for the absence of this kind of research and the apparent lack of an empirical basis for treatment policies lies in the nature of the relationship between clinical practice and research in this period. The notion that research findings should strongly influence clinical practice is a relatively new concept. Since the 1990s 'evidence-based medicine' has gained ground. Recent guidelines on good clinical practice (including those on the treatment of addiction) have made use of evidence derived from research, but this was largely not the case in the 1970s and 1980s when these were much more closely based on clinical practice and experience.[58] Treatment policy evolved from the clinical setting and was directed by those psychiatrists actually involved in the treatment of addiction, not social scientists tasked with evaluating these.

There appears to have been a good deal of tension between those engaged in treatment and those conducting research. At the same time as the ARU was established, Connell created the Drug Dependence Clinical Research and Treatment Unit, also based at the Maudsley.[59] The unit provided both inpatient and outpatient treatment for addiction as well as promoting research.[60] There was obviously a degree of competition between this unit and the ARU. Discussions among Ministry of Health officials over a proposed visit by the Duke of Edinburgh to the Maudsley stressed that if the Duke were to visit the hospital he must see both Edwards's and Connell's units 'as there is a certain amount of rivalry between the two and a visit to one and not the other might cause difficulty'.[61] Connell's dislike of the Institute of Psychiatry, and his motives for setting up his own unit, were revealed in an interview he gave to the *British Journal of Addiction*. He asserted that including the term 'research' in his unit's name meant that research could be 'funnelled to the unit under my direction, rather than things having to go through the Institute of Psychiatry, which I later learned to my cost was interested in furthering its own research and service interests rather than trying to make a contribution to a very complex and unrewarding field'.[62] This suggests that Connell was not opposed to research per se; indeed, he had outlined the need for research into addiction on a number of occasions throughout the late 1960s, but rather he objected to research conducted by someone else into matters he did not consider important.[63] For Connell and other clinical psychiatrists there was a sharp distinction between the research conducted by epidemiologists, sociologists and other social scientists 'to produce by careful research, data relating to the causes of drug taking, methods of spread and suggestions relating to prevention' and 'the challenge to physicians to produce hard data relating to treatment programmes in order that [the] most effective methods can be delimited'.[64] The implication was that social scientists investigated the 'social' side of addiction but the 'medical' side—research into and the development of treatment methods—was to be left to psychiatrists.

THE DEVELOPMENT OF CLINICAL PRACTICE IN THE TREATMENT OF HEROIN ADDICTION

Going to the Clinic

A consideration of the development of clinical practice in the treatment of addiction strongly supports the notion that such a divide existed. Treatment policy between 1968 and 1979 developed under the direction of psychiatrists with little input from social scientists, politicians, government officials or any other bodies and individuals. This should not, however, necessarily be read as a victory for the 'medical' over the 'social'; these two forces continued to interact and work together to shape the treatment of addiction. This can be observed in the way the DDUs operated and the way they dealt with their addict-patients. When the clinics opened in April 1968, the doctors running them were woefully inexperienced. As has already been noted, there was a distinct lack of expertise in dealing with drug addiction, and subsequently many clinic doctors had never encountered a heroin addict prior to the establishment of the DDUs.[65] The first problem that presented itself to clinic staff was how to determine if a patient was addicted to heroin, and if a patient was, how much should be prescribed. Gardner and Connell at the Bethlem and Maudsley found that a positive urine test for the presence of opiate drugs could assist in diagnosis, but this did not prove that the patient was an addict, nor did it indicate what dose was required to prevent the onset of withdrawal symptoms.[66] Determining the correct amount to prescribe to an addict was a crucial decision, but there was no reliable test on which to base this assessment.[67] In their study of DDU practices Stimson and Oppenheimer found that, in order to arrive at a dose, clinic psychiatrists questioned addicts about their use of drugs, checked for needle marks and conducted urine tests but that the most reliable method for assessing dosage level was to admit the addict to hospital where reactions to different amounts of opiates could be closely monitored; however, this seemed to be a rare occurrence, as inpatient admission was costly and time-consuming, and many DDUs lacked the facilities to admit patients for this purpose.[68] The most common way of determining the amount to prescribe, according to Stimson and Oppenheimer, was for the doctor to ask the addict what they would like to be prescribed and then divide it by two. This decision was based not on any 'scientific' evidence but on 'a simple rule of thumb'.[69] It is likely that these unreliable methods of dosage determination, coupled with doctors' inexperience, led to the overprescription of heroin to addicts attending clinics in the first year of their operation.[70]

Doctors working at DDUs found that addicts were unlike patients they had encountered in other areas of medicine. Margaret Tripp, a psychiatrist who ran the DDU at St Clement's Hospital between 1968 and 1971, noted that many addicts did not consider themselves 'sick'.[71] This observation paralleled an American study of methadone patients, which found that while 95 per cent of doctors thought their addict-patients were mentally ill, the 'vast majority' of addicts disagreed.[72]

This had implications for the doctor-patient relationship (between clinician and addict) and the treatment offered. Being, or allowing, oneself to be labelled as 'sick' conferred certain attributes. In *The Social System* Talcott Parsons developed one of the most important models describing the social expectations and obligations of taking on the sick role.[73] He found that becoming sick allowed an individual to be excused from the performance of normal social obligations and also exempted that person from responsibility for their own state. However, these were contingent on two obligations: to want to get well as soon as possible, and to seek technically competent help and cooperate with medical experts.[74] Although Parsons's formulation remains a central concept in medical sociology, it has been frequently criticised, principally because it appears to lack empirical validity.[75] There were a large range of conditions in which the sick role did not seem to apply. Addiction was clearly one of these: addicts often failed to fulfil the obligations expected of them, principally because many addicts did not believe they were sick. For critics of the disease-based notion of addiction, such as Thomas Szasz, '"addiction" refers not to a disease but to a despised kind of deviance. Hence the term "addict" refers not to a bona fide patient but to a stigmatised identity, usually stamped upon a person against his or her will.'[76]

Indeed, there was clearly a distinction between the sick role and the patient role in the treatment of addiction. Stimson and Oppenheimer found that addicts frequently went to clinics because they wanted a clean, legitimate, regular supply of drugs 'but such attendance did not, for many, commit them to seeing that they needed "treatment" in the sense of medical help, a "cure", and eventual abstinence'.[77] What is more, addicts were often in direct conflict with DDU doctors, demanding, cajoling, threatening and pleading with staff to be prescribed more drugs.[78] Here it could be suggested that addicts were behaving in some ways like patient-consumers. The notion of patient as consumer was beginning to gain ground in healthcare more generally during the late 1960s and early 1970s.[79] Although this concept was to have little direct impact on the actual delivery of addiction treatment services until the 1990s, elements of a more consumerist approach can perhaps be discerned in the willingness of addicts to make demands of treatment services and the health professionals offering these.[80]

The powerful demands that addict-patients made of treatment services, coupled with the apparent unwillingness of some addicts to want to get well, combined to make addicts 'difficult' patients, but also, more fundamentally, called into question the role of the psychiatrist in treating him or her. Questioning the sickness of the addict threatened the disease-based nature of addiction and thus the doctor's role in 'treating' this. Many doctors working in clinics raised these same issues, as they were unsure what treatments to offer or even what 'treatment' meant in the context of addiction. 'Treatment' in the early years of the DDUs varied widely from clinic to clinic.[81] Some clinics prescribed intravenous heroin, others prescribed intravenous methadone, others would only give addicts oral methadone. There were even variations within clinics, with some patients receiving prescriptions for heroin and others methadone. Still others were not offered drugs at all but instead were given psychotherapy, group therapy and/or occupational therapy.[82] The rationale behind these treatments was also deeply significant. Stimson and Oppenheimer noted that 'treatment' was 'often a euphemism for other goals and we have to look not just at what was done to or for the patients, but also at the clinicians' motivations in so acting'.[83] They found that many of the psychiatrists they spoke to in 1976 regarded their work as 'control' or 'containment' of the drug problem and talked about the 'benefits to society' of their work. Therapy was still a concern, but Stimson and Oppenheimer felt it was unusual to see such a concern for social control within medical practice.

Treatment of the addict and social control of addiction through clinical practice came then not just from the stated dual purpose of the clinics but also from the treatment setting. Doctors found that it was difficult to 'treat' a 'patient' who did not accept that he or she was sick. Their work then took on the function of social control; however, some clinicians were uncomfortable with their role as social controllers. A clinic doctor interviewed by Stimson and Oppenheimer said that doctors resented having to act like 'policemen with white coats on'.[84] If psychiatrists were simply handing out prescriptions to addicts with no attempt to get them off drugs they could be said to be 'overpaid grocer[s]' or 'dealers by appointment to H.M. Government'.[85] Many

DDU doctors disliked prescribing heroin to addicts on a maintenance basis because it conflicted with 'therapeutic ideals, for patients who were maintained, it was argued, were not being cured of their addiction'.[86] Prescribing heroin to heroin addicts might benefit society, but it did not appear to cure the individual addict of the disease.

The Introduction of Methadone

A change in the prescription polices of the DDUs in the early 1970s suggested a rejection of the social control of addiction through maintenance as well as a resurgence of a more 'medical' form of treatment directed towards the 'cure' of addiction. There was a discernable shift away from the prescription of injectable heroin, first to injectable methadone and then later to orally administered methadone. In July 1968, 2,690 grams of heroin was prescribed to patients attending DDUs. By December 1970, this amount had fallen to 1,358 grams.[87] In 1968 it was estimated that between 60 and 80 per cent of addicts were receiving prescriptions for heroin, or heroin and methadone, compared to 31 per cent of addicts in 1970.[88] At the same time as the amount of heroin being prescribed and the proportion of addicts receiving prescriptions for this drug were falling, the amount of methadone prescribed and the percentage of addicts taking opiate substitutes increased. In August 1969, 918 grams of methadone was prescribed by clinics to addicts, but just sixteen months later, in December 1970, this increased to 1,131 grams.[89] This meant that, in 1970, 51 per cent of addicts were receiving prescriptions for methadone or other heroin substitutes. Over the decade this trend continued so that, by 1978, 71 per cent of addicts were being prescribed methadone, and just nine per cent were receiving prescriptions for heroin, or heroin and methadone.[90] A similar pattern was replicated on the micro-scale. A study of the prescription records from the Maudsley DDU between 1968 and 1983 found that, for the first five years of the clinic's life, more than half the prescriptions issued were for heroin, but by 1973 oral methadone was increasingly prescribed so that by the early 1980s it accounted for two thirds of prescriptions.[91]

There was a definite move away from the prescription of heroin to addicts and towards the prescription of substitute drugs, such as methadone during the 1970s, but this shift was not based on a policy decision taken by government ministers, civil servants or advisory bodies such as the ACDD; it evolved through clinical practice.[92] Clinic doctors gradually began to prescribe less heroin and more methadone to their addict-patients. This development requires explanation on two levels: firstly, to explain how methadone replaced heroin as the main drug being prescribed to addicts and secondly, to understand why this change took place. Prescribing methadone rather than heroin did have a number of advantages. Its longer half-life meant that it could be taken less frequently, allowing the addict a more 'normal' life without the constant interruptions of having to inject.[93] Injectable methadone was cheaper than injectable heroin, although surprisingly little reference is made to this in the contemporary literature, suggesting that this was not a major factor in the decision to adopt the drug.[94] Methadone could also be administered orally, thus removing the dangers of infection that came with intravenous injection.[95]

Methadone's 'image', however, was as important as the practical benefits its use conferred. The opioid substitute methadone was developed by German scientists in the 1940s and had been used as part of inpatient withdrawal treatment in American hospitals during the early 1950s.[96] But it was not until the 1960s that methadone was trialled on a maintenance basis. Vincent Dole and Marie Nyswander gave methadone to heroin addicts and found that they behaved 'better' while taking the drug; they were more likely to be in work or education, less likely to be committing crime and, crucially, they seemed to avoid taking heroin while on methadone.[97] Dole and Nyswander argued that long-term use of heroin resulted in structural changes in the body's metabolism, and another drug (methadone) was required to regulate these changes.[98] This biological view of addiction as a problem requiring a pharmacological solution concurred with the more general resurgence of biological psychiatry and the pharmacological revolution. According to Courtwright, for supporters of methadone treatment, 'Methadone was to addiction what insulin was to diabetes, a medically appropriate answer to a genuine disease'.[99] Methadone maintenance did become more widely used in addiction treatment in the USA during the 1970s but primarily as a result of its perceived benefits in reducing drug-related crime, not because of a wholesale endorsement of the biological view of addiction. Outpatient methadone maintenance was first trialled by Jerome Jaffe in Chicago in 1968. The apparent success of Jaffe's work—and a similar programme adopted by Robert DuPont in Washington, DC, where over a four-month period only 2.6 per cent of methadone patients had been arrested, compared to the 26 per cent who had tried to become abstinent and the 50 per cent of those who had dropped out—convinced the Nixon White House of the potential value of methadone maintenance.[100] In 1971 Jaffe was appointed to run the Special Office for Drug Abuse Prevention (SODAP) and tasked with rolling out methadone maintenance across the country.[101]

Interest in the American approach to drug addiction among an emerging group of British drug addiction specialists was high. Edwards visited America in the late 1960s and brought back with him the idea of introducing a drug-free residential therapeutic community for the rehabilitation of addicts, similar to Synanon, Daytop and Phoenix House.[102] Bewley also went to the USA on a WHO fellowship to study treatment methods in 1967. He reported his findings to the MRC and in an article in the *Bulletin on Narcotics*.[103] Bewley was impressed by the range of treatments offered but was particularly convinced of the value of methadone prescription. After his visit Bewley thought that 'we should change over to methadone by a process of gradual evolution. Vincent Dole was the most intelligent and rational person I met on my trip and I thought he had shown very clearly the value of a long-acting opiate.'[104] Yet Dole and Nyswander's experiment initially seemed to offer little in terms of direct applicability to treatment in DDUs. Firstly, Dole and Nyswander gave addicts methadone orally, which had to be taken in front of the doctor or nurse, whereas in the early days of the clinics, British addicts were accustomed to prescriptions of injectable heroin to be consumed in private.[105] Secondly, Dole and Nyswander claimed that if methadone were taken at sufficiently high doses, it would saturate the addicts' nerves and prevent them from getting 'high' if they took heroin while also being prescribed methadone.[106] British experts were sceptical about this 'methadone blockade' and suggested that this would not work with British addicts, as they were already accustomed to higher doses of heroin.[107] For DDU psychiatrist Martin Mitcheson, Dole and Nyswander's experiment's real importance for British drug treatment was that it gave methadone a 'respectable image'.[108] According to a group of psychiatrists and psychologists, methadone was 'in public and professional eyes' a 'medicinal drug', whereas heroin was a 'drug of abuse'.[109] Prescribing addicts methadone had the appearance of being a more medical approach, having acquired this status from its use in the USA and also because it was not the drug most addicts were taking before they presented themselves for medical treatment. Prescribing methadone thus differentiated what DDUs were prescribing from addicts' own self-medication with illicit heroin.

A study evaluating the prescription of methadone and heroin to addicts appeared, to many DDU psychiatrists, to endorse the prescription of methadone to addict-patients. In 1972 Martin Mitcheson and Richard Hartnoll conducted a randomised controlled trial at University College Hospital DDU to compare the prescription of injectable heroin to addicts with the prescription of oral methadone. Over a three-year period a total of ninety-six addicts were randomly allocated into two groups; the first were prescribed heroin on a maintenance basis (HM), and the second were prescribed oral methadone on a maintenance basis (OM).[110] Hartnoll and Mitcheson assessed patients at the end of the trial period on drop-out rate, illicit opiate use, frequency of injection, non-opiate use, involvement with drug subculture, employment, health and criminal activity. Among the most significant of their findings was that 90 per cent of the HM group were still injecting heroin one year later, compared to 57 per cent of the OM group.[111] Hartnoll and his colleagues interpreted this to mean that prescribing heroin to addicts maintained the 'status quo', with the addict showing little sign of change in lifestyle or in coming off drugs, whereas prescribing methadone to addicts instead 'may be seen as a more active policy of confrontation that is associated with greater change'.[112] There were, however, other consequences of refusing to prescribe heroin to addicts and giving them methadone instead. Hartnoll and Mitcheson noted that 70 per cent of the OM group were convicted of a crime during the trial period, compared with only half of the HM group.[113] They also found that 76 per cent of the HM group were still visiting the clinic one year later, whereas only 29 per cent of the OM group were regularly attending.[114] This would indicate that prescribing heroin led to less criminal activity among addicts and also resulted in more of them remaining in contact with treatment services when compared with prescription of methadone. This contradicted the American studies that seemed to show that methadone prescription resulted in crime reduction, but in the USA the prescription of heroin to addicts was prohibited, and so methadone was being prescribed in a very different context.

Hartnoll and Mitcheson were guarded in their conclusions. They argued that their findings should 'contribute to a more informed discussion' of treatment options 'rather than provide an unequivocable [sic.] answer' and that these findings needed to be considered in conjunction with the desired treatment outcome and who it should benefit—society or the individual.[115] This was not, however, how the study was received. Mitcheson observed that his research was 'perceived by many staff in London clinics as clear evidence for replacing injectable heroin maintenance with oral prescribing' and 'this probably reflected the already formulated opinion that the policy of prescribing injectable drugs was, either or both, unhelpful to the patient and/or insupportable to therapeutically inclined staff.'[116] This assertion is supported by the relative amounts of heroin and methadone being prescribed; the figures quoted above indicate that methadone was already beginning to replace heroin as the primary drug prescribed to addicts before the study was published in 1980. As Hartnoll and Mitcheson presented their findings prior to publication, it is likely that many clinic doctors knew of the study and its results as early as 1976, but this was still after the switch to methadone had been made.[117] Indeed, Mitcheson felt the study was 'used as an after-the-decision confirmation'.[118] Stimson and Oppenheimer found that although most DDU doctors had heard of the study, few had actually read it, nor did they appreciate the caution that Hartnoll and his associates had expressed about the direct applicability of their results to a treatment situation. Instead, 'What concerned them more, as several consultants indicated, was that here was scientific justification for a policy change that was already emerging from the work context.'[119]

This remark hints at another reason for the change from the prescription of heroin to the prescription of oral methadone—clinical frustration. Psychiatrists working in treatment centres began to question the value of prescribing heroin to addicts on a number of grounds. By the mid 1970s it was clear that clinics were no longer able to undercut the black market by prescribing heroin to addicts.[120] Illicit 'Chinese' heroin could be bought in London's West End from 1967, but its popularity grew as clinics took over the treatment of addicts and the availability of pharmaceutical heroin decreased.[121] There were other concerns that sprang directly from the treatment situation. As already indicated, addicts could be 'difficult' patients, and this coupled with the lack of therapeutic success resulting from treatment (Stimson and Oppenheimer found that only 38 per cent of their sample of addict-patients had become abstinent in ten years) led to 'battle-fatigue', 'stagnation' and 'frustration' among 'demoralised' clinic staff.[122] This prompted a move towards the prescription of methadone instead of heroin to addicts, as methadone was seen to be more 'respectable', 'therapeutic' and could be used in a more 'confrontational' treatment response designed to provoke change in addict behaviour.[123] The introduction of methadone, it was hoped, would 'cure' addicts.

A greater emphasis on the 'cure' of addiction was given additional importance by the changing administrative context in which the DDUs operated. Increasing evaluation of the DDUs encouraged a response that more readily moved addicts through the clinic system, resulting in a 'cure'. In 1975 the ACMD set up a working group to review the treatment facilities provided by the DDUs, producing an interim report in 1977.[124] Though the report made few recommendations, recognising that a much wider investigation of treatment services was required (the resulting report, *Treatment and Rehabilitation* is discussed in more detail in Chapter Four), it represented a more evaluative approach to the work of the DDUs. As drug use began to increase exponentially, attention refocused on the success or otherwise of the DDUs in dealing with drug addiction. An editorial in *The Lancet* in 1982 opined that the policy of long-term prescription to some patients left the DDUs 'in a position akin to that of a geriatric ward with its beds blocked'.[125] Addict-patients were not leaving the DDU as they were not being 'cured'. The prescription of oral methadone on a fixed term basis seemed to offer a chance to reverse this trend by providing a more 'confrontational' response, provoking change in the addict, leading to a 'cure' and the addict's subsequent removal from DDU patient lists. The administrative and financial implication of this was not lost on Mitcheson; he noted that the 'prior introduction of time limited prescribing [in the 1970s] may . . . have subsequently enabled clinics to respond to the increased number of new referrals [in the early 1980s], without necessitating increasing staff and budgets'.[126]

Despite these non-medical factors involved in the adoption of the prescription of methadone by the DDUs, this was largely interpreted as a more 'medical' response because of its emphasis on 'cure'. Moreover, it was an approach that was not just 'medical' but seen as specifically 'psychiatric'. In her study of DDU practices, Smart found that 90 per cent of the clinics surveyed thought that individual psychotherapy was either a 'very important' or an 'important' part of the treatment they offered, compared to the 97 per cent who believed heroin maintenance was not important or not their policy.[127] Lart asserted that this was indicative of a shift in emphasis on the part of DDU psychiatrists from trying to contain the epidemic of drug use to focus on the addicts they saw. Methadone was thus a way of 'Challenging those patients therapeutically, and perhaps changing some of them . . . "curing" them of the disease of addiction, was more important than trying to control society's drug use'.[128]

This characterisation, however, ignores the retention of a strong social dimension to the treatment provided by the DDUs. DDUs did not just offer treatment for addiction: they attempted to control the spread of this condition by placing strict controls on the behaviour of addict-patients. Addicts were required to pick up prescriptions on a daily basis so they would never have a surplus that could be sold to other addicts.[129] Addicts were asked to sign 'contracts' agreeing to attend regular treatment sessions, reduce their drug dosage by fixed amounts and be drug-free by a certain date.[130] The introduction of these methods would suggest that DDU psychiatrists did not entirely reject their role as social controllers, but at the same time enhanced control measures also had some value as 'treatment', providing the addict with a structure, stability and targets.[131] Treatment and control, the 'medical' and the 'social', were thus bound even more tightly together through DDU practices.

CONCLUSION—GROWING HOMOGENEITY IN THE TREATMENT OF ADDICTION

In contrast to their early heterogeneous response to addiction, the DDUs gradually became more homogenous so that by the end of the 1970s all clinics offered essentially the same treatment to addict-patients.[132] Replacing intravenously administered heroin with oral methadone became the orthodox method of treatment for new patients at DDUs from 1976/7.[133] In 1978 Stimson and Oppenheimer found that there were only three clinics in London that would prescribe injectable drugs to new patients.[134] Consensus on this issue was based around an informal code of practice and maintained through peer pressure within the group of London DDU consultants.[135] These doctors met regularly from 1968 onwards, first at the Department of Health and Social Security and later at the Home Office, to discuss treatment policies.[136] Spear, who attended these meetings, stated that ceasing the prescription of injectable drugs to addicts was first mooted in 1975 when the proposal was greeted with general acceptance among clinic psychiatrists.[137] Although some doctors continued to prescribe injectable heroin to addicts during this period, this became less and less common. James Willis, consultant psychiatrist at Guy's Hospital DDU, argued that the situation deteriorated into a 'race' to see who could prescribe the least heroin.[138] Influential DDU psychiatrists such as Connell called for 'a uniform approach' to the prescription of drugs to stop addicts from 'shopping around' for extra, or larger, supplies of drugs.[139] Uniformity on prescription rapidly turned into uniformity on treatment as all DDUs offered essentially the same approach. But, as clinics narrowed the range of treatment they also narrowed the range of addicts who could be treated successfully. A handful of doctors recognised that greater uniformity in DDU treatment policies might discourage some addicts from attending clinics altogether.[140] Stimson and Oppenheimer spoke to a consultant who prescribed only oral methadone but admitted that this was something of a 'cul-de-sac' response, as it disregarded individual difference and treated all addicts the same.[141]

TABLE 1 SOURCE OF FIRST NOTIFICATIONS OF HEROIN ADDICTION, 1970, 1975, 1980 AND 1981

	1970	1975	1980	1981
Treatment Centres (DDUs)	163 (46%)	202 (40%)	463 (39%)	602 (36%)
GPs	20 (6%)	118 (23%)	499 (42%)	791 (48%)
Prison Medical Officers	170 (48%)	191 (37%)	219 (19%)	267 (16%)

Source: ACMD, *Treatment and Rehabilitation: Report of the Advisory Council on the Misuse of Drugs* (London: HMSO, 1982), 120.

Addicts who did not find the treatment response put forward by the DDUs suitable sought drugs, and/or treatment, elsewhere. The ACMD's 1982 report, *Treatment and Rehabilitation*, found that, in 1970, 46 per cent of notifications of heroin addiction came from treatment centres, 48 per cent from prison medical officers and just 6 per cent from GPs. By 1981 the proportion of notifications from treatment centres had fallen to 36 per cent and those by prison medical officers to 16 per cent, but GPs now accounted for 48 per cent of notifications (see Table 1).[142] This shift towards the generalist was, stated the report, an 'unplanned development' over which there were a 'number of causes for concern'.[143] The issues raised by this development require thorough exploration and will be dealt with in Chapter Four, but it is clear that there was a growing trend towards the involvement of doctors outside the DDUs in treating addiction from the late 1970s and into the early 1980s. The very homogeneity of the clinic response led to heterogeneity in the treatment of addiction outside the DDU.

The Heroin Explosion and the Re-intervention of the Generalist, 1980–1987

In 1985–1986 the government-run Central Office of Information launched an anti-drug campaign targeting would-be heroin users. Designed by top advertising agency Yellowhammer and costing £2 million, the campaign consisted of advertisements in teenage magazines, billboard posters and even a 30-second television commercial.[1] Based around the tag line 'Heroin Screws You Up', the advertisements depicted the consequences of heroin use in graphic detail. One image, entitled 'Your Mind Isn't The Only Thing Heroin Damages', depicted a pale, sick-looking young man in a sweat-soaked shirt, sitting hunched over on the floor. Surrounding him were labels indicating some of the physical complications of intravenous heroin use, including skin infections and blood diseases as well as the symptoms of withdrawal, such as aching limbs and wasted muscles. The images were clearly designed to shock, drawing heavily on contemporary fears about the consequences of heroin use. Yet the 'Heroin Screws You Up' campaign was also deeply contentious. Some advisors to the government (including members of the Department of Health and Social Security) warned that it was doubtful whether the advertisements would make a significant impact on those already using heroin and would dissuade only those unlikely to take the drug in any case from doing so.[2] The campaign appears to have backfired. Some young people read the staunchly anti-drug message as an example of government hypocrisy and displayed the posters on their bedroom walls as signs of their anti-establishment rebellion.[3]

Despite its dubious outcome, 'Heroin Screws You Up' was representative of some key changes in the approach taken to dealing with heroin addiction during the

1980s. The very existence of this public health promotion campaign illustrates the extent to which heroin had become a problem of seemingly national significance. Heroin use had remained largely static during the early 1970s, but towards the end of the decade and into the 1980s, this increased dramatically. There were 2,016 known heroin addicts in 1977; by 1987 there were 10,389.[4] Moreover, heroin addiction appeared to be spreading across the country. Previously heroin use had been found almost solely in London but was now being reported in cities throughout Britain. To combat this growing crisis, a greater range of actors became involved in addressing different aspects of the heroin problem. The 'Heroin Screws You Up' campaign was part of a much more sustained interest in drug issues from the central government than had been seen in previous years. But it was not just politicians and civil servants who became more involved in dealing with heroin. A range of other bodies, such as voluntary organisations, joined what Berridge has described as the 'policy community' around illegal drugs.[5] Drug addiction treatment could not remain unaffected by these developments. Increasing numbers of addicts meant that an increasing number of doctors were required to treat them; however, many of these doctors were to be found not in the specialist DDUs but outside these, in private and general practice.

Examined here are the reasons why addicts sought out treatment away from the DDU, looking particularly at the re-intervention of the general practitioner. The role played by private doctors in the treatment of addiction will be considered in Chapter Five, but it is important to note that the involvement of both types of doctor posed a threat to the newly created specialist status of the DDU psychiatrist. These threats were slightly different, and so will be dealt with separately. GPs had been pushed aside by the creation of the DDUs, but in the 1980s they returned, albeit in fairly small numbers. Their participation in the treatment of addiction threatened the very nature of the specialist approach: if a GP could treat an addict, why were specialists required? The reaction of specialists to this threat was to attempt to re-iterate their expert status by arguing that GPs should be afforded only a limited role in the treatment of addiction. This approach can be discerned through a close analysis of the ACMD's 1982 report, *Treatment and Rehabilitation*. While *Treatment and Rehabilitation* claimed to present a pluralist view of addiction treatment, encouraging a range of medical and non-medical agencies to become involved in dealing with what it described as 'problem drug use', the report contained a powerful subtext that reinforced the specialist nature of treatment for heroin addiction. Under the influence of DDU psychiatrists, the ACMD recommended that though GPs might have a role to play in the treatment of addiction, this should only be under the close supervision of experts in the field. This could be seen as an essentially defensive move, as drug addiction specialists sought to protect their expert status by affording the generalist a fairly limited role and insisting that such a role be under their direction.

Tensions between specialists and generalists within medical practice were, of course, nothing new, but the divide between the hospital-based consultant and the community-based GP was strengthened in this period. There was something of a resurgence of generalism in the 1970s and 1980s after a long drift towards specialism. General practice was revitalised through its encounter with biographical medicine, which placed the patient instead of the disease at the centre of therapeutic endeavour. Here attention focused less on the diagnosis of disease than on the meaning of illness, less on the body and more on the patient him or herself. This gave the work of the GP new meaning and significance, helping reinvigorate general practice and elevate its status. Increasingly self-confident and self-reliant, GPs therefore posed a greater danger to the authority of the specialist than they had done previously, particularly in areas such as addiction, where the nature of that specialism was tenuous and already under threat from other bodies and authorities. Moreover, biographical medicine encouraged GPs and other community-based doctors to 'see' the 'disease' of addiction in a different way than their hospital-based, specialist colleagues. This resulted in further conflict between these groups—this time over treatment methods—a dispute that will be explored in greater detail throughout the rest of this book.

THE CHANGING NATURE OF HEROIN ADDICTION IN THE 1980s

The Changing Pattern of Heroin Use

Heroin addiction in the 1980s appeared to be a very different problem than the one encountered in previous decades. Gone was the confidence of the mid-1970s when addiction seemed to have 'fizzled out, like Hong Kong "flu"'.[6] The first indication that the pattern of heroin use was altering came in the form of an increase in the numbers of notified addicts. David Turner, of the voluntary organisation the Standing Conference on Drug Abuse (SCODA), told the *Daily Telegraph* in 1979 that Britain was on the brink of a heroin epidemic.[7] This assertion was repeated by SCODA's chairman, the Earl of Denbigh, in the House of Lords and echoed by Sir Bernard Braine MP (Conservative, Essex South-East) in the House of Commons later that year.[8] Braine and Denbigh found evidence for this 'heroin epidemic' in a sudden rise in the number of addicts notified to the Home Office.[9] The number of known heroin addicts had remained relatively static in the early 1970s, increasing by a few hundred between 1971 and 1973, and even decreasing between 1974 and 1976 (see Chart 1).[10] But from 1977 onwards, the number of known addicts rose from 2,016 to 2,402 in 1978 and to 2,666 in

1979.[11] This trend continued into the 1980s. Between 1980 and 1981, the number of notified addicts increased by almost a thousand.[12] This represented a 44 per cent increase in the number of new notifications— a rise, Bing Spear argued, that could not just be attributed to more accurate data collection.[13] Notifications to the Home Office continued to rise throughout the decade so that by 1987 there were 10,389 known addicts.[14] Despite better reporting of addiction, official figures were notoriously unreliable so the 'real' number of drug addicts could have been as much as five or even ten times greater than the reported figures.[15]

CHART 1   NUMBER OF KNOWN ADDICTS, 1958–1996

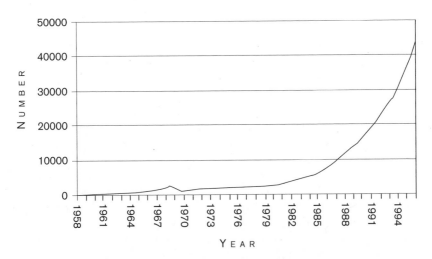

Sources: Ministry of Health, *Drug Addiction: Report of the Interdepartmental Committee* (London: HMSO, 1961): Ministry of Health, *Drug Addiction: The Second Report of the Interdepartmental Committee* (London: HMSO, 1965); ACMD, *Treatment and Rehabilitation: Report of the Advisory Council on the Misuse of Drugs* (London: Home Office, 1982); Home Office, *Statistics of Drug Addicts Notified to the Home Office, United Kingdom, 1996* (London: HMSO, 1996).

Heroin addiction was not just increasing numerically; it also appeared to be spreading geographically. When the second Brain Committee reported in 1964, it was thought that heroin addiction was largely confined to London.[16] By the end of the 1970s, it was clear that this was no longer the case. Denbigh, in his speech to the House of Lords on drug addiction in 1979, stated that over the past seven years there had been a 127 per cent increase in the number of addicts notified who resided outside the London area.[17] Manchester, Merseyside and Glasgow were particularly affected, but opiate use was increasingly to be found in urban areas throughout the UK.[18] Although drug use researchers Geoffrey Pearson and Mark Gilman argued that the 'heroin epidemic' of the 1980s was not truly a 'national' problem, pointing to considerable regional differences in heroin use, the broader implications of heroin addiction were being felt on a national scale for the first time.[19] This was recognised by the ACMD in their report *Treatment and Rehabilitation* when they noted that by 1982 notifications of addiction were received from most parts of the country, reinforcing the view that this was no longer a problem experienced by Greater London alone.[20]

The rise in heroin addiction in 1980s Britain was not necessarily confined to any particular social grouping. Stimson argued that as drug use became less associated with Bohemian or counter-cultural groups it became more 'common' and not associated with any particular view on life.[21] While some commentators pointed to a link between rising drug use and increased urban deprivation and unemployment, others stressed that drugs were an evil to be found at all social levels.[22] The nature of the relationship between deprivation and drug use was complex and, according to Susanne MacGregor, rapidly politicised. Those on the Right tended to stress 'the corruption of young people by outside elements—pushers and dealers'. Consequently, 'criminal subversive elements were the root of the problem, together with the moral weakness of some young people who had not been brought up to say no'.[23] Individuals who supported this argument asserted that drug use was to be found at all levels of society; it was not deprivation that caused drug addiction but moral corruption.[24] This view was often reinforced by the media. Marek Kohn explored tabloid stories of upper-class and working-class drug use and concluded that heroin was seen as a problem of the estates, the country ones and the council ones.[25] An alternative view was frequently put forward by those on the Left. Labour MPs, often in deprived, Northern, urban constituencies, were quick to suggest there was a strong link between unemployment and addiction. Allan Roberts, Labour MP for Bootle, told the *Yorkshire Post* in 1984: 'The Thatcher years are "the hard-drug years" . . . A whole generation is being sacrificed. The Government are directly responsible . . . unemployed youngsters and teenagers with no hope or stake in their future are easy prey to the drug pusher'.[26] Attributing escalating drug addiction to deprivation allowed the Left to blame the Conservative government and attack its poor record on unemployment and public spending. Any potential link between drug use and unemployment, crime or social deprivation remained politically sensitive despite widely reported clusters of addiction in areas with high rates of unemployment, such as Glasgow and Liverpool.[27] Connecting drug use with deprivation remained controversial throughout the 1980s and for much of the 1990s. Griffith Edwards, chair of the working group that produced the ACMD's 1998 report *Drug Misuse and the Environment*, noted that this was 'the first occasion on which the ACMD had told the government that deprivation is a strongly relevant item on the drug policy agenda'.[28]

Heroin use in the 1980s expanded in scale at the same time as the black market in illegally produced and distributed drugs grew. Illicit 'Chinese' heroin could be bought in London during the late 1960s and early 1970s, but it was thought that most of the illegally produced drugs that reached Britain's shores at that time were in transit for distribution elsewhere; however, in 1979 the domestic market for illicit drugs expanded dramatically.[29] This was partly due to changes in supply. Heroin from Iran flooded the market, as exiles from the revolution sought ways to move capital out of the country.[30] The amount of heroin seized by police and customs, likely to represent a fraction of the total smuggled into the UK, rose considerably. The authorities seized just 3.3 kilograms of heroin in 1973, compared to 93.4 kilograms seized in 1981.[31] At the same time, demand increased as DDUs cut down on the amount of heroin prescribed to addicts, replacing it with methadone instead. Buying drugs on the black market was an attractive proposition for addicts who disliked methadone, as illicitly produced heroin at that time was both relatively pure and relatively cheap. In real terms, the price of black market heroin fell by as much as 25 per cent between 1980 and 1983.[32] By the mid-1980s it was clear that a large, organised black market in illegally produced and distributed heroin existed, in contrast to the 'grey' market in traded pharmaceutical opiates of previous decades.[33]

The influx of heroin from Iran, and later Afghanistan and Pakistan, had an important impact on the character of the British heroin problem and may have led to an increase in addiction quite apart from the usual issues of supply and demand. Heroin imported from these countries was particularly well suited to smoking rather than injecting.[34] Subsequently, there was an increase in 'chasing the dragon' (smoking heroin) in Britain during the 1980s. In 1979 most heroin users first took the drug intravenously, but by the end of the 1980s Strang and his colleagues found that the majority of new users began taking the drug by inhalation.[35] This was significant: smoking heroin did not carry the dangers and stigma of injection and may have resulted in some individuals taking the drug who were repelled (at least initially) by intravenous use.[36]

Quantifying how important this change in the mode of administration was to the rise in heroin addiction overall is of course difficult, but the increase in the smoking of heroin needs to be seen in the context of an increasingly 'poly-drug' problem.[37] Heroin users were not just injecting heroin; they were often taking a range of other drugs by a variety of routes. As the prescription of heroin to addicts became more strictly controlled, many users turned to other opiate drugs that could be obtained from doctors without a license to prescribe heroin. The synthetic opiate Diconal was particularly popular during the 1970s and early 1980s.[38] Prescribed in tablet form, which was then crushed and injected, Diconal use grew until 1984 when it was added to the list of drugs for which a doctor required a license to supply to addicts.[39] Heroin addicts were also increasingly using non-opiate drugs in addition to, or as a temporary substitute for, heroin. Barbiturates, amphetamines and benzodiazepines could be acquired from doctors or bought on the 'grey' market of legally produced but illegally distributed pharmaceutical drugs.[40] These drugs presented their own problems. Barbiturate use led more readily to overdose than opiate drug use, resulting in greater numbers of users presenting to accident and emergency departments, particularly in central London.[41] Injecting drugs not meant for intravenous use could lead to more complications, such as injection site sores and blood clots.[42] Individuals attempting to help barbiturate users found them difficult to work with, as barbiturates frequently made patients aggressive.[43] The use of other drugs by heroin addicts became so extensive that The Lancet noted in 1979, 'Poly-drug abuse, rather than dependence on a single drug, is now the entrenched pattern of drug abuse' and that it was 'misleading to speak of opiate addicts and poly-drug abusers as two separate populations requiring different treatment approaches'.[44] This holistic approach to the treatment of drug addiction was apparently not one adopted by the DDUs. Street agencies and casualty departments were increasingly encountering poly-drug users who were not catered to by the treatment centres.[45] There was, according to another editorial in The Lancet in 1982, 'a near total preoccupation with opiate dependence' at DDUs.[46] Clinics were reluctant to take on poly-drug users or those using only drugs other than heroin as this could not be treated through the prescription of methadone. Treatment facilities established in the late 1960s were not designed to cope with the changing nature of the drug problem in the 1980s.

This did not escape the notice of those outside the medical community. Political interest in the drugs issue heightened over the period, spurred on by an apparent 'panic' over heroin use. As MacGregor has shown, increased drug use was described as a problem, a crisis, an epidemic and a plague by the media and politicians.[47] According to Kohn, articles in the popular press 'loaded with sensationalism, titillation and moral indignation . . . convinced the public that the nation's youth was threatened by a plague of heroin'.[48] The broadsheets did not escape the sense of hysteria. In 1985, 61 separate stories in The Times specifically concerned heroin (more than one a week), and many more appeared on related issues such as the traffic of drugs and the prevention and treatment of addiction.[49] Compared to the 25 heroin stories in the same newspaper two years before, it would seem that 1984–1985 were the peak years of the heroin panic.[50] Kohn found an explanation for the timing of this in the contemporary socio-political context. Heroin became the focus of attention during the miners' strike.[51] Kohn argued that as the strike deepened social divisions and began to turn people against the Thatcher government, it became important to find an issue that could re-unite the country. He asserted, 'Heroin is the consensus issue *par excellence* [his italics]. Everybody is against it. Even most junkies are against it.'[52] It was hoped that a war on heroin, like the recent war in the Falklands, would bring people together against a common enemy.

Kohn's line of analysis suggests there was a 'moral panic' over the use of heroin similar to those described by Stanley Cohen in his classic work *Folk Devils and Moral Panics*.[53] A strong moral element was clearly at work in much of the debate about heroin in this period. MacGregor analysed some key contemporary newspaper reports and found the emphasis on the decay, corruption and hopelessness of heroin addiction betrayed a distinctly moral tone.[54] Nicholas Dorn and Nigel South assessed the validity of applying the term 'moral panic' to the furore surrounding heroin in the 1980s. They argued that the significant increase in drug use in Britain at that time, coupled with long held fears about the abuse of the body and the use of drugs for 'selfish pleasure', suggested deeper forces were at play than could be explained by the notion of a 'moral panic'.[55]

The 'Heroin Screws You Up' campaign clearly tapped in to—and enhanced —the climate of fear and moral unease concerning heroin. Yet, however misguided, 'Heroin Screws You Up' was evidence of a growing concern about the drugs issue emanating from central government. Legislative and political interest in drugs during the 1970s had been scant. The Misuse of Drugs Act, passed in 1971, had largely consolidated earlier pieces of legislation concerning heroin, such as compulsory notification and the requirement that doctors prescribing heroin to addicts be in possession of a licence. The Misuse of Drugs Act and the Misuse of Drugs Regulations (1973) introduced some new measures. 'Dangerous drugs' were now called 'controlled drugs', and these were separated into three categories: Class A, Class B and Class C. Class A drugs included heroin and cocaine; Class B included cannabis and some amphetamines; Class C contained benzodiazepines. Different penalties for offences connected to these drugs were attached to each category. For example, possession of a Class A drug such as heroin could result in seven years' imprisonment, a fine or both. In contrast, possession of a Class C drug met with two years' imprisonment, a fine or both.[56] During the 1980s these penalties and the whole approach to drug use was re-evaluated by the Conservative government. In July 1984 the Ministerial Group on the Misuse of Drugs was set up under the chairmanship of a Junior Home Office Minister, David Mellor. The group's report, *Tackling Drug Misuse*, stated that 'the misuse of drugs is one of the most worrying problems facing our society today' and suggested 'a coherent strategy which attacks drug misuse by simultaneous action on five main fronts'. These were: 'reducing supplies from abroad'; 'tightening controls on drugs produced and prescribed in the UK'; 'making policing more effective'; 'strengthening deterrence'; and 'improving prevention, treatment and rehabilitation'.[57] *Tackling Drug Misuse* concentrated predominantly on controlling the production and supply of drugs, a move Stimson saw as representative of a decline of the 'medico-centric' view of drug policy and the emergence of a new emphasis on control, in what he termed the 'criminal-economic model'.[58]

This enhanced emphasis on law enforcement reflected international developments, particularly in the USA. American drug policy in the late 1970s and early 1980s moved away from treatment and towards a greater emphasis on enforcement. Methadone programmes introduced during the Nixon administration fared poorly under Presidents Ford and Carter. High inflation ate away at limited federal resources for treatment, resulting in a steady reduction of funds in real terms.[59] Yet money was found for the escalating 'war on drugs', targeting not just heroin but also cannabis and cocaine. The Reagan administration's 'Just Say No' campaign at home was matched by an aggressive attempt to reduce the drug supply by destroying cocaine labs and breaking up drug cartels in Central and South America.[60] British law enforcement agencies, assisted by the armed forces, adopted many of the tactics of the American Drug Enforcement Administration (DEA) and also began to target drug traffickers and their assets, as well as substituting and eradicating drug crops in other countries.[61] Furthermore, as in the US where mandatory minimum sentences for drug offences were introduced, domestic penalties for drug crimes were stiffened; the maximum sentence for trafficking in Class A drugs (such as heroin) was increased to life imprisonment.[62]

Party-political and parliamentary involvement in drug issues also grew in the mid-1980s. Drugs were on the agenda of the Conservative Party Conference in 1984; the leader of the Social Democratic Party (SDP), David Owen, discussed drugs in conjunction with unemployment in a speech in 1985; and the Labour party included drugs in their statement on health produced in 1986.[63] According to MacGregor, drugs were often described as a particularly Conservative issue, allowing the government to demonstrate concern about a social issue they could not be blamed for causing.[64] Cross-party committees also began to inquire into the 'misuse' of drugs in 1985. The House of Commons Home Affairs Committee examined the production and traffic of illegal drugs, and the Social Services Committee concentrated on the treatment and rehabilitation of drug 'misusers'.[65] The Social Services Committee found that: 'The misuse of drugs, and particularly misuse of heroin and cocaine, is a serious and growing problem. It demands an immediate, determined response from Government and society as a whole.' The committee further asserted: 'Existing services are woefully inadequate to cope with the increasing pressure. Treatment facilities are few, underfunded, often inaccessible and always have long waiting lists.'[66] Interest in drug issues was clearly not limited to law enforcement and trafficking; treatment remained an issue of paramount importance.

The Changing Treatment Response

Treatment, though, was in turmoil. DDUs, which had formed the cornerstone of heroin addiction treatment policy since 1968, were increasingly unable or unwilling to respond to the needs of some patients. An editorial in *The Lancet* in 1982 branded the British System as 'failing', arguing that 'the "clinic system" which is the focal point of the response to drug dependence in the UK, is now completely inadequate.'[67] The DDUs faced two main difficulties in dealing with heroin addiction in the 1980s. Firstly, they were under-resourced and understaffed. Tight controls on public expenditure exercised by the Conservative government meant that spending on the NHS grew very slowly in the 1980s.[68] Over the decade, spending on hospital and community health services rose by just ten per cent in real terms.[69] Drug addiction treatment facilities were not in a good position to compete for scarce resources within the health service, as they were traditionally accorded a low priority.[70] Despite Department of Health and Social Security guidance to local health authorities asserting that the improvement of services for drug addicts was to be accorded the 'highest priority' (along with improvements to other so-called 'Cinderella' services such as provision for the mentally ill and the elderly), money did not always get through.[71] As MacGregor and Ettore remarked, 'Health Authorities find it difficult to put services for drug misusers ahead of those for, say, kidney transplants or old people.'[72] DDUs consequently lacked the resources to deal with an influx of new patients. Waiting lists for treatment at clinics lengthened: many addicts had to wait more than six weeks for a first assessment appointment at a DDU.[73] Long waiting periods, as the Social Services Committee noted, could prove a disincentive to those seeking treatment.[74]

Those who did manage to be seen at a DDU often found the treatment offered did not suit them. This was the second major problem encountered by the DDUs: they had failed to adapt to changing patterns of drug use in the 1980s. DDUs had altered their prescription policies over the previous decade. Clinics stopped prescribing injectable heroin to new addict-patients, giving addicts (first injectable and later oral) methadone. Prescriptions were usually over a short period and directed towards total abstinence from drugs rather than indefinite maintenance. All the London DDUs were the same; 'the resultant uniformity of treatment', according to *The Lancet*, had 'stultified research into different treatment options.'[75] Indeed, the form of treatment on offer at the DDUs did not meet the needs of all addicts. Psychiatrist John Strang argued that the restrictions placed on those seeking treatment at a DDU for the first time meant that 'it is virtually impossible for some new patients to obtain service of any valuable nature from the drug clinics.'[76] DDUs were inflexible, homogeneous and simply unable to cope with the influx of addicts in the 1980s.

Addicts subsequently began to seek treatment elsewhere. In 1982 *The Lancet* observed that 'many drug abusers now prefer to stay outside the system and approach non-clinic doctors', a move the journal attributed to a greater willingness on the part of doctors outside the DDUs to prescribe injectable opioids.[77] Yet, more generous prescriptions were not the only reason for addicts' abandonment of DDUs. One addict who had left his local clinic in favour of a private practitioner asserted that he would have been 'quite happy to attend [NHS clinics] if they were any good'.[78] He complained that not only was he prescribed an inadequate dose of methadone at the DDU but he was being forced to reduce this to nothing over a period of six months, was required to pick up his prescription on a daily basis, which made working difficult, and had to attend counselling sessions that he found to be 'arrogant and patronising'. In contrast, he asserted that the treatment provided by the private doctor enabled him to 'hold down my job and live a reasonable life' in addition to 'reduc[ing] my intake of injectable and oral methadone at a rate which I can cope with'.[79] Non-clinic doctors were undoubtedly encountering greater numbers of addicts. Notifications of addiction to the Home Office from GPs rose steadily as notifications from DDUs declined. In 1970 just 6 per cent of notifications of addiction came from GPs, 46 per cent from DDUs and 48 per cent from prison medical officers. In 1981 48 per cent of notifications came from GPs, 36 per cent from DDUs and 16 per cent from prison medical officers (see pg. 61).[80] This trend continued over the decade with over half of all new notifications coming from GPs throughout the period (see pg. 65).[81]

In a national survey of GPs conducted in 1985, Alan Glanz and Colin Taylor of the ARU found that one in five GPs saw a patient addicted to opiate drugs over a four-week period, amounting to between 30,000 and 44,000 new cases of opiate use presenting to general practitioners a year. These figures were far higher than the Home Office notification statistics and were inflated by some duplication of addict names, but in other ways may actually have been more accurate, as they accounted for under-notification of addicts by GPs.[82] Whatever the precise numbers involved, the trend towards increasing involvement of the GP in the treatment of addiction was obvious. This led Glanz and Taylor to conclude that the role of the GP should be 'given serious consideration in the development of a national strategy for responding to the current drugs problem'.[83] Yet, the increasing involvement of non-clinic doctors in the treatment of addiction was, according to the ACMD, an 'unplanned development' that they viewed with 'some concern'.[84] How the GP came to play a greater role in the treatment of addiction and the reasons why this was regarded with 'concern' by the ACMD and others requires further consideration.

TREATMENT AND REHABILITATION—
A SPECIALIST OR A GENERALIST APPROACH?

The ACMD's 1982 report *Treatment and Rehabilitation* played an important role in setting the parameters of the debate over the treatment of heroin addiction in the 1980s. It has been viewed in two slightly different ways. Stimson argued that the transition from the 'addict' of the 1960s Brain reports to the 'problem drug taker' described by *Treatment and Rehabilitation* indicated the emergence of a more 'diffuse understanding [of drug taking] . . . with medicine taking a much less central position in the response'.[85] For MacGregor too the report marked the acceptance of a 'reformist' rather than 'medical' model for drug policy.[86] Other commentators, however, pointed to the retention of a strong medical influence, particularly over the report's recommendations on the treatment of addiction. Moreover, the view on treatment presented was that of a particular section of the medical community, the DDU psychiatrist. These doctors felt threatened by the intervention of other agencies and individuals, especially general and private practitioners. *Treatment and Rehabilitation* represented a defence of the specialist's role in the treatment of addiction. Spear suggested it was not 'over-fanciful' that 'the more politically motivated and forceful members' of a group of consultants at the London DDUs 'saw in the Advisory Council's review of treatment services an opportunity to regain the influence they feared they were in danger of losing'. He asserts that these psychiatrists made 'The elimination of both the independent doctor and the NHS general practitioner from the field' their 'primary objective', and to do this they persuaded the working group to listen to their views and include them in the final report.[87] Spear's opinion was endorsed by some contemporary analysis of the report. Rowdy Yates, a project coordinator at the Manchester-based street agency the Lifeline Project, asserted that the ACMD's recommendations effectively extended the power of DDUs over non-specialist services so that GPs would be allowed to treat addicts only in conjunction with advice from clinic doctors.[88] This proposal led Mike Ashton, of the Institute for the Study of Drug Dependence (ISDD), to argue that, 'It took little imagination to see the Advisory Council's recommendations as an attempt to legislate the non-hospital doctor out of addiction treatment.'[89]

Such a view would seem to contradict the diffuse model of treatment policy found in *Treatment and Rehabilitation* by Stimson and MacGregor; however, these two approaches are not necessarily contradictory. Indeed, the one explains the other: the very diffusion of the general response to drug use put forward by the ACMD encouraged the purveyors of the main medical response (the DDU psychiatrists) to defend their specialism from the encroachments of the GP and the private practitioner.

The DDU psychiatrist faced two kinds of threat to their position as the authority on drug problems: from external non-medical agencies, such as voluntary organisations, politicians and local authorities who threatened the powerful position of medicine in defining and shaping the response to drug use; and from internal alternative medical agencies, such as general and private practitioners who threatened the existence of the treatment of addiction as a psychiatric specialty. To retain a role in the 'policy community' the DDU psychiatrist needed to present a unified, cohesive 'medical' approach. In order to do this, the GP and the private practitioner (the issues surrounding private practice will be dealt with separately in Chapter Five) needed to be removed from the treatment of addiction, or at least marginalized, so that psychiatrists could present a powerful claim to authority within the increasingly diverse 'policy community' based on their specialist status.

A close analysis of *Treatment and Rehabilitation* supports such a notion by revealing the presence of both currents: the move away from a purely medical approach to drugs towards a more diffuse response; and within the specialist medical approach, a reaction to this diffusion in the form of an attempt to reduce the role of the generalist. The Treatment and Rehabilitation Working Group of the ACMD was set up in 1975 to 'undertake a comprehensive review of the treatment and rehabilitation services for drug misusers and to make recommendations for dealing with both immediate problems and the situation generally'.[90] The composition of the working group reveals the increase in the range of bodies and individuals interested in drug addiction and, at the same time, pointed to the continued importance of the clinical psychiatrist. There were social workers, probation officers and representatives from voluntary agencies suggesting a broad view of drug problems and their consequences; however, the persistence of a strong medical view was indicated by the continued dominance of doctors. There were six doctors on the committee and of these, four were psychiatrists involved in the treatment of addiction, the largest group.[91] They were: D.J. Parr, a Brighton consultant psychiatrist; Anthony Thorley, a consultant psychiatrist at Newcastle Hospital and director of the Parkwood House Alcohol and Drug Dependence Unit; most crucially of all, Thomas Bewley, consultant psychiatrist at St Thomas' Hospital; and Philip Connell, director of the DDU at the Maudsley, the leading facility on the treatment of addiction. It is highly likely that Connell and Bewley were the 'medical politicians' darkly referred to by Spear.[92] The presence of these men on the ACMD working group points not only to the continued importance of psychiatry in responding to drug use but also hints at a potentially powerful political incentive for Connell and Bewley who, in order to preserve their expert status, needed to diminish the importance of the generalist in the treatment of addiction.

In order to gather evidence for their report, the working group visited a number of treatment centres and took evidence from groups and individuals 'concerned with the problems of drug misuse'.[93] In 1977 they produced an interim report recommending some immediate action but also suggested that a more wide-ranging study of drug 'misuse' was necessary.[94] The group examined the available data on drug use and sent questionnaires to 34 treatment centres in England and Wales. In addition, they spoke to voluntary workers about rehabilitation facilities for recovering addicts. They published their findings in *Treatment and Rehabilitation* in 1982. The report considered the shortcomings of the current services in light of the changing pattern of drug use and proposed 'a new approach to the problems of the drug misuser and a framework under which services could be developed'.[95] They examined the implications of the increased involvement of the private and general practitioner and made recommendations on safeguards for prescribing controlled drugs. The report also looked at the need for training and research as well as the difficulties of funding services for drug misusers.

Treatment and Rehabilitation noted changes in drug use and the response to this already apparent to many of those working in the field. The report discussed the increasingly poly-drug problem: the overall rise in number of people using drugs, the geographical spread of this use, the increased availability of illicit drugs, the growing proportion of those first notified who claimed to be addicted to heroin rather than any other drug and the increased proportion of addicts being notified by doctors in private and general practice.[96] The ACMD also noted that treatment and rehabilitation facilities were largely inadequate in many areas.[97] To address these problems and improve services, *Treatment and Rehabilitation* presented a new way of looking at drug users. They also appeared to be questioning elements of the disease-based notion of addiction or dependence by stating that 'Most authorities from a range of disciplines would agree that not all individuals suffer from a disease of drug dependence. While many drug misusers do incur medical problems through their use of drugs, some do not. The majority are relatively stable individuals who have more in common with the general population than with any essentially pathological sub-group.'[98] The working group thus shifted emphasis away from a purely medical, or treatment-based, approach to the problem of addiction. They found no evidence for the existence of a 'typical' addict or person with drug problems. There should, therefore, be a range of treatment and rehabilitation services available to suit each individual. To this end, the report suggested that services should not be orientated towards specific client groups, heroin addicts, amphetamine users, barbiturate takers and so on. But, according to the working group, the needs of different types of drug users were also similar, so 'Services in the future need to be geared to solve common problems rather than be merely substance or diagnosis centred.' The approach should be 'problem orientated'.[99]

Here the ACMD were drawing on the findings of the Advisory Committee on Alcoholism (the Kessel Committee) who published a report in 1978 detailing *The Pattern and Range of Services for Problem Drinkers*.[100] This report marked a shift from dealing with 'alcoholics' to providing for a wider group of 'problem drinkers'.[101] Similarly, *Treatment and Rehabilitation* represented a transition from the 'addict' to the 'problem drug taker'. The problem drug taker was defined as: 'a person who experiences social, psychological, physical or legal problems related to intoxication and/or regular excessive consumption and/or dependence as a consequence of his own use of drugs or other chemical substances (excluding alcohol and tobacco)'.[102] Problem drug takers were, therefore, not just 'addicts' but any individual who experienced problems with drug use. According to Stimson, the adoption of this definition indicated 'a major shift away from the disease model and the opiate addict'.[103] Lart concurred, noting that the use of the term 'problem drug taker' resulted in a move 'away from the narrow conception of addiction' which 'open[ed] up the range of aspects of a drug user's life of legitimate concern to services'.[104] Subsequently, services were to be developed with the 'problem drug taker' in mind. The ACMD stated that these should recognise the medical, legal and social problems resulting from drug taking for the individual and for the community. Responses to the 'problem drug taker' could come from hospital-based treatment services, detoxification services, street agencies and various other voluntary and non-statutory agencies.[105] Official sanction was therefore given to the involvement of a range of bodies and authorities. Stimson saw the report as indicating that service provision would be less dominated by doctors and instead involve 'workers with many different skills'.[106]

Despite stressing a multi-disciplinary view of the problems of those using drugs, *Treatment and Rehabilitation* paid particular attention to the role of the doctor, suggesting the persistence of medical approaches to drug use. The report stated that 'for the majority of problem drug takers, treatment by doctors will be an important component of the help they receive'. This was because 'only doctors may prescribe drugs and they will be expected to treat the physical and psychological consequences of problem drug taking'.[107] The emphasis on treatment led Tony Slater, of the therapeutic community Phoenix House, to comment in the *British Journal of Addiction* that the report seemed to be 'very heavily slanted towards supporting the medical model of treatment' and did not 'understand all of the needs facing the "problem drug taker" and his or her subsequent rehabilitation'.[108] This paralleled criticism of the Kessel Committee's report on problem drinkers. Thom notes that although the committee believed they had rejected medical understandings of alcoholism in favour of a community-based notion of the problem drinker, some critics found evidence for the continued existence of the medical model through the emphasis placed on treatment.[109] By placing a strong emphasis on the 'treatment' offered by doctors rather than the 'rehabilitation' offered by other agencies, *Treatment and Rehabilitation* appeared to be prioritising the medical approach over the more 'social' alternatives.

The nature of this medical approach is revealed by the recommendations of the ACMD on prescribing safeguards, which betrayed a less than inclusive view of who should be offering treatment to 'problem drug takers'. The report highlighted the trend towards drug users seeking medical help from doctors not based at hospitals and noted that according to the Home Office, doctors working at the DHSS and the views expressed in a number of medical journals, this gave rise to 'a number of causes for concern'.[110] These fell into four categories. Firstly, the ACMD were worried that doctors working with problem drug takers lacked sufficient training and expertise to treat addicts adequately in isolation from specialist advice. Secondly, the committee feared that drugs supplied to problem drug takers might be diverted to the black market, noting that only DDUs tended to prescribe to addicts on a daily basis as they had special forms that allowed drugs to be dispensed in this way. Thirdly, concerns were expressed about the pressure that doctors who prescribed to addicts might become subject; aggressive and persuasive addicts could exploit elderly doctors or those working alone. Finally, the report noted that few doctors had access to the kind of support staff and facilities available at the DDUs.[111] The consequence of this was that controlled drugs were being prescribed 'injudiciously', giving rise to two major problems. The first was that liberal prescribing encouraged some patients to leave DDUs and obtain larger doses of drugs from non-clinic doctors. The second was that the amount of legally manufactured drugs on the black market had risen considerably.[112] This last assertion does not appear to have been backed up with any figures, but it led the ACMD to contend that there had been a recurrence of the same problems that caused concern for the second Brain Committee, in which doctors were providing addicts with drugs in too liberal a manner, thus feeding the black market. The ACMD therefore recommended that a role could be afforded doctors outside DDUs in the treatment of addiction only with 'strict safeguards'. These included close liaison with hospital-based services, links with other agencies such as social services and opportunities for further training. The working group were not convinced that these measures alone would be sufficient. They subsequently recommended that guidelines be established on good practice, the possibility of extending licensing for the prescription of all controlled drugs to addicts be examined and wider use be made of the tribunal system for irresponsible prescription.[113]

Some of those who read *Treatment and Rehabilitation* felt these recommendations would do little to encourage GPs and private practitioners to become involved in the treatment of addiction and actually might dissuade many. Yates argued in the *British Journal of Addiction* that the report ignored 'any discussion of enhancing the *positive* [his italics] role of General Practitioners in the treatment of addiction'. He went on to note that *Treatment and Rehabilitation* did not deal with the fact that the majority of GPs were reluctant to see drug users and its recommendations were 'tantamount to a green light to GPs to continue to avoid any responsibility for this group'.[114] This, it could be argued, was exactly what some members of the ACMD working group (the DDU psychiatrists like Connell and Bewley) wanted. *Treatment and Rehabilitation* recognised that GPs and private practitioners were increasingly involved in the treatment of addiction, and while it purported to represent a 'community-based' response and advocated the participation of a range of bodies in dealing with the 'problems' of drug users, its recommendations on treatment were a good deal less inclusive. By raising the problems associated with the treatment of addiction in private and general practice and not considering the possible benefits, the report was making a covert attack on this mode of treatment. What is more, it drew lines for battle by recommending a number of measures that became key issues in the dispute over who should treat the addict (generalist, specialist or private practitioner) and also how the addict should be treated (short-term withdrawal or long-term maintenance), such as the need for guidelines on good practice. *Treatment and Rehabilitation* thus had a vital role to play in setting the parameters of the debate between specialists and generalists in the treatment of addiction.

THE REVITALISATION OF GENERAL PRACTICE AND THE TREATMENT OF HEROIN ADDICTION

Generalists and Specialists: An Old Divide Renewed?

A divide between community-based general practitioners and hospital-based consultants or specialists existed in Britain as early as the mid-nineteenth century. According to Anne Digby, this divide was not, however, necessarily a clear one as the respective roles of the specialist and the generalist were ill-defined throughout the Victorian period, leading to 'intra-professional disputes'. It was not until the 1930s that formalised definitions of specialist and generalist emerged. A consultant or specialist was defined as a doctor who 'confines himself [sic.] entirely to "consultation" work' in relation to a particular part of the body and was usually on the staff of the local hospital. Significantly, Digby found that 'within the profession the status of the GP was lower than that of the consultant'.[115] The creation of the NHS in 1948 perpetuated this divide.[116] Consultants were given privileged status and allowed to continue private work, and the 'difference between general practitioners and consultants' was underlined by the 'increasing difficulty of crossing the divide between them'.[117] GPs were not controlled by the Regional Hospital Boards but by their own executive councils and were employed by the local authorities, not the NHS directly. A considerable gulf developed between specialists and generalists as medical and technical developments led to the creation of specialist knowledge about particular diseases and conditions. The status of the GP declined as more and more of their original functions were transferred to hospital-based specialists.[118] According to Margot Jefferys and Hessie Sachs, by the late 1950s and early 1960s this had the effect of 'giving the public, as well as both branches of the medical profession the impression that general practitioners, when compared to hospital based consultants, were second-class doctors'.[119] Furthermore, it was not just the general public who viewed general practice with some disdain; a survey of final year medical students between 1961 and 1966 found that only a quarter gave this as their first choice of career.[120] General practice reached something of a nadir during the 1960s, and there was 'tension and mutual suspicion, if not hostility' between the two branches of medicine.[121]

But by the end of the decade, and into the next one, there were signs that general practice was beginning to fight back. In 1967 GPs' pay was increased to roughly that of some hospital-based specialists, helping improve status.[122] Elimination from the hospital made GPs increasingly aware of their own collective identity and practices. Through the Royal College of General Practitioners (founded in 1953) a new approach to general practice and a different way of seeing medicine and disease emerged.[123] This placed the patient and the patient's symptoms rather than the disease itself at the centre of the medical gaze. Although the notion of seeing the 'patient as a person' rather than as a disease had existed since the early twentieth century, this approach was most fully realised in Dr Michael Balint's *The Doctor, His Patient and The Illness* in 1957.[124] Balint was a Hungarian psychoanalyst who began working with GPs in 1950. He applied psychotherapeutic techniques to the general practice setting, and this resulted in a shift of focus from the diagnosis of disease to the meaning of illness, from the illness to the patient, and from the patient to the doctor-patient relationship.[125] Armstrong argues that for Balint, 'the medical gaze was no longer to be directed to the silent interior of the body but to the patient's biography and environment'. This approach, which Armstrong describes as 'biographical medicine,' did not deny the existence of organic pathology but reduced its significance, paying more attention to the symptoms of disease as experienced by the individual patient. The patient was no longer the 'passive receptacle of organic pathology' but transformed into the 'centre of the medical problematic'.[126] Balint's work influenced GPs who attended the seminars he hosted, and his ideas were communicated to the wider field of general practice when these doctors became leaders of the Royal College of General Practitioners.[127] These same GPs were also key figures in the publication of the college's iconic teaching manual *The Future General Practitioner* in 1972. According to Professor of General Practice Marshall Marinker, this marked 'a massive breaking-away from intellectual and emotional chains of a predominately instrumental and reductionist hospital-orientated medicine'.[128] *The Future General Practitioner* adopted the ideas of Balint and placed the patient and the patient's social environment at the centre of therapeutic endeavour. Balint's work thus provided a new epistemological basis for general practice, one that was gradually internalised through the use of *The Future General Practitioner* in the training of new GPs throughout the 1970s and 1980s and was crucial to the foundation of an ideology of general practice independent of hospital specialism.[129] The divide between specialist and generalist was thus reinforced as GPs became more confident in their own worth and the services they could offer as distinct from the hospital-based consultant.

General Practitioners and the Treatment of Addiction

The social scientist Alan Glanz has argued that this context of an improving position for general practice within medicine was crucial to the re-intervention of the GP into addiction treatment in the late 1970s and early 1980s. Through biographical medicine, 'the whole position of general practice had been strengthened and the GP could meaningfully be called upon to play a significant role in the treatment of drug misuse'.[130] While the specific consequences of biographical medicine for the methods used in the treatment of addiction in general practice will be dealt with in more detail in Chapter Six, it is sufficient to note here that the confidence of GPs in their own abilities and outlook allowed them to take on, and even challenge, a previously specialist domain. In addition, there were a number of more practical reasons why the GP became more involved in the treatment of addiction during the 1980s. The growing scale of the drug problem meant that specialist facilities were overloaded and, failing an expansion in these, addict-patients would have to be seen elsewhere by other doctors. The GP was a natural and an obvious choice. General practitioners were to be found all over the country and were often the first source of medical help turned to by addicts. Psychiatrist John Strang also suggested that as the numbers of drug takers increased and they became more 'normal', it was logical that treatment services become more 'normal' in response.[131] Involving the GP was thus, at least in part, a pragmatic reaction to the changing nature of drug use in this period.

Attempting to assess why addicts approached GPs for treatment highlights the politicised divide between those who supported the growing involvement of the GP in the treatment of addiction and those who opposed it. Those specialists who criticised the treatment of addiction in general practice argued that addicts went to GPs because they more readily prescribed opiate drugs than DDUs. It was a commonly held concern among DDU psychiatrists that GPs working alone with limited knowledge of the wiles of the addict, and no access to diagnostic testing facilities, could be put under pressure to overprescribe.[132] Connell and Mitcheson expressed an oft-repeated fear when they asserted that unlike most treatment centres, where a team approach was practiced, the single-handed doctor 'who has little or no experience of addicts is a vulnerable target for the drug seeker'.[133] GPs, it was strongly implied, were more easily duped than DDU staff into prescribing inappropriately large doses of opioids. DDUs, therefore, were the best place for the addict to receive treatment, as specialists were less likely to overprescribe drugs that would feed the 'grey' market.

In contrast, those who were critical of the DDUs, such as the private practitioner Ann Dally, argued that the practices of the clinics were driving addicts to GPs. She asserted that giving addicts no other option than reduced doses of oral methadone and refusing to treat them as individuals encouraged them to seek treatment elsewhere, either with GPs or sympathetic private doctors like herself.[134] Some reports published in the medical press also suggested that psychiatric services were inappropriate for the treatment of addiction. A survey of referrals to psychiatric services in Scotland (there were no DDUs in Scotland) from a general practice in Edinburgh for the treatment of addiction was revealing. The research team found no evidence to 'indicate that patients receiving treatment from the psychiatric drug treatment service have a higher rate of abstinence than those not starting treatment, casting doubt on the value of this kind of service'.[135] Furthermore, the study's authors took the high rates of non-attendance among the patients referred to these services to mean that 'patients find the service both uncomfortable and inappropriate'.[136] This was, at least in part, because few of the patients encountered considered themselves to be suffering from a psychiatric illness. This led the researchers to argue that 'The relevance of referral for every drug abuser is debatable, particularly if treatment is largely limited to withdrawal.' Instead, they contended that 'General Practitioners may be in the best position to cope with the extended management of drug users, and certainly community based treatment seems more likely to maintain contacts [with the drug user].'[137]

Similar conclusions were reached in another report produced by some of the same researchers. A study of the medical facilities used by a group of addicts found that general practice was 'the main interface between the drug users and the medical establishment (even accounting for selecting the study group through general practice)'. The authors felt this had not been sufficiently taken into account in the response to drug addiction, leading them to argue that 'the historical emphasis placed on intervention based in hospital (normally psychiatric) for the education and general management of drug users appears to be inappropriate.'[138] Taken together, these studies could be construed as a counterattack on the specialist nature of the treatment of addiction. If psychiatric services were of little use in treating addiction, then the generalists' position was automatically enhanced at the cost of the 'expertise' of the psychiatrist.

However, examining the actual role played by the GP in the treatment of addiction at first seems to indicate that this was insignificant in the mid-1980s, posing little real threat to the authority of psychiatry in this area. A national survey of a random sample of GPs conducted by Glanz in 1985 found that two-thirds of GPs referred addict-patients on to either a DDU or general psychiatric services.[139] Furthermore, they noted that many GPs were not keen about taking addicts on as patients; less than a third of the GPs surveyed said they would take on opiate users as willingly as other patients, and two-thirds thought the treatment required by addicts was beyond the competence of the general practitioner.[140] Yet, the flip side of this research would indicate that there was a sizeable minority of GPs who were interested in addicts and their problems, GPs who did not simply refer opiate users on to the specialist services. Taking Glanz and Taylor's more conservative estimate of 30,000 'new' cases of opiate misuse presenting to GPs a year, at least 10,000 addicts were not being seen by specialists.[141] This would suggest that there was not a total monopoly of the treatment of addiction by clinical psychiatrists. Indeed, not all GPs were completely averse to addict-patients: 55 per cent of those surveyed said they thought they could play a positive role in the treatment of addict-patients even if they were not prepared to come off drugs.[142] Moreover, positive attitudes towards the treatment of addict-patients were often found in those GPs most recently qualified. Around 40 per cent of GPs surveyed who qualified in the 1970s and the 1980s said they were prepared to treat addict-patients as willingly as any other patient, compared to just 25 per cent of those who qualified before this period.[143] This would suggest that the new generation of GPs, trained in the principles of biographical medicine, were more amenable to treating addicts. This needs further investigation, as does what happened to the third of addicts who remained under the care of general practitioners. Glanz's study was not designed to answer this question, and his figures do not really allow for direct comparison, but he found that those GPs who did prescribe to addicts were just as likely to prescribe opiate drugs on a long-term basis (over two weeks) as on a short-term basis.[144] The involvement of the GP with maintenance and the impact of biographical medicine on the treatment offered in community-based practice will be discussed in more detail in Chapter Six, but it is clear that the GP could and did play a significant role in the treatment of addiction, which in turn posed a threat to the expert status of the psychiatrist in this field.

CONCLUSION—SPECIALIST VERSUS GENERALIST—
AN ONGOING BATTLE?

This threat was particularly potent when placed in the overall context of a burgeoning 'policy community' around drugs. As the number of actors interested in drug problems increased, psychiatrists had to defend their claim to a powerful position in this community by pointing to their expertise in treatment. Yet their claim was also being challenged. A new generation of self-confident GPs revitalised by biographical medicine were less willing to accept that addiction was inherently an area of specialist knowledge. When combined with existing problems in catering to a growing number of increasingly diverse drug users, it was unsurprising that more GPs were becoming involved in the treatment of addiction. This brought them into conflict with hospital-based psychiatrists, particularly those in DDUs, who felt their position was being threatened. In response, a group of psychiatrists attempted to reduce the role played by the generalist in the treatment of addiction by trying to bring the GP under the control of the DDU, a recommendation made in *Treatment and Rehabilitation*. In addition, clinic psychiatrists tried to discourage GPs from becoming involved in this area by outlining some of the 'difficulties' involved with the treatment of addiction in the pages of medical journals and elsewhere, thus reinforcing the notion that this was a specialist area of medical knowledge.

There were, therefore, particular reasons as to why there was a conflict between the specialist and the generalist in the treatment of addiction, but this can also be read as a manifestation of the old divide between specialist and generalist redrawn. General practice, reinvigorated through its encounter with biographical medicine, was reinventing itself and taking an interest in areas that had previously been considered solely the domain of the specialist, such as addiction. Indeed, biographical medicine was to bring GPs involved in the treatment of addiction into further conflict with the specialist. The community-based physician came to view disease and its treatment in a different way. Subsequently, many GPs and private practitioners who treated addicts offered a different form of treatment than that found in the DDUs, one that drew on the principles of biographical medicine and placed the patient at the centre of the endeavour. This led to additional conflict between the specialists and the generalists over the treatment of addiction, a conflict that will be discussed in Chapter Six. However, before moving on to discuss this conflict, it is first necessary to consider another conflict involving the DDU psychiatrist, this time with the private practitioner. As will be seen in Chapter Five, the conflict over territory was intertwined with another dispute over treatment methods, adding a further dimension to the debate over the treatment of addiction in this period.

Disputed Territory

The Treatment of Heroin Addiction

in Private Practice, 1980–1987

The GP was not the only doctor treating addicts away from the DDUs. Some addicts abandoned publicly funded treatment on the NHS altogether, preferring instead to seek treatment from private doctors. This development resulted in a heated debate. In 1982, the ACMD noted that for 'many members of the medical profession' the prescription of controlled drugs to addict-patients by private doctors raised 'moral and ethical aspects' that gave 'grave cause for concern'.[1] An editorial published by *The Lancet* in the following year suggested that the treatment of addiction in private practice should be banned because 'the prescription of a dependence-producing drug in return for a fee smacks so strongly of legalised drug-dealing'.[2] Numerous DDU addiction specialists were sympathetic towards the opinion expressed by consultant psychiatrist John Strang that 'most addicts view the payment of [a] fee as being direct payment for the prescription of drugs and not for any medical, psychiatric, or psychotherapeutic service'.[3]

This was a view vigorously contested by doctors engaged in the treatment of addiction in private practice, such as Ann Dally. Dally asserted that there was 'something terribly wrong in the official drug clinics' resulting in 'an increasing need for general practitioners and psychiatrists to treat drug addicts outside drug dependence units'.[4] The mid-1980s subsequently witnessed an intense dispute between those who supported the treatment of addiction in private practice as an alternative to 'failing' NHS services and others who regarded this as undesirable and unethical. This dispute was played out in the letters and comment pages of leading medical journals, in government committees investigating the response to heroin addiction and in the General Medical Council's (GMC) hearing of charges of serious professional misconduct relating to the prescription of drugs to addicts by leading private practitioners, including Dally herself.

On the surface, this was a specific argument conducted between a handful of doctors about the practical and ethical dilemmas resulting from the treatment of heroin addiction in private practice. However, beneath the rhetoric, issues of deeper significance were being contested: about how heroin addiction should be treated, about what kind of doctor should be responsible for this and about the wider role of medicine in addressing the burgeoning social problems surrounding drug use. Although private healthcare undoubtedly continued to arouse strong passions (seen for example in the row over private beds in NHS hospitals during the 1970s), the position of many doctors, including those involved in the treatment of addiction, was often more equivocal.[5] Private medicine never disappeared with the creation of the NHS, and during the 1970s and 1980s it began to expand. This presented opportunities for many NHS doctors: a survey conducted in 1984 found that 85 per cent of NHS consultants also practiced privately.[6] Similarly, some drug addiction specialists employed in NHS DDUs did private work, including those who were outwardly critical of the treatment of addiction in private practice.[7]

What this suggests is that the apparent focus on private doctors in this debate was something of a smoke screen: the problems of treating addiction in private practice provided a convenient way of attacking the treatment of addiction away from the DDU, whether this was in private or in general practice. The specialist status of the DDU psychiatrist was increasingly under threat as general practitioners became involved in the treatment of heroin addiction. The intervention of private doctors heightened this threat still further, although the nature of this challenge was slightly different than that posed by the GP, as many of the doctors treating addicts privately were psychiatrists, or psychiatrically trained. Instead of challenging the treatment of addiction as an area of psychiatric expertise per se, these doctors were presenting an assault on the actual practices of the DDU and those who developed them. The existence of the private practitioner suggested there was an alternative locus of expertise on addiction, one situated away from the DDU and NHS care provided. This was construed, therefore, as a more personal attack on the knowledge, methods and expertise of a group of individuals (the DDU psychiatrists) who, until recently, had been unchallenged in their position as the leading authority on drug users and their problems but were now facing threats to their status and position from all sides.

The contested role of the private practitioner in the treatment of addiction needs to be viewed from both the public and private perspectives. This will be achieved through a detailed examination of the work of

Ann Dally. Dally provides a particularly important and interesting case study not because her practice was the only or even standard model for the private treatment of addiction, but because it exemplified the central challenges to the specialist status of the DDU psychiatrist. The critique of the private treatment addiction offered by the DDU specialists will also be examined here. There were some very real problems associated with the treatment of addiction in private practice, particularly surrounding the prescription of substitute drugs and the payment of fees. But, as an analysis of the GMC's case against Dally for serious professional misconduct in 1983 demonstrates, it is hard to separate some of the difficulties surrounding private treatment for addiction from the broader debate about what kind of doctor should be involved in the treatment of addiction, where their expertise lay, and what methods should be used.

THE TREATMENT OF ADDICTION IN PRIVATE PRACTICE, DR ANN DALLY

The increase in private treatment for addiction paralleled a more general growth in private medicine in this period, but there were a number of anomalies between the overall pattern of private health care provision and the treatment of addiction in private practice that suggested there were different reasons for expansion in this area. Private health-care services had co-existed with state provision since the foundation of the NHS but expanded considerably during the 1980s, spurred on by the Thatcher government who believed that 'the private sector was more efficient, better managed and more responsive to the consumer than the public sector.'[8] A review of spending in 1983 resulted in policies designed to achieve greater efficiency within the NHS and also encouraged the development of health insurance and private care to exist alongside collective provision.[9] A rapid growth in the private sector followed, so that by 1988 there were around 200 private or voluntary hospitals in Britain, treating 8 per cent of all inpatients.[10] Private medical services were most commonly used for elective repair surgery for non-life-threatening conditions, particularly when there were waiting lists for similar services in NHS facilities.[11] Much of this care was provided through health care insurance policies. Subscriptions to medical insurance policies rose steadily over the decade: in 1979 2.7 million Britons (just under 5 per cent of the population) were insured by such schemes, compared to 6.2 million Britons (around 10 per cent of the population) in 1989.[12] Treatment for addiction, however, was rarely, if ever, provided for under such schemes.[13] Addicts generally paid for treatment at the time of service, paying fees directly to the doctor concerned. So while the increase in private treatment for addiction was concomitant with an upsurge in private medicine, it was not necessarily part of the more general pattern in terms of the way services were provided.

Yet the relationship between public and private provision of health-care does provide some clues as to why the private treatment of addiction expanded in the 1980s. Despite the ideological fury sometimes aroused by the issue of private practice, social policy analyst Rudolf Klein saw the relationship between the NHS and the private sector as essentially a symbiotic one. He argued that for the NHS the private sector was a 'safety valve' catering to patients' demands not met by state provision, and for the private sector, the NHS offered services that could not be provided in private medicine, or at least not at a profit.[14] In this way, the private market in health care could be used to gauge where the NHS was lacking, or perceived to be lacking, by those who could afford to opt out of the state system.[15] The existence of private treatment for addiction in this period might, therefore, suggest that the NHS was 'failing' some of its addict-patients. This was the view of Lyn Perry, Assistant Director of drugs advice charity Release, who said in a statement supporting Dally in 1986, 'In many areas, only private practitioners are prepared to offer flexible treatment options, and are stepping into the breach where state services are patchy or inadequate'.[16] This argument requires further exploration. Addicts, like any other patients, must have had good reasons for leaving free public services to pay for private treatment. The services offered by private practitioners therefore need investigation.

The work of Ann Dally provides a particularly pertinent example. Dally was one of the most prominent private practitioners working in the field. Her private papers (held at the Contemporary Medical Archive Centre at the Wellcome Library for the History and Understanding of Medicine in London) are a uniquely detailed source of information on this area. She was an outspoken critic of the DDUs and established an organisation, the Association of Independent Doctors in Addiction (AIDA), in 1981 to support and promote the role of the 'independent' (private or NHS, but non-DDU) doctor in the treatment of addiction.[17] Dally, as the president of AIDA, sat on the Department of Health and Social Security (DHSS) working group tasked with drawing up guidelines on good clinical practice in the treatment of addiction in 1984 and gave evidence to the House of Commons Social Services Committee investigating drug misuse in 1985.[18] In 1983, and again in 1986/7, Dally came before the GMC charged with serious professional misconduct as a result of irresponsible prescription to addict-patients. These cases reveal much about the debate surrounding the treatment of addiction in this period, exemplifying tensions over the defence of the DDU psychiatrists' specialist status and the wider debate over treatment methods.

Dally practiced privately in rooms off Harley Street from 1963 onwards.[19] She had a medical degree, although she had no formal qualifications in psychiatry. Dally regarded herself as a psychiatrist and not a general practitioner, maintaining that she had gained training and experience wherever possible.[20] In her previous work Dally had encountered heroin addicts but stated that after 1979 she was referred increasing numbers of this type of patient by GPs.[21] This was the result, she argued, of serious deficiencies in the treatment offered by the DDUs.[22] Dally asserted that 'all clinics are geared to the addict who is young, recently addicted, unemployed, single and male.'[23] She believed that DDUs concentrated on young, 'new' addicts as they felt that there was a greater likelihood of 'success' in getting them off drugs.[24] This meant that clinics favoured a prescription policy concentrating on withdrawing drugs from the addict, with abstinence as a clear, immediate goal. Dally thought this was unrealistic for those who had been addicted to heroin for a long time. She found some truth in the notion that 'it takes as long to wean an addict off drugs as the time he has been taking those drugs'.[25] Long-term addiction, in her opinion, required long-term treatment.

This view was at the heart of Dally's treatment philosophy, and it was this that set her approach apart from that of the DDUs. This was most clearly displayed in her prescription policies. Dally asserted that the treatment she offered was directed at a series of clear, mutually dependent goals: 'to improve their [the addicts] general health and social situation and to help them reduce their drug need, with the hope that they would eventually become drug free'.[26] To achieve this, Dally prescribed sufficient opiate substitutes (usually methadone) to prevent withdrawal and had regular sessions with the patient directed towards helping the patient acquire greater self-confidence and a more 'stable' life, at which point work could be undertaken to reduce the dosage of drugs.[27] Prescription could occur over a prolonged period. She did not, however, regard this treatment as 'maintenance'. Dally disliked the term and thought 'that the idea of simply giving an addict a regular dose of a drug forever and not doing any more to help him is quite wrong, or at least not the function of a doctor'.[28] Instead, she preferred to think of this as a 'stabilisation dosage' and her treatment as 'long-term detoxification'.[29] Dally summarised her prescription policy as being 'to prescribe as little as possible and to reduce the dose as fast as possible, but only within the capacity of the individual patient'.[30]

This focus on the individual was in contrast, Dally argued, to the policies of the DDUs.[31] Addicts who came to Dally told her that they were not treated as individuals by clinics and disliked the attitudes of the staff who worked there. One patient commented, 'the treatment provided by the NHS is at best dogged by an excess of very generalised and rigid rules and regulations, which take little or no account of an individual's needs and expectations'.[32] Another felt they were 'treated like a criminal rather than a patient'.[33] Many addicts told Dally that the way clinics operated, with daily prescription collection and treatment sessions during office hours, made it impossible to continue in paid employment.[34] In contrast, addict-patients initially saw Dally once a week, but when they were 'stable', or she felt that they could be trusted, they came once every few weeks or even once a month.[35] She also allowed addicts to collect their prescriptions once a week instead of daily. Dally argued that this meant the patient had to take less time off from work to attend treatment sessions.

For Dally, this was an appropriate response to the needs of what she regarded as a different group of patients than those seen by the DDUs. She asserted that, on average, her patients were older, had been addicted to heroin for a longer period of time and were more likely to be in employment than those attending clinics.[36] Establishing that the patient had a guaranteed source of income was vital for Dally, not only because she needed to ensure that he or she was able to pay her fees but also to guard against the likelihood of a patient selling prescribed drugs to a third person. Like most private practices in the treatment of addiction, addicts paid their fees directly to Dally; private health insurance rarely covered the cost of treatment for drug addiction.[37] Dally charged addict-patients £30 a session, and in addition patients had to pay for their prescriptions privately, usually at a higher price than the NHS flat rate.[38] The cost of private treatment was not, therefore, insubstantial; but as Dally pointed out, it was cheaper than buying drugs on the black market.[39] Her means of treating addicts, she felt, was the only other alternative for addict-patients who found the clinics unsuitable. In an interview she even went as far as to say, 'I don't think private practice is a good way to treat addiction. But there simply wasn't anything else; they [addicts] had no other alternative except the clinics, which were so dishonest.'[40]

This attack on the DDUs and their methods was in keeping with Dally's outspoken criticism of clinics' practices and her strong advocacy for the increased involvement of what she termed the 'independent' practitioner in addiction. Dally argued that doctors 'independent' of the DDUs, be they GPs or general psychiatrists, in private practice or working for the NHS, had a role to play in the treatment of heroin addiction.[41] To strengthen this claim, and to campaign for the wider involvement of the 'independent' doctor, Dally established the Association of Independent Doctors in Addiction (AIDA) in 1981. Its purpose was to: 'promote high standards of practice among doctors (both National Health Service and private) who are interested in treating drug addicts outside clinics and to encourage and teach National Health Service general practitioners to look after their own addicts'.[42] Dally canvassed support for her organisation by persuading medical journals to insert notices about AIDA.[43] She claimed that she received several hundred replies from doctors all over the world, but AIDA's membership was actually quite limited.[44] In a document prepared for her lawyers prior to the 1986/7 GMC hearing, Dally stated that AIDA had ten 'active' members and a further thirty members 'world-wide'.[45] Elsewhere Dally conceded that many of the practising doctors rarely attended meetings, and 'some of [the] membership [is] really a mailing list'.[46] Those who joined AIDA, according to Dally, were 'doctors like myself who were trying to help addicts and to treat them in a humane and effective way and who wished to meet and discuss with others of like mind'.[47] Despite Dally's protestations, AIDA was frequently seen as an organisation consisting purely of private doctors. A researcher who had observed the work of the DDUs noted in a letter to *The Lancet* that 'most' members of AIDA were private doctors.[48] Dally was quick to reply that 'Private practitioners form a substantial minority [of AIDA's members], but it is a minority.'[49] The accuracy of this is unclear. Of the ten 'active' members, including Dally herself, listed in 1986, six practised privately (some in addition to NHS work) and only one practised exclusively within the NHS.[50]

AIDA's reputation was not enhanced by being associated with a number of doctors who had their names deleted from the GMC's register of licensed medical practitioners. A former AIDA member, Dr Ali Khan, was struck off in 1982 for irresponsible prescription to addicts.[51] Dally stated that this happened before the organisation had really got going and that they had persuaded Khan to change his prescription practices, but by then it was too late.[52] Dally maintained that he was the only member of AIDA to be struck off by the GMC, but this was not necessarily widely understood. At a meeting of the DHSS Working Party on Drug Misuse constituted to create guidelines on good clinical treatment of addiction in 1984, Bewley confidently asserted that members of AIDA had been struck off.[53] Dally admitted that there were other doctors of dubious clinical reputation who became associated with AIDA. Dr Peter Tansey, Dr Rai and Dr Rahman had all been found guilty of irresponsible prescription by the GMC and were all 'cited by our critics as being members', although Rai and Rahman attended only one meeting.[54]

AIDA did, however, have a number of more positive associations. According to Dally, Bing Spear was 'enthusiastic', and he felt that an organisation like AIDA had 'long been needed and offered help'.[55] Spear initially allowed AIDA to meet at the Home Office, giving Dally the impression of support, allowing her to boast in a letter to *The Lancet* in 1982: 'We are meeting regularly together with observers from the Home Office and the Department of Health and Social Security.'[56] They were later forced to reconvene at Dally's home after protests about AIDA meeting at the Home Office came from what she described as the 'drug dependency Mafia' led, she alleged, by Bewley.[57] Dally believed that 'meeting there [at the Home Office] had given us a respectability that was unacceptable in some quarters.'[58] This may have been more than paranoia: Spear noted that 'the London consultants did not take too kindly to the contact the Drugs Inspectorate had with AIDA and individual private practitioners.'[59] However, Spear viewed AIDA more equivocally than perhaps Dally realised. He noted that his contact with the organisation was 'perfectly consistent with our [the Home Office Drugs Inspectorate's] long-established policy of keeping in contact with anyone working in the drug dependence field. It did not imply approval, or disapproval, of the clinical judgements of those concerned.'[60] Spear's interest in AIDA, therefore, did not necessarily equate with support for its members or their goals.[61]

The work of AIDA was primarily advisory. There was an attempt to provide a practical solution to some of the problems in the treatment of drug addiction identified by AIDA when the organisation tried to establish its own non-profit clinic. This clinic would 'try to help the large numbers of addicts who do not benefit from the NHS but cannot afford private treatment'.[62] Patients would be seen on referral from their GPs, and the addict would pay a small fee 'in accordance with their means' for treatment.[63] AIDA applied to the DHSS for a grant to pay staff working at the clinic on a per session basis. Dally maintained that they did not hear anything about the success or otherwise of their application, and AIDA's attempt to set up a clinic never came to fruition.[64] The greatest potential for AIDA to influence the development of drug addiction treatment came in 1984 when they were asked to send a representative to sit on the working party of drug addiction experts tasked with drawing up guidelines on the good clinical treatment of addiction by the DHSS. AIDA elected Dally as their representative, and another AIDA member, Dr Dale Beckett, also sat on the working party.[65] A more extensive discussion of the working party and the guidelines produced will take place in Chapter Six, but it is clear that Dally and Beckett were very much minority voices on the committee. They were unable to have a significant influence on the content, wording or style of the final guidelines, to the extent that AIDA felt moved to produce their own comments on the document.[66]

AIDA were also asked to give evidence to the House of Commons Social Services Committee in 1985.[67] AIDA submitted a memorandum and gave verbal evidence raising a number of issues with current drug treatment policies. They stated that the 'proper person to treat most addicts is the general practitioner' and suggested that some kind of additional payment could be made to GPs willing to take on addict-patients.[68] There is some evidence to indicate that the committee took on board this suggestion, as they recommended that the DHSS examine the feasibility of such a scheme.[69] In fact the committee commended the role of the GP in the treatment of addiction more generally and suggested that there was no reason why GPs should not treat addicts with gradually diminishing doses of oral methadone on a short-term basis, provided they were properly trained and had access to specialist support and advice.[70] It is unlikely, however, that AIDA were solely responsible in shaping this recommendation, as the committee heard evidence from a number of bodies and individuals who stressed the role of the GP in the treatment of addiction, including the Royal College of General Practitioners.[71]

AIDA was very much Dally's organisation. She was its founder and president and believed that she did most of its work, complaining she was the only doctor in the organisation who spoke out or criticised the DDUs.[72] Most of the documents produced in AIDA's name were drafted entirely by Dally, and it is almost impossible to differentiate between AIDA's collective views and Dally's personal opinions. It is revealing, for instance, to compare the written comments Dally sent to Dr Dorothy Black at the DHSS on the *Guidelines of Good Clinical Practice in the Treatment of Drug Misuse* (the *Guidelines*) and those sent out under the auspices of AIDA.[73] The two documents make almost identical points, and though similarities might be expected, nothing separated the supposed 'consensus views' of AIDA from Dally's own beliefs.[74] Dally was without doubt AIDA's most vocal representative, but the other members did play a role in the organisation's work. Dr Tessa Hare was an AIDA member and NHS GP who treated addicts in a similar fashion to Dally, emphasising the need for helping addicts develop a stable life. In an interview with *General Practitioner* in 1983, she mentioned her membership in AIDA, and she and Dally gave evidence jointly on behalf of the organisation to the Social Services Committee on the Misuse of Drugs in 1985.[75] AIDA members were called upon to support Dally when she faced the GMC on charges of irresponsible prescription to addicts in 1983 and again in 1986/7, but there was no broad-scale campaign to publicise her case or her position. Dr Beard, an AIDA member, submitted written character evidence in support of Dally at her 1983 hearing, and Beckett appeared as a witness for the 'defence' in the second GMC case in 1986/7.[76] Beckett was one of Dally's greatest supporters, but whether this was as a friend or as a fellow AIDA member is unclear.

Questions can therefore be raised about the extent to which AIDA had any significant impact on heroin addiction treatment policy in this period. Though they gave advice to both the DHSS committee on the production of the *Guidelines* and the Social Services Committee, their views were largely ignored. Most of the membership, apart from Dally, Hare and Beckett, showed little sign of becoming actively involved in the organisation's work or the broader debate over the treatment of addiction. Yet AIDA was important for two reasons. Firstly, AIDA's true significance lay in the fact that it existed at all. The presence of an organisation founded to support and defend the role of NHS GPs and private practitioners interested in the treatment of addiction indicated that these doctors were playing an increasing role in this area, and this was provoking conflict with the DDUs. AIDA was created because a broader debate was taking place over who could most effectively treat the addict: the DDU psychiatrist, the GP or the private doctor. Secondly, Dally, as AIDA's founder, president and prime activist, dramatically raised her own profile in the field through the organisation. This enhanced her claim to be an 'expert', something she was later to rely on in her GMC disciplinary hearings, but her high profile also made her a target for those keen to eliminate the 'independent' doctor from the treatment of addiction. AIDA was thus significant for Dally personally and the private practitioner more generally.

'LEGALISED DRUG DEALING'—THE CRITIQUE OF THE TREATMENT OF HEROIN ADDICTION IN PRIVATE PRACTICE

An organisation such as AIDA had much to contend with when it came to improving the position of the private practitioner in the treatment of addiction. The image of private treatment for heroin addiction had been somewhat tarnished by the activities of some notorious 'prescribers,' doctors who prescribed controlled drugs to addicts freely, seemingly without limitation. The infamous Lady Frankau discussed in Chapter Two had, of course, been in private practice, and when she died in 1967 she was simply replaced by other doctors. Dr John Petro took over many of Frankau's patients, and he easily equalled his predecessor in terms of notoriety among addicts and also the wider newspaper reading public.[77] Petro had his name struck off the Medical Register in 1968, but 'prescribers' like Dr Christopher Michael Swan continued to overprescribe controlled drugs to addicts until he too was struck off and sentenced to fifteen years imprisonment in 1970.[78] Strong connections were thus made between private practice and dubious prescribing practices.

Tales of ludicrous overprescription by private doctors fed into attacks directed at the private treatment of heroin addiction in the 1980s. Those who opposed the treatment of addiction in private practice saw the connection between prescribing drugs and the payment of fees direct to the doctor as little short of 'legalised drug dealing'. This appeared to be the central issue in the debate over the treatment of addiction in private practice. According to *The Lancet* there were 'potentially enormous financial rewards' to be had by prescribing privately to addict-patients.[79] This assertion was supported by an article by Bewley, in which he estimated a doctor seeing 20 such patients a day 'could receive over £100,000 a year solely by prescribing controlled drugs to addicts'.[80] This statement suggested that doctors involved in private practice were not interested in treating addicts but only in giving out drugs and receiving their fee; but it is unclear if this practice was widespread during the 1980s. There was no suggestion, for example, that Dally had been financially motivated in offering treatment to addicts.[81]

In many ways the issue of fees was a surface concern, one that masked a deeper conflict over what kind of doctors should be responsible for the treatment of addiction and what methods should be used. Bewley's paper represented an attack on the position of the private practitioner in the treatment of addiction.[82] A number of individuals took issue with Bewley's claims. A.B. Robertson, an addict receiving private treatment, wrote to the *British Medical Journal* arguing that he did not 'consider that I am being sold a batch of drugs at every visit. Doctors must charge fees, or how else are they to live?'[83] Private psychiatrist and AIDA member Dale Beckett also wrote to the *British Medical Journal* protesting about the article by Bewley and his colleague, consultant psychiatrist A. Hamid Ghodse, stating that their assertion about being able to earn £100,000 made him 'angry' as in his practice 'a session with an addict lasts an hour, and usually I spend a long time afterwards writing out prescriptions'.[84] Dally argued in her book *A Doctor's Story* that those who viewed private medicine as a 'money-making racket' were unaware of the expenses of private practice. Annual rents on rooms from which a doctor could practice in the Harley Street area coupled with other expenses, including a secretary, led Dally to argue that a doctor who gave up two NHS sessions had to earn at least £1,000 a week to cover costs and compensate for loss of earnings.[85]

The precise amount that a private doctor could earn by prescribing to addicts was less of an issue than how addict-patients were to find the money to pay for this. Bewley stated that if the patient was unemployed, he or she might sell some of the drugs prescribed to support themselves and to pay the doctor's fee.[86] This suspicion was seemingly confirmed by social anthropologist Angela Burr, who observed the operation of the black market in legally prescribed but illegally sold drugs in the Piccadilly area.[87] She found that 'most' drug users who were prescribed drugs on a private basis sold some of their supply to pay doctors' and chemists' fees. Burr asserted that if addicts had a surplus left over, then private practitioners were clearly prescribing addicts larger amounts of controlled drugs than was necessary for the alleviation of withdrawal symptoms.[88] A survey of addict-patients conducted by Bewley and Ghodse supported Burr's assertion. They asked 69 addict-patients why addicts went to see private doctors, and survey results suggested that private practitioners: prescribed injectable drugs, prescribed more than one drug, prescribed weekly, prescribed in larger doses and were easier to con.[89] According to *The Lancet* private practitioners and those working outside the clinics 'may be casual in the quantities that they prescribe and what they overprescribe [sic.] can readily find its way to the black market'. This led the journal to conclude that while these doctors might be well intentioned, 'many people well placed to judge the consequences of their actions argue that they [non-clinic doctors] are aggravating an already grim scene'.[90] Bewley and Ghodse suggested that there were only two ways to remedy the situation: Home Office tribunals or the GMC should act to stop private doctors deliberately overprescribing to addicts and, failing that, the licensing system for the prescription of heroin to addicts should be extended to include all controlled drugs.[91] Either option would result in the effective exclusion of the non-clinic doctor, as licenses for the prescription of heroin were generally limited to DDU psychiatrists.

The studies conducted and editorials penned certainly painted a bleak picture of the work of the private practitioner in the treatment of addiction. The impression given was that private doctors overprescribed opiate drugs to their addict-patients either unwittingly, due to a lack of experience, or deliberately in order to make money for themselves. Regardless of motive, this overprescribing had the consequence that more drugs found their way onto the black market as addicts sold their surplus —sometimes to help fund private treatment. However, over-spill of legitimate drugs onto the illegitimate market came from NHS doctors as well as private practitioners. Burr found that drugs bought and sold in Piccadilly came from DDUs as well as from private doctors.[92] Furthermore, the significance of this 'grey' market in pharmaceutical drugs may well have been exaggerated: illicitly produced, imported and traded drugs were freely available by the early 1980s, and this black market easily exceeded the 'grey' market in terms of size.[93] Other studies, such as Bewley and Ghodse's, were based on somewhat questionable evidence. Bewley and Ghodse asked addict-patients attending DDUs a series of rather leading questions, such as if they considered private doctors were more easily 'conned' than clinic doctors, or if private practitioners prescribed larger doses than could be obtained from DDUs.[94] However, as only 50 per cent of the 69 respondents had actually consulted a private doctor, half of the responses were not based on personal experience but rather on rumour and supposition. This article subsequently came in for a good deal of criticism. Beckett asserted that 'the *BMJ* has published propaganda disguised as a scientific paper'.[95] For Spear, 'the true purpose of the paper' was an 'establishment attack on the private sector'.[96]

This 'attack' on the treatment of addiction in private practice was caused by more than the particular problems facing private treatment in this field. Though it may be tempting to suggest that this could be read as a more generalised assault on private medicine, examining the actions of some of the key protagonists indicates this was unlikely. Dally believed that Bewley was totally opposed to private medicine. She asserted that 'Bewley had a strong dislike of private practice and made no attempt to hide it.'[97] Yet in response to a direct question about his views on the private treatment of addiction in an interview with the *British Journal of Addiction*, Bewley replied: 'I don't see any objection in principle to the private practice treatment of addicts', although he did note, 'It can be difficult for a single-handed practitioner.'[98] Bewley himself did not practice privately, but other leading DDU doctors, such as Philip Connell, did.[99] Connell told the House of Commons Social Services Committee that he even treated a few addict-patients privately, although he stated, 'I personally would not prescribe drugs to a patient in private practice unless it was very clearly on a withdrawal scheme that was stuck to whatever happened'.[100]

Connell's response to the Social Services Committee suggests an alternative motivation behind the sharp criticism directed towards the treatment of addiction in private practice during the 1980s. His comment indicated that he believed short-term withdrawal was the preferred method of treatment for addiction. The fact that private practitioners such as Dally were prepared to offer treatment on a longer-term basis presented an alternative to this, one that appeared to contradict and conflict with the methods of the clinics. The attack on private practice appeared to be the result not of an ideological opposition to private practice or even necessarily a dislike of addiction treatment conducted in this manner but because of the potential threat posed by private practices to the authority of a group of DDU doctors. Spear asserted: 'The intrusion of the independent practitioner into the drug addiction treatment field was seen as a direct challenge to the pre-eminence and prestige of a few influential clinicians, whose personal views and prejudices dominated treatment policy in London.'[101] Spear's contention may be correct in spirit, but he offers no explanation as to how and why the DDU doctors felt sufficiently threatened to try and push out private doctors. To understand this, it is necessary to look to the position of the treatment of drug addiction as a specialty within medicine and also within the 'policy community' surrounding drugs.

As already noted, the establishment of the DDUs in the late 1960s and the gradual 'psychiatrisation' of addiction facilitated the development of the specialist status of the DDU psychiatrist, but this remained fairly fragile. Despite the growing confidence of psychiatry in general during this period, it remained a relatively low status specialty. Within psychiatry, the treatment of addiction was even more poorly regarded.[102] The growing number of GPs becoming involved in the treatment of addiction called into question the relevance of the specialist approach, but there were other attacks on the specialist status of the DDU doctors. There was, as Virginia Berridge has noted, a move to 'bring drug services out of hospitals and into the community' by involving GPs and other non-medical actors.[103] This more diffuse response to drug use can be detected in the ACMD's 1982 report *Treatment and Rehabilitation*. By placing emphasis on the range of difficulties encountered by the 'problem drug taker' rather than the disease of the 'addict', *Treatment and Rehabilitation* paved the way for the involvement of a wider group of agencies. This was gradually realised through the introduction of a dedicated funding stream for drug services, the Central Funding Initiative (CFI), from 1983 to 1989. The aim of the CFI, according to Berridge was 'to displace the old hospital-based London-focused specialist treatment system'.[104] Such a claim is supported by the pattern of grants awarded under the CFI: not only did a significant proportion of the funds go the regions instead of the capital but just 18 per cent of grants went to DDUs or hospital-based services, with the rest of the grants going to community-based services within the statutory and non-statutory sector.[105]

The London-based drug addiction specialists were thus in an increasingly precarious position, with their status and authority as the experts on drug use under attack from two sides: from within medicine by general and private practitioners and from outside medicine by a growing range of interested authorities. In order to retain both the treatment of addiction as a specialist area and a powerful position in the expanding 'policy community' around drugs, it was necessary for DDU psychiatrists to demonstrate a continued relevance for specialist treatment. This could be achieved by pointing to the problems associated with non-specialist treatment, most clearly evidenced in the treatment of addiction in private practice.

THE GMC VERSUS DR ANN DALLY, 1983

It is in this context that the GMC's case against Dally in 1983 needs to be seen. This case highlighted some of the problems connected with the treatment of addiction away from the DDU and in private practice in particular, but it was also representative of a more practical attempt to remove Dally, and private practitioners in general, from the treatment of addiction. The General Medical Council (GMC) is a statutory body granted powers by Parliament to regulate the medical profession. It was created as a result of the Medical Act in 1858 to administer a single register of all medical men and was designed to differentiate between the qualified practitioner and a range of unqualified healers.[106] In essence, the function of the GMC has remained the same since its establishment. The GMC controls who may enter the register of licensed medical practitioners by deciding what qualifications are necessary to practice medicine and can remove those deemed unfit to continue. To this end, it approves medical schools and investigates complaints or convictions against licensed medical practitioners. It has no inspectorate and relies upon complaints or convictions reported to the GMC to learn of suspected instances of serious professional misconduct. The GMC is responsible to the Privy Council, and appeals against the GMC's findings are heard there. The GMC is a self-regulating professional body but has included lay, or non-medical, members as a statutory requirement since 1950.[107] It is independent of the NHS and the government and is funded directly by its members.

A re-examination of the GMC's role came in 1975 with the Merrison Enquiry. Merrison found that the GMC was not a complaints machine for patients but existed to protect the public from unqualified practitioners. Its purpose, therefore, was not to punish doctors but to maintain the standards of the profession.[108] Merrison endorsed the position that doctors could only be removed from the register if they had been convicted of a criminal offence that suggested they were unfit to practice or if they were found guilty of serious professional misconduct.[109] Serious professional misconduct was defined by the Medical Act in 1969 as being 'serious misconduct judged according to the rules, written or unwritten, governing the profession'.[110] In order to clarify what kinds of behaviour could be constituted as serious professional misconduct, Merrison suggested that the GMC's guidance to doctors, *Professional Conduct and Discipline: Fitness to Prescribe*, known as the 'Blue Book', should be expanded.[111] According to the 'Blue Book', professional misconduct fell into four categories. The first was neglect by doctors of their professional responsibilities to patients for their care and treatment. The second was the abuse of professional privileges or skills. The third concerned the personal behaviour of the doctor and encompassed conduct seen to be derogatory to the reputation of the medical profession. The last prohibited the advertising of professional services by doctors.[112]

When answering charges of serious professional misconduct, doctors were allowed legal representation and the same standards of proof were required as in a court: the charge had to be proven beyond reasonable doubt.[113] If the charge was proved, the council had four basic options open to them: they could simply conclude the case if they felt the doctor had already suffered enough; they could admonish the doctor and then conclude the case; they could suspend the doctor for a fixed period of time (up to a year); and, finally, they could have the doctor's name erased from the register, meaning that he or she would no longer be able to practice medicine.[114] The GMC were also able to make continued registration conditional on whatever they deemed appropriate for a maximum period of three years.[115]

The GMC had traditionally been reluctant to play a role in disciplining doctors believed to be overprescribing opiate drugs to addicts. The Rolleston Committee recommended that tribunals be established to deal with doctor-addicts and those who dispensed drugs to addicts too freely.[116] The Dangerous Drugs Regulations of 1926 provided the statutory basis for tribunals, permitting the Home Secretary to remove the doctor's right to prescribe controlled drugs if found guilty, but these were never used.[117] When the first Brain Committee examined the issue in 1961, they were not convinced that tribunals were either practical or necessary given 'the infrequency of these irregularities'.[118] The overprescription of drugs to addicts by a handful of doctors prompted the second Brain Committee to reconsider; however, they decided that should disciplinary proceedings be necessary, the appropriate tribunal would be the Disciplinary Committee (later the Professional Conduct Committee) of the GMC.[119] If the charge was proved, the GMC should have the authority to remove the doctor's right to prescribe controlled drugs.[120] According to Smart, the GMC refused to take on this responsibility.[121] The President of the GMC at that time, Lord Cohen, did not believe that the Council should act as 'a police authority for the medical profession'.[122]

To deal with doctors who prescribed drugs to addicts in an irresponsible manner, Home Office tribunals were to be revived under the Misuse of Drugs Act, 1971.[123] It was not until 1974 that these came into being, by which time the GMC had changed its stance on the issue and were increasingly prepared to consider 'the prescription of drugs other than in the course of bona fide treatment' as being serious professional misconduct.[124] Why the GMC changed its position is unclear, but they heard 39 cases of improper prescribing between 1972 and 1984, resulting in 18 doctors having their names erased from the medical register.[125] Home Office tribunals were not widely used to pursue cases of irresponsible prescription until the early 1980s; between 1974 and 1982 just nine tribunals were held.[126] The ACMD were critical of this, noting that a narrow and legalistic approach had been adopted, resulting in only those cases where there was clear evidence of gross irresponsible prescription being heard.[127] Stung into action, the Home Office tribunal prohibited three doctors from prescribing controlled drugs in 1983, another three in 1984, and a further three were prevented from doing so on a temporary basis.[128] This meant that there were two separate bodies pursuing the discipline of doctors prescribing irresponsibly to addicts: the Home Office tribunals and also the GMC. The two differed in the charge they could levy and the punishment they could exact but were effectively trying the same offence. Tribunals tried doctors for irresponsible prescription and, if found guilty, could remove the doctor's right to prescribe controlled drugs. The GMC assessed whether or not a doctor's prescription of drugs to an addict was part of bona fide treatment and, if they decided it was not, could charge the doctor with serious professional misconduct and censure him or her in whatever way they saw fit.

To confuse matters still further, the two systems were not in contact with one another, and there did not seem to be a clear reason why a doctor should face a tribunal and not the GMC or vice versa. Being found guilty of irresponsible prescription by the Home Office did not automatically lead to a GMC hearing on charges of suspected serious professional misconduct.[129] The two systems existed because of the GMC's initial reluctance to become involved in disciplining doctors thought to be prescribing in an inappropriate manner, so the Home Office instigated their own methods. By the time these had been put into place, the GMC were more amenable to the idea of considering overprescription to addicts as serious professional misconduct, so there were two pieces of machinery to deal with the same problem. Deciding which body a doctor should face probably depended upon the peculiarities of the individual case. Unravelling the reasons behind this is less revealing than the overall upward trend in the use of both tribunals and GMC hearings. By 1983 there was a more general willingness to use these bodies to pursue doctors believed to be prescribing to addicts irresponsibly.[130] According to Mike Ashton, editor of the journal *Druglink*, the disciplinary mechanisms were being 'oiled-up and put to use'.[131] This suggests that either more doctors were prescribing irresponsibly and/or there was more interest in these cases, resulting in a greater number coming before the Home Office and the GMC. Dally's hearing was thus part of a more general increase in the use of the available machinery to discipline doctors thought to be prescribing to addicts irresponsibly.

The case that actually brought Dally before the GMC centred on her treatment of one addict-patient, Brian Sigsworth. The charge laid against Dally was that between June and November of 1981 she abused her position as a medical practitioner by issuing prescriptions for controlled drugs (the opiate substitutes Ritalin and Diconal) other than in the course of bona fide treatment. The GMC's main contention was that 'Even if it be right in rare cases to prescribe large quantities of controlled drugs to acknowledged addicts so as to forestall their obtaining those drugs on the black market and with a view to ultimately reducing the dosage and therefore weaning them from their addiction, that course of treatment should be done only in the strictest of conditions.'[132] Dally, the GMC's barrister Timothy Preston argued, had not observed these conditions. He suggested: that precautions should include not issuing prescriptions to a third person; a clinical examination of the patient be carried out to check that he was not injecting the drugs prescribed; and the doctor should check to ascertain if these drugs were being taken at all. Preston also drew the committee's attention to the fact that Dally was treating Sigsworth privately and the special responsibilities that this placed on the practitioner. He noted that the fee charged should not be so great as to tempt the patient to sell the drugs prescribed in order to finance treatment, which he argued was particularly pertinent in the case of a patient like Sigsworth, who had a criminal record. Preston's concern was that Sigsworth, as an unemployed student living on a grant, travelling from Coventry to London to see a private doctor who charged £30 a consultation, paying an average of £7 to have his prescription filled, would find the temptation to sell some of his prescription to raise money too great. The question, therefore, was whether it ought to have occurred to Dally that Sigsworth might sell some of the Diconal she prescribed him.[133] If Dally had 'closed her eyes to that possibility' or 'given the circumstances of this case probability' that the patient might sell drugs to a third party, that would be treatment in bad faith and would, therefore, constitute serious professional misconduct.[134]

Dally defended her treatment of Sigsworth by arguing that her prescription to him had not been excessive, she had been able to reduce his dose and she believed that he could afford her fees by taking on extra work if necessary.[135] She could not accept that Sigsworth would sell some of his prescription in order to pay her fees, as he, in her opinion, needed the drugs prescribed. Dally's barrister, Adrian Whitfield, argued that there was no suggestion of bad faith in Dally's prescription of Diconal to Sigsworth, and even if she was guilty of prescribing too liberally, this did not in itself constitute serious professional misconduct. He noted that there were not many cases in which allegations of irresponsible prescription were made and members of the Drugs Inspectorate, such as Bing Spear, could be called upon to defend the practitioner concerned. He concluded, on examining the facts of the case, 'this lady appears as one who was doing her best'.[136]

Before the committee retired to consider their verdict, the Legal Assessor was asked to provide more evidence on how irresponsible prescription could be considered to be serious professional misconduct. He determined that a doctor could be found guilty of such an offence if that doctor knew, or did not care if, controlled drugs prescribed by them were being sold by a patient.[137] Dally believed that the wording of the charge was being changed so as to find her guilty, an assertion supported to some extent by reports of journalists overhearing a person 'associated' with the GMC or its lawyers remarking that the 'prosecution' were unlikely to win their case because of the wording of the charge, and subsequently this was altered.[138] After consideration, the committee decided that Dally had been prescribing Diconal to Sigsworth not in the course of bona fide treatment and was, therefore, guilty of serious professional misconduct. The President told Dally that, as the medical profession had been given special responsibilities in relation to the prescription of controlled drugs to addicts, the GMC were 'bound to take a serious view of a case such as yours where it has been proved to their satisfaction that you have disregarded those special responsibilities'.[139] The committee found that Dally had prescribed large amounts of drugs to a patient, and the circumstances in which the prescriptions were issued did not amount to a sufficient level of supervision. They believed that she had not taken satisfactory steps to establish adequate therapeutic reasons for prescribing Diconal to Sigsworth, and she did not monitor his progress well enough. The committee took into account 'the many references and representations made' on Dally's behalf and decided to admonish her and conclude the case.[140]

Examining the evidence presented and the verdict reached in Dally's case raises some key points about the treatment of addiction and the role of the private practitioner. Dally's handling of Sigsworth was flawed given the climate of opinion among specialists about the treatment of addicts. In contrast to the DDUs, she prescribed large doses of an opiate substitute on a weekly basis, did not carry out extensive clinical examinations and saw her patient somewhat infrequently. Furthermore, there were specific issues that related to the treatment of addiction in private practice. As a private doctor Dally charged Sigsworth a fee for consultations. In order to fund this treatment, as an addict-patient on a low income who had committed criminal acts in the past to get money for drugs, it was perfectly possible that Sigsworth could or would sell some of the pills prescribed by Dally. Of course, Sigsworth could just as easily have sold drugs prescribed to him by an NHS doctor, but he would not have had to pay for treatment, nor would he have had to pay as much for his prescription. There was less of an inducement, as there was less of an incentive.

Viewing the case on its merits alone, however, would suggest that to find that Dally had acted in bad faith when prescribing to Sigsworth was something of a curious verdict. *The Lancet's* legal correspondent, barrister Diana Brahams, found that the evidence submitted during the hearing fell 'well short of proof of a lack of good faith', setting her analysis of the case against the 'background of concern about the role of private doctors in the treatment of drug dependence'.[141] In order to explain this verdict, the wider context in which it was delivered needs to be considered. Views on the private treatment of addiction were increasingly polarised, and a powerful, well-supported group of DDU psychiatrists wanted to eliminate the private practitioner from the treatment of addiction. Dally was a figurehead for the private doctor treating addicts and, therefore, an obvious target in the dispute over drug addiction treatment.

Evidence for this view can be found in the reaction to the GMC's verdict in the medical press and elsewhere. Dally's case had a number of significant implications not just for those treating addicts but also for the methods used. The GMC, it appeared, was not above conducting 'political' trials. Jean Robinson, a former chairperson of the Patients' Association, sat on the GMC as a lay member during the 1980s. She argued that although the members of the disciplinary committee tried to do an honest job, in the end they 'merely become instruments for the occasional ritual sacrifice'.[142] For Michael O'Donnell, doctor, medical commentator and member of the GMC, this was clearly what happened in the Dally case. O'Donnell asserted that without the 'background political noise' surrounding the treatment of addiction the case would not have been brought. O'Donnell could well understand the view of journalists watching proceedings that 'this was a political trial in which the "establishment" was out to "get" Dr Dally because of her heretical views'. Because Dally had dared to 'question the party line on the management of drug addiction', she was subjected to a 'trial' by the GMC.[143]

O'Donnell and Dally both referred to the dismay of journalists in the public gallery at the GMC's verdict, yet none of this outrage spilled out into articles in the broadsheet press.[144] Most newspapers just confined themselves to the details of the case; only *The Guardian* hinted at wider political reasons for the hearing, stating that Dally had 'publicly set herself up in opposition to the government-run clinics for drug addicts', suggesting that the case might be about adjudicating a debate over treatment.[145] The medical press covered the case in more detail. O'Donnell's attack on the Dally 'trial' appeared in the *British Medical Journal*, and *The Lancet* devoted an editorial to the case, noting that there was 'speculation' about 'the motives behind the charge' and that the evidence against Dally was not 'compelling'.[146]

There was some attempt on the part of the GMC to fight back against the criticism directed at their findings. Sir John Walton, chairman of the GMC and of the panel that heard the Dally case, wrote to the *British Medical Journal* defending his committee's verdict and challenging some of the allegations made by O'Donnell. He argued that the GMC did not take such decisions lightly and 'least of all vindictively'. The case, he maintained, was not about the benefits or drawbacks of a particular method of treating addicts but about determining whether or not Dally had abused her position as a medical practitioner by issuing prescriptions to a patient other than in the course of bona fide treatment. According to Walton, that alone was the issue on which the GMC adjudicated and found the charge to be proved to their satisfaction.[147] Yet, the climate in which the case was brought clearly helped shape its outcome. Ashton pointed out that debate about the involvement of the private doctor in the treatment of addiction had reached its height just a few months before Dally appeared before the GMC.[148] He argued that what mattered was not so much whether the judgment against Dally was 'right' or 'wrong' but the significance this verdict held in terms of the controls placed on the prescription of drugs to addicts. For Ashton the decision represented 'a tougher line on addiction treatment'.[149]

IMPLICATIONS

Taken as a whole, these articles indicate that the Dally case was about more than Dally. And, when viewed in context of the debate about the role of the private practitioner in the treatment of addiction that took place immediately prior to the hearing, it is difficult not to conclude that Dally was the 'sacrificial lamb' referred to by O'Donnell. Prescribing drugs to addicts was always likely to be a risky business. Whether in private practice or working at an NHS DDU, drugs prescribed legitimately by doctors did find their way onto the black market. The risks were, of course, greater with private prescription as the costs involved increased the likelihood that drugs could be sold to finance treatment, but these drugs constituted just a small proportion of those available to addicts wishing to buy drugs illegally; most drugs by the 1980s came from illicit sources. This, however, was not widely acknowledged by those who wished to halt the intervention of the private doctor in the treatment of addiction. Flagging up the problems of private practice in *Treatment and Rehabilitation* and in countless letters and articles in medical journals had not stopped the involvement of private doctors and GPs in this field. But, by finding a key private practitioner treating addicts guilty of serious professional misconduct, the Dally case could also serve as a warning to other private doctors and prevent them from becoming involved. The GMC were, therefore, assuming a position in the conflict over the role of the private practitioner in the treatment of addiction through this verdict. It was no coincidence that this position was broadly that of the DDU psychiatrists, the respected 'experts' in the field who had strong links to the medical establishment and even the GMC itself. Both Connell and Bewley had an extensive list of honours and memberships: Bewley was the president of the Royal College of Psychiatrists, and Connell even sat on the GMC. That is not to say there was necessarily a 'campaign' to 'get' Dally, rather the position and authority of the leading DDU doctors allowed them to indirectly influence the GMC's decision.[150]

To some extent the GMC hearing can be said to have 'failed'. It did not stop Dally practising and treating addicts, nor did it completely halt the intervention of the private doctor. Moreover, astute commentators recognised the political significance of the GMC's findings. As well as raising the well-aired concerns about what kind of doctor should treat the addict, Dally's case pointed to a number of other issues around which the treatment debate continued to revolve. The hearing demonstrated that there was a great need for guidelines on the treatment of heroin addiction, both to help practitioners determine the correct course to follow and also as a standard against which doctors thought to be prescribing to addicts irresponsibly could be held. Running through the case was an undercurrent concerning not just private practice treatment of addiction but all treatment of heroin addiction. Some of the criticisms directed at Dally's treatment methods were not just attributable to her status as a private doctor but raised issues with her underlying treatment philosophy. Indeed, the debate within the treatment of addiction moved away from issues of whether or not private or general practitioners should be involved in the treatment of addiction and instead began to focus on the type of treatment offered. It is the consideration of this issue that will be examined in the next chapter.

Disputed Methods

Maintenance and Withdrawal, 1980–1987

'**K**halid' was a self-employed roofer who had been addicted to heroin for eleven years. He was a patient of Dr Ann Dally's from 1982 until 1985. During this time Dally prescribed Khalid injectable methadone on a slowly reducing basis so that by the end of the three-year period he had cut his drug intake by around a half, something Dally regarded as 'a good result'. Problems arose, however, when Khalid's wife contacted Dally and told her that her husband was currently unemployed and was selling some of the methadone ampoules Dally had prescribed; however, Dally was unconvinced by Mrs Khalid's allegations as Dally believed Khalid needed the drugs prescribed.

Dally became concerned when solicitors acting on behalf of Mrs Khalid sent her a letter setting out the claim in more detail. At her next consultation with Khalid in December 1985, Dally showed him the solicitor's letter and told him that she would be unable to continue treatment until the matter was resolved. In the meantime, Dally told Khalid to go to his GP for help. Dally wrote in Khalid's notes that she had discharged him, but she failed to write to the patient's GP. She argued that she did not want 'to write a discharge letter only to find that Khalid and his wife returned in a week or two and I would have to write another letter'. Khalid went to his GP, who referred him to a DDU. But Khalid did not go to the clinic and turned instead to the black market. He was arrested for selling heroin a few weeks later.[1]

Dally's handling of Khalid came to the attention of both the Home Office and the General Medical Council, and in 1986 she was called before the GMC to answer the charge of serious professional misconduct. However, the charges made against Dally concerned more than just one patient: they called into question the very appropriateness of maintenance as a form of treatment for heroin addiction. This suggests that Dally's case, like her first hearing in 1983, needs to be set in the context of a much wider debate taking place in this period about the methods used in treating heroin addicts. In the 1980s tension existed not only between DDU psychiatrists and private and general practitioners involved in the treatment of addiction but also between those doctors who offered short-term, abstinence-orientated withdrawal treatment and those who prescribed for addicts on a long-term, or maintenance, basis. Director of the Liverpool DDU, John Marks, asserted, 'The debate about controlled drug prescribing has split the profession down the middle.'[2] Those who supported the rapid withdrawal of drugs from addicts prescribed diminishing doses of an opiate substitute (usually orally administered methadone) over a short period of time (usually between three and twenty weeks), at the end of which the addict would be 'abstinent' or 'drug free'.[3] It could then be said that the addict was 'cured', as he or she was, officially, no longer taking their drug of addiction. Doctors who supported maintenance prescribed drugs to addicts over a much longer period (of several months or even years) and were less inclined to reduce the dose. This treatment was aimed not so much at getting the addict off drugs but was instead targeted at enhancing the social functioning of the patient, improving relationships, employment and general health. The treatment offered by the respective groups thus differed in the duration of prescription but also in the expected outcome.

The position and the type of medicine practised frequently separated advocates of short-term withdrawal and those who offered maintenance. Supporters of short-term, abstinence-oriented treatment were largely to be found in NHS DDUs, whereas those who called for long-term maintenance were often found in private or general practice. This division was no coincidence; indeed, it can be used to explain why disputes over the treatment of addiction were so bitterly fought. The relative position of these groups, the environment in which they existed and the types of medicine they practised fundamentally affected their understanding of addiction and its treatment. DDU psychiatrists saw addiction as a disease to be treated and paid less attention to the social situation of the individual addict-patient. Addicts were examined, and, if the diagnosis of addiction was made, treatment was offered. Doses of opioids were reduced as rapidly as possible, as this 'treatment' was more likely to result in 'cure'—i.e. the patient being drug-free.

In contrast, private and general practitioners operating outside hospitals frequently practiced biographical medicine. Here, emphasis was placed more on the patient rather than the disease. Through biographical medicine, attention was paid to the experience of the sick individual and not just to ridding them of disease.[4] This goes some way towards explaining why private and general practitioners treating addicts were less concerned with the rapid removal of the drug from the body of the addict. These doctors were more aware of the context in which the addict and the addict's illness resided and therefore were more interested in improving social functioning rather than withdrawing the drug. It is, therefore, argued that conflict over the treatment of addiction during the 1980s was caused as much by a clash between different approaches to sickness and disease as by specific concerns about who should treat the addict (specialist or generalist, NHS doctor or private practitioner) or how the addict should be treated.

Caution, however, should be exercised. The distinction between the different groups and their positions can be too tightly drawn. There were exceptions to the rule: some DDU psychiatrists were more amenable to maintenance, and some GPs offered addict-patients short-term withdrawal treatment. Moreover, maintenance and withdrawal had existed as suggested forms of treatment since at least the nineteenth century.[5] Those who worked with drug addicts were divided over which method was to be preferred during the 1920s and in the 1960s, but the clash between maintenance and withdrawal occurred anew, and with added vehemence, in the 1980s. The case for withdrawal and the case for maintenance will be examined here in more detail, taking into account the position and outlook of key protagonists. It will then move on to look at how this debate was articulated, particularly in the GMC's case against Dally in 1986/7. A close analysis of this case demonstrates that although maintenance was to remain a controversial treatment approach in dealing with heroin addiction, it could not be completely discredited, particularly as AIDS loomed into view.

THE CASE FOR SHORT-TERM WITHDRAWAL

It is almost impossible to distinguish short-term withdrawal from the practice of the DDUs. DDU doctors were its strongest advocates, and it was at clinics that the method was most widely practised. In 1982 a survey of the treatment offered at DDUs found that clinics ranked 'help with withdrawal' as their most important treatment policy. In contrast, they did not believe that maintenance played a significant role in the treatment they offered. An overwhelming majority of the DDUs surveyed (97 per cent) believed that heroin maintenance was either not important or not their policy, 84 per cent thought the same about maintenance with injectable methadone and 29 per cent found that maintenance with oral methadone was not acceptable either.[6] By the mid-1980s, few clinics were prepared to prescribe new addict-patients opioid drugs over a long period of time. In 1984, Strang stated that all of the last 100 patients treated at his DDU in Manchester had been placed on a withdrawal regime to be completed in a fixed period of between three and twenty weeks. In every case the drug prescribed was to be administered orally.[7] Short-term prescription of oral drugs (usually methadone) aimed at abstinence was the method of treatment offered by most DDUs and championed by many drug addiction experts.

Explaining why this was adopted and how it became the orthodox method of treatment is as much about the perceived disadvantages of maintenance as the advantages of short-term withdrawal. There were six main arguments put forward against maintenance and in support of rapid withdrawal. The first was that prescription of a drug to an addict maintained the addiction. Psychiatrists at a DDU in Sheffield felt that 'prescribing drugs of addiction [to an addict] comes close to colluding with and maintaining the habit'.[8] The choice of words in this statement is particularly interesting. 'Collusion' suggests that by prescribing drugs to an addict, a doctor was complicit in perpetuating a 'habit', not providing treatment for a medical condition. Maintenance was, therefore, unacceptable as it fed a habit and did not treat the disease. This belief was underlain by an essentially moral objection to maintenance. Connell told the Social Services Committee in March 1985 that maintenance might be suitable for a small group of 'chaotic' individuals, under very strict control, but as a whole this method was not appropriate. By posing the rhetorical question, 'Is society required to provide something like a sweet or a drug because somebody wants it?' and countering that 'Those who are trying to treat this seriously are a little worried about adopting this view, which is of course the view that the person dependent upon the drug likes to put forward', Connell implied that giving an addict a drug simply because he or she asked for it was unacceptable.[9] Moreover, he suggested that prescribing addicts drugs of addiction was not treating the condition 'seriously'. This was the second argument made against maintenance: as maintenance perpetuated the disease of addiction, it did not constitute treatment and was not, therefore, the role of the doctor. This was not a new argument, but it was frequently repeated. Dr Strachan of the Royal Edinburgh Hospital asserted at a meeting of the Northern Drug Addiction Psychiatrists in 1985 that 'NHS facilities should be used for those who want treatment not sociomedical [sic.] control nor prevention of crime.'[10] Even if maintenance had advantages in terms of controlling addiction or reducing crime, it was not the responsibility of a doctor to prescribe drugs to addicts.

Similar arguments had been made twenty years earlier when the Ministry of Health tried to determine the function of the DDUs and the treatment they should offer. Maintenance was tentatively endorsed because civil servants and doctors alike wanted to avoid the development of a black market in drugs and thought this could be prevented by providing addicts with a legal supply through the clinics.[11] The third argument raised by those who opposed maintenance was that this reason for long-term prescription was redundant by the 1980s. According to addiction specialist J.S. Madden, maintenance therapy 'had not fore-stalled an expansion of the drug market'.[12] Furthermore, it was widely argued that addicts prescribed drugs on a maintenance basis frequently sold their drugs to other addicts or bought illegal drugs to supplement their legal supply, the fourth and fifth arguments made against long-term prescription. A study of the Piccadilly drug scene in 1983 by an-thropologist Angela Burr found a thriving market in the illicit trading of drugs prescribed by DDUs and GPs.[13] Many drug addiction specialists, such as Connell and Bewley, were anxious about overspill from the pre-scription of drugs to addicts to the black market. Consequently they en-couraged the development of restrictions as to when an addict could be prescribed drugs and under what conditions in an effort to reduce over-prescription.[14] Other doctors involved in the treatment of addiction, such as Jenner and Gill, contended that they adopted a non-prescribing policy when treating addicts because they were 'frequently being misled and cheated'.[15] The simplest way to avoid this was not to prescribe to addicts at all, or to do so over a very short period.

The final argument put forward against maintenance was essentially an economic one. The ACMD noted in *Treatment and Rehabilitation* that maintenance treatment offered to 'old' existing patients at DDUs 'may be a factor in blocking the ready access of new patients to the clinics'.[16] This view was endorsed by Strang, who noted that the 'constant flow of patients into the clinic system was not matched by any equivalent flow of patients out of the system'. As clinics were faced with static or dimin-ishing resources they 'found it necessary to look at shorter, more cost ef-fective (and perhaps more appropriate) types of response'. Adopting short-term prescription instead of maintenance was, therefore, 'a prag-matically derived approach'.[17] Short-term prescription was cheaper than long-term maintenance as fewer drugs were required over a shorter pe-riod. What is more, resources were being applied to those most likely to be 'cured' of addiction; when asked what happened to the majority of addicts who did not want treatment at a meeting of the Northern Drug Addiction Psychiatrists, Strachan replied that there were enough pa-tients who wanted withdrawal to keep DDUs busy.[18] Furthermore, in the increasingly evaluative context in which the DDUs were operating where 'results' were expected, withdrawal offered a tangible outcome in the form of 'cure'. The potential benefits of maintenance for the indi-vidual and for society were much more difficult to assess. In addition, maintenance was expensive, 'blocked' clinics from those most likely to benefit from their services and, it was argued, was not cost-effective.

The case against maintenance was, therefore, a powerful one, covering a range of arguments and supported by many doctors credited with ex-pertise in the treatment of addiction. Maintenance did not cure addicts of their addiction and could not therefore be considered 'treatment' and the responsibility of the doctor. The experiment with maintenance that

DDUs flirted with in the 1960s and early 1970s had not prevented the development of a black market, nor had it stopped addicts from selling the drugs they were prescribed. And in addition to being seen as ineffective, it was expensive. Arguing against maintenance prescription was easy, but this did not necessarily amount to an automatic endorsement for short-term withdrawal. There were far fewer positive assertions portraying the benefits of short-term treatment than negative comments about maintenance. Those who supported rapid withdrawal tended to concentrate on the damaging effects of maintenance rather than the plus points of short-term treatment. This can be attributed, in part, to a lack of 'evidence' to support either short-term prescription or maintenance. The Hartnoll-Mitcheson trial comparing injectable heroin to oral methadone (published in 1980) compared the drugs, not the method of treatment, as both drugs were prescribed on a maintenance basis. The study did indicate that prescribing oral methadone to addicts was associated with greater change and that those prescribed methadone were more likely to be abstinent from drugs than those prescribed injectable heroin.[19] These findings were used to explain the widespread adoption of oral methadone as opposed to injectable opioids in the DDUs, but this change also indicated a shift in the orientation of the treatment offered in clinics towards abstinence. Strang noted in 1984 that the service offered to addicts at his DDU was now 'predominantly geared towards helping the drug taker to become and remain drug free'.[20] It had long seemed counter-intuitive to many doctors to prescribe a drug that perpetuated a medical condition, and this view was strengthened by disillusionment with maintenance as a method of treatment for addiction. A new emphasis was placed on helping the addict become abstinent from drugs by withdrawing the drug in the shortest time period possible.

This method fit with the view of disease and its treatment that arose from the clinical context and operational environment of the hospital-based DDU psychiatrist. Through their rejection of maintenance and adoption of short-term withdrawal, psychiatrists were returning to their expected clinical role: to diagnose disease and to treat it. The therapeutic optimism imbued in psychiatry by the pharmacological revolution encouraged psychiatrists to believe that they were able to successfully treat psychiatric conditions, and, in this context, maintaining the condition of addiction instead of trying to rid the addict of their disease appeared to be a contradiction for many psychiatrists. Short-term withdrawal treatment using methadone appeared to offer a 'confrontational' response that would lead the addict to come off drugs and so be cured. The irony was that the treatment of addiction, unlike the treatment of other psychiatric conditions, involved the removal of a drug rather than the prescription of one. Yet as short-term, abstinence-oriented treatment was directed towards the 'cure' of addiction, it conformed more readily to the principles of clinical psychiatry and thus became the 'orthodox' method of treatment advocated by the leading specialists in the field.

The emergence of short-term withdrawal as the 'orthodox' method of treatment was facilitated by the perceived 'expert' status of those who promoted short-term treatment and their connections to the medical and psychiatric 'establishment'. Connell was probably the leading expert on drug addiction in Britain during the 1980s, closely followed by Bewley. Both men were advocates of rapid withdrawal, both were considered to be experts in the field and both held powerful positions within the medical establishment as well as advising the government on drug addiction related issues.[21] It has been suggested that Connell had particular influence in political as well as medico-political circles. Dally contended that Connell had the 'ear' of the Home Office Minister in charge of drugs issues, David Mellor, and was thus partly responsible for what she saw as Mellor's 'prohibitionist' attitudes.[22] Connections such as these allowed men like Connell and Bewley to control the direction of drug addiction treatment policy within central government, which was becoming more involved in drug issues in this period; however, their influence within the medical community was just as important, if not more so, as this was where most of the crucial changes in drug addiction treatment were initiated. Here, the support Bewley and Connell received from other DDU doctors, particularly in London, was vital. Consultant psychiatrists at London clinics all advocated the short-term withdrawal of opioid drugs from addicts, at least in public. Regular meetings of the London DDU doctors ensured a high degree of uniformity of practice across clinics in the capital. Furthermore, these doctors were regarded as 'experts' in their own right, particularly those who held posts at teaching hospitals that commanded higher status than those in non-teaching facilities.[23] Thus there appeared to be a high degree of expertise in favour of short-term withdrawal, encompassing the leading figures in drug addiction treatment at a practical and advisory level. This meant that short-term withdrawal was rapidly becoming the dominant treatment method for addiction.

THE CASE FOR MAINTENANCE

A small but vocal group of doctors continued to advocate the long-term prescription of drugs to addicts despite the climate of powerful opposition to the use of this method within medico-political circles. Support for maintenance treatment came mainly, but not exclusively, from doctors operating outside DDUs. Some of these doctors, like Dally and Beckett, worked in private practice. Others, such as Banks and Hare, were NHS GPs. There were also a few psychiatrists working in NHS DDUs who advocated the long-term prescription of opioid drugs to addicts. The most prominent of these was Dr John Marks, consultant psychiatrist at Liverpool DDU. A handful of other supporters of long-term prescription to addicts could be found in provincial DDUs, particularly in the north of England. In Scotland there were no DDUs, so treatment for addiction was carried out either within general psychiatric services or, more often, in general practice.[24] As a result, there was often more criticism of short-term withdrawal and support for maintenance in these areas. Marks estimated that around 25 per cent of regional clinics offered some form of long-term prescription to addicts, with the remaining 75 per cent following the London DDUs and advocating rapid reduction.[25] It is significant that support for maintenance treatment by DDU doctors occurred away from the capital. Local differences in the heroin 'problem' might account for the differences in approach, but it is more likely that the relative remoteness of regional DDUs from the power networks of London doctors and drug addiction experts allowed them a degree of autonomy not afforded clinic doctors in the capital.[26] This permitted a few regional clinic doctors to adopt an 'unorthodox' line and offer maintenance prescription to some addict-patients.

Those doctors who advocated the long-term prescription of opioid drugs, whether working at a DDU or in private or general practice, held a common view of addiction and the addict. They felt that addicts usually took drugs as a result of other psychiatric problems and could only be taken off drugs when they were able to deal with these. Marks asserted that 'Addicts give up when they are ready to and special detoxification units do little to expedite this.' Instead, treatment should 'discover why addicts abuse drugs or alcohol and then work with them to seek alternative methods of dealing with the problems muffled by drug dependence'.[27] There was a feeling that withholding drugs from addicts did not result in them becoming abstinent. Dr Sefari stated at a meeting of the Northern Drug Addiction Psychiatrists in 1986 that 'the natural history of drug addiction suggests that people will continue to take drugs one way or another, legally or illegally, whether there is prohibition or not'.[28] Marks, too, argued that heroin addicts tended to maintain their addiction themselves if they were not prescribed drugs.[29] Furthermore, as authors of a study of drug addiction in Edinburgh pointed out, withdrawal from heroin or another opioid drug constituted a minor part of treatment because, 'heroin abuse, like alcohol abuse, is a remitting and relapsing disorder, with users spontaneously abstaining with little or no medical intervention.' Abstinence, they argued, did not always equate with 'cure'.[30]

Nonetheless, abstinence was the ultimate goal of treatment involving long-term prescription, just as it was with more rapid withdrawal. Dally argued that her philosophy was to prescribe a minimum dose to her addict-patients and to reduce this gradually 'with the aim of eventually achieving a drug-free life'.[31] GP Dr Tessa Hare (an AIDA member) also asserted that it was her policy that addict-patients 'come off the drug sometime'.[32] At the Liverpool DDU the first stated goal was 'to return the patient to a drug free life style'. Where those who offered maintenance differed from those who advocated rapid withdrawal was over the time period after which abstinence was expected. At Marks's clinic a drug-free lifestyle might be a 'short, medium or long-term goal according to age, previous drug history and motivation of the patient'.[33] Dally also stressed the reduction of a patient's drug intake but only within an individual's capacity.[34] Her policy differed from that of many DDUs that set a fixed time limit on the duration of prescription.

Getting the addict off drugs might have been the hoped for outcome of treatment, but those who advocated maintenance asserted that this was not to be achieved at the cost of the social functioning of the patient. The treatment offered by the Liverpool DDU under Marks was aimed at improving the health and quality of addicts' lives. The idea was to switch injecting heroin addicts to oral methadone and to reduce drug consumption so long as this did not compromise the social functioning of the patient. Treatment was intended to: improve the physical and mental health of the addict, stabilise the addict's lifestyle, improve family relationships, decrease the amount of black market drugs being bought, reduce the level of criminal activity of the patient and increase the employment prospects of the patient.[35] In order to achieve these goals, prescription of an opioid drug was permitted while the problems hidden by addiction were dealt with. This did not result in blanket maintenance prescriptions for all addict-patients attending the Liverpool DDU. Between 1985 and 1987, 17.5 per cent of patients were prescribed oral opioids on a maintenance basis after the first consultation, and just 6.2 per cent were maintained on injectable drugs. The majority of patients, 58.9 per cent, were placed on some sort of withdrawal regime, but arbitrary limits of the amount prescribed and the duration of prescription were not set.[36] Reduction was achieved on an individual basis. Dally used a similar justification for maintenance prescription for some of her addict-patients. She argued that she prescribed the minimum dose necessary for the individual patient to lead a 'normal' life: earning a legal living, looking after a family and children and so on.[37] Once more, stress was placed on the individual patient rather than on a specific treatment programme designed for all.

The emphasis on the individual was indicative of a change in the perceived function of maintenance treatment. During the late 1960s, maintenance was described as a form of social control; it was seen as a way to prevent the development of a major heroin addiction problem by providing addicts with drugs so that they would not need to buy these on a black market. It was argued that this would reduce the social problems associated with addiction and at the same time prevent the spread of the disease of addiction within the community by limiting the contact between infected persons (addicts) and healthy individuals. Maintenance was seen as largely being for the good of society rather than the good of the addict. In the 1980s, those who supported maintenance spoke not of social control of addiction but of the social functioning of the addict. The explanation for this shift lies partly in the public health context in which the condition was being described. In the 1960s, addiction was located in the relationships between people, leading it to be described as a social disease. Twenty years later public health looked not at the relationships between people as a source of disease but to individual behaviours. The 'new public health' was concerned with 'lifestyles' and the potential 'risks' to individual health through voluntary actions such as drinking, smoking and taking drugs.[38] The discourse about maintenance in the 1980s drew on some of these concepts by placing the behaviour of the individual at the centre of treatment. Long-term prescription, when intended to improve social functioning, concentrated on enhancing the 'lifestyle' of the addict and reducing the risk of drug taking to their general health, relationships, employment and so on. Individual behaviour was thus not just a cause of disease but also its potential cure.

Those who practised short-term withdrawal were not immune to the increased attention being placed on individual behaviour. Here too there was talk of social functioning. Strang argued in 1985 that the 'pure medical component of therapeutic intervention' into heroin addiction had reduced in recent years so that treatment was now about 'practical management of the physical complications that may accompany drug withdrawal', facilitating 'family, social, and occupational rehabilitation to take place'.[39] This was one area of common ground between the two different treatment philosophies, as was the hope by those who offered maintenance that their addict-patients would one day achieve a drug-free life. What separated short-term withdrawal and long-term prescription was the priority accorded social functioning and abstinence. For advocates of rapid withdrawal, it was most important for the addict-patient to become abstinent from drugs in a short period of time. For supporters of maintenance, social functioning was the primary concern. Only once this had been improved could abstinence be achieved. Conflict, therefore, was about more than the duration of prescription; it was about what treatment should be expected to achieve. This debate went to the very heart of what 'treatment' meant within the context of addiction and in medicine more generally.

Signs of a different approach to addiction in community-based practice and hospital medicine were apparent as early as the late 1960s, a divide that was accentuated by the growth of biographical medicine. In 1967 the *British Medical Journal* published a collection of articles on the proposed centres for the treatment of addiction. Comparing the outlook of Bewley, who argued that 'special centres' based in hospitals had 'advantages', and Chapple, a GP interested in the treatment of addiction who asserted that this was best conducted in the community, is instructive. Bewley noted that the establishment of clinics and cooperation between these would allow for the development of 'standard practice' when dealing with addicts.[40] Chapple, however, asserted, 'Institutional treatment has been an almost complete failure . . . because it has created a situation where the patient finds himself in conflict with his doctors—often forced to relinquish drugs against his will—but also because it fails to face the real problem, which is that of teaching the addict-patient to live in society without using drugs.'[41] According to Lart, the gap between these views 'reflects that between the perceptions of "hospital medicine" and "biographical medicine"'. The GPs' view was that the treatment of the addict could only be successfully undertaken in the community, as this would be more accessible to the addict than clinical treatment.[42]

These differing perspectives reflect the greater sensitivity to the social context of illness found in general practice, a trend that continued into the 1970s and 1980s as biographical medicine began to make a more significant impact upon community-based medicine. Biographical medicine revitalised general practice, but it also brought GPs into further conflict with specialists by providing them with a contrasting view of disease. For the community-based doctor, the disease could not be abstracted from the patient, and in turn the patient could not be removed from the social context in which he or she resided.[43] In a study based on interviews with GPs during the 1970s, sociologists Margot Jefferys and Hessie Sachs found that these doctors were conceptualising their work in a different way from hospital-based consultants. GPs saw their approach as taking into account social situations that hospital doctors ignored. Jefferys and Sachs reported: '"Ideally in general practice" one doctor reflected, "each patient is recognised as a unique distillation of his physical, psychological and social experiences."' This approach was contrasted with the 'ready-made' service provided by hospital consultants. General practice, Jefferys and Sachs's respondents claimed, was 'tailored to the needs of the individual'.[44] This focus on the individual and his or her social setting was reflected in the kinds of treatment community-based physicians offered addicts. Maintenance focused on the whole addict rather than just on the disease. Doctors who prescribed opioid drugs to addicts over a longer period took into account the situation of the addict and focused on improving the addict's social functioning before 'curing' the disease by removing the drug.

The emergence of biographical medicine provided an alternative way of seeing and responding to disease, bringing it into conflict with hospital-based clinical medicine. The existence of this clash can be observed in debates about the treatment of addiction. Examining the arguments of leading protagonists suggests that their views were shaped by their respective positions and the type of medicine practised. Hospital-based

DDU consultants saw the disease of addiction and not the addict him or herself. DDU doctors, therefore, largely advocated the rapid withdrawal of drugs from addicts, wanting to cure the patient as quickly as possible by making them abstinent. To achieve this, clinical methods were employed: blood tests, urine tests and physical examinations resulting in the same programme of treatment being prescribed for all. In contrast, the community-based GP or private practitioner saw the patient and their symptoms. This led the community doctor to focus on the experience of addiction, on the social, physical and psychiatric problems that the individual addict faced rather than the 'disease' itself. To this end, they advocated the long-term prescription of opioid drugs in order to combat these problems and improve the social functioning of the addict. Attention was paid to the condition of the individual rather than the disease (addiction). It would seem, therefore, that short-term withdrawal represented a hospital-based clinical view of disease, and its treatment and maintenance represented a community-based biographical view. But biographical medicine's influence was not limited to general practice. By providing an alternative way of seeing and treating disease away from the disciplinary mechanisms of the hospital, biographical medicine reinvigorated other types of community-based medicine, including those in private practice. The individual patient had always retained more significance in private practice because, as Porter commented, 'private doctors must, within limits, give patients what they want.'[45] Private practitioners dependent upon fees for their livelihoods were more amenable to the needs of the patient and not necessarily so concerned with the disease. Such an approach was sanctioned by biographical medicine that placed the patient at the centre of the conceptualisation of disease and its treatment. A divide thus existed between those who treated addicts within the community and those who treated addicts in hospital-based specialist facilities.

As indicated above, caution must be exercised as this divide can be too tightly drawn. There were DDU doctors who maintained addicts, just as there were GPs who practised short-term withdrawal. These positions were not as entrenched as at first may appear, with both methods of treatment sharing some common ground. It is also possible that the treatment approaches of the DDU doctors and the community-based physicians may have been partially influenced by the type of patient they saw rather than their philosophical outlook. Maintenance was considered an acceptable form of treatment for the middle-aged, middle-class addicts of the 1920s but not for the younger, recreational addicts of the 1960s and 1970s. If the addicts seen by GPs and private practitioners were more like the addicts of the Rolleston era, it would be understandable if these doctors responded to older, middle-class addicts in the same way as their predecessors had done sixty years earlier, with maintenance. Dally repeatedly stated that she treated a different kind of patient than those seen at DDUs. She asserted that her patients were older, employed, middle-class, stable addicts in contrast to the younger, unemployed, chaotic, working-class addicts more likely to be seen at a DDU.[46] Confirming this assertion is difficult. Detailed data of patient profiles is not available for a sufficiently large number of private and general practitioners to compare these to the DDUs.[47] Even if a comparison between patient profiles were feasible, it would not be possible to extrapolate how important this was for the individual doctor in making the decision to offer short-term withdrawal or long-term maintenance.

It is also difficult to assess the extent to which community-based physicians treating addicts were influenced by biographical medicine. Though biographical medicine was the 'dominant ideology' within the Royal College of General Practitioners in this period, its adoption in the field was not necessarily so widespread.[48] GP and writer Julian Tudor-Hart noted that in 1986 the RCGP had 13,000 members, which was only just over a third of all GPs.[49] Tudor-Hart was a leading proponent of another ideological approach that influenced general practice: epidemiology.[50] Here the focus was not on the individual patient, as with biographical medicine, but on the pattern of disease within the patient-cohort seen in general practice, suggesting a different focus of therapeutic endeavour. Despite changing theoretical outlooks, many GPs continued to show little interest in treating addicts, often preferring to refer them on to specialist services; however, those who did treat addicts were often younger doctors who had qualified in the 1970s and 1980s, when biographical medicine was at its most influential.[51] It is possible, therefore, that these doctors used this approach in their work, enabling them to view the disease of the addict in a different way from their specialist, hospital-based colleagues.

This view helps account for the high degree of conflict over the treatment of addiction. The dispute was rooted not just in intra-professional battles between DDU psychiatrists jealously guarding their speciality from private and general practitioners who threatened their autonomy and status but also in a deeper conflict concerning opposing philosophies of medicine and its treatment. That is not, however, to deny the significance of addiction in this wider battle. Indeed, the clash between clinical medicine and biographical medicine could only take place in an arena like that of addiction, where the field was relatively 'open'. The socio-medico status of the 'problem' of addiction facilitated the emergence of a range of approaches to providing a 'solution'. As no one could agree on what that solution should be, there was no conclusive evidence to 'prove' that any method 'worked'. Judgements about what was the most appropriate method of treatment for addiction therefore came to be based on other elements, such as the position of the doctor and his or her pre-existing ideas about disease and its treatment. The presence of these alternative views on the treatment of addiction presented a challenge to hospital-based clinicians advocating short-term withdrawal. Yet DDU psychiatrists were able to counter this challenge by reiterating the need for a specialist approach to the problems of addiction and confirming rapid withdrawal as the orthodox method of treatment.

THE GMC VERSUS DR ANN DALLY, 1986/7

A further opportunity to confirm the orthodoxy of withdrawal treatment came with the GMC's case against Dally for serious professional misconduct in 1986/7. The case revolved around Dally's actions in dealing with one patient, Khalid, but also called into question her more general treatment methods and the practice of maintenance in particular. Dally had continued to treat addict-patients following her 'conviction' for serious professional misconduct in 1983. She was perfectly at liberty to do so, as she had merely been admonished for her conduct by the GMC; however, the Home Office Drugs Branch and Inspectorate continued to closely monitor her prescription of controlled drugs, as they did with many other doctors involved in the treatment of addiction.[52] Though these visits may have been routine, one inspector in particular, Donald McIntosh, raised some issues about Dally's prescribing habits, especially her prescription to addict-patients who lived at some distance from her surgery.[53] At the same time, Dally also reported that during these visits other inspectors, including Spear himself, had warned her that the 'drug dependency establishment' were trying to 'make trouble' and get her charged before a Home Office tribunal.[54]

In the end, it was the GMC that acted, not the Home Office. On 2 September 1986 Dally received a letter from the Registrar at the GMC alleging that she had abused her position as a medical practitioner on two separate grounds. The first charge was that she had issued 'in return for fees, numerous prescriptions for methadone hydrochloride in an irresponsible manner'. The second related to Khalid. It was also alleged that Dally had prescribed for Khalid in an irresponsible manner and, furthermore, that she had failed to conduct a 'conscientious and sufficient physical examination', did not monitor his progress adequately and discharged him without making proper arrangements for his ongoing treatment.[55] The GMC's charges were based on information received from the Home Office. Much of this had come from the Inspector's interviews with Dally, but the information on Khalid came from Dally herself. She knew that Spear liked to be informed of interesting cases, so she sent him copies of the correspondence with Mrs Khalid's solicitors. Dally thought that this was then passed on to someone interested in 'damaging' her.[56] Indeed, Dally saw the whole case as part of a conspiracy to impose a particular method of treatment for addiction and stop her and other 'independent' doctors from treating addicts. She had long maintained that the treatment of addiction was being controlled by a powerful clique of London-based DDU consultants.[57] This group, led, she argued, by Connell and comprised, among others, of Bewley, Ghodse and Mitcheson, sought to impose their system of treatment even if it was 'failing'.[58] This (according to Dally) was to be achieved in two ways. The first was to get 'themselves elected to every powerful committee that is in any way relevant to the problem and then, with the power gained, [impose] an orthodoxy'.[59] The second was to eliminate the 'independent' doctor from the treatment of addiction, either through the Home Office tribunals or the GMC's Professional Conduct Committee (PCC).[60] Dally told her defence team that the DDU consultant group built the case against her and were using the GMC to remove her from the field.[61] She argued, 'Strongly influenced by the Connell-Bewley faction, the GMC has got itself into a power game which few of its members understand or are even aware of . . . They do not realise they are being used for political ends by a particular group of doctors.'[62] Dally felt that 'everyone at the GMC who has any connection with drug dependency is either Connell's stooge or his disciple on the subject.'[63] She stated in the diary she wrote during the 'trial' in 1986/7 that she had heard that the GMC's solicitors, Waterhouse, had been instructed to look for 'dirt' on her so that a case could be brought.[64]

There is evidence to suggest that this was not simply paranoia. Dr David Marjot, a former NHS DDU consultant and ally of Dally's told her that a private detective working for the GMC had telephoned him asking for the names of addict-patients to check if any of Dally's patients were also receiving prescriptions from him.[65] Dally's defence team and an interested freelance journalist found that the GMC had indeed employed a private detective called Dave Kingham, a former policeman who had worked for the drugs squad inspecting pharmacists' records.[66] Although the GMC were not acting outside their remit by bringing in the services of a private investigator, they were perhaps acting contrary to their usual stance.[67] In 1975 the Merrison Committee had recommended that the GMC set up an investigation unit to examine alleged instances of serious professional misconduct, but the proposal was rejected by the GMC, who felt that this was not part of their role.[68] Likewise, the circumstances in which the case was brought, while not unprecedented, were perhaps unusual. The GMC called doctors to answer charges of serious professional misconduct either as a result of a reported criminal conviction or when a complaint was made about a doctor's conduct. This might come from other doctors, officials or members of the public.[69] In Dally's case no specific complaint was made about her; information was passed on to the GMC by the Home Office about her prescription of controlled drugs. This was probably fairly common with cases of suspected irresponsible prescription, but it helped fuel Dally's notion that she was being 'persecuted' by the GMC itself rather than facing charges as the result of an individual complaint.[70]

This notion of persecution and the allied belief that there was a conspiracy between DDU consultants and the GMC to besmirch Dally's reputation and stop her from treating addicts requires careful consideration. The 'evidence' for the existence of this conspiracy was predominately based on hearsay and comes from material found in the Dally papers—largely her own writing on the subject—rather than any independent, corroborative source. Moreover, it was clearly vital for Dally to locate her case in a bigger battle. She needed to show that she was not guilty of serious professional misconduct, and pointing to a wider conspiracy to 'get' the independent doctor shifted focus from her own behaviour. Yet there was much that could have brought Dally to the attention of the GMC without a 'conspiracy'. At a meeting of the GMC in May 1985, the Professional Standards Committee directed doctors to consider three issues when prescribing to addicts: firstly, not to ignore warnings from the Home Office or the police about the effects of prescribing in some areas; secondly, that it was inadvisable to prescribe to patients who lived a long distance from their surgery, especially when there were other facilities available; and, thirdly, the danger that prescribing privately to an addict without sufficient funds would lead him or her to sell part of that prescription to a third party.[71] Dally, it could be argued, ignored all three of these warnings. As well as disregarding general advice, she also failed to recognise the seriousness of the cautionary words spoken by Home Office Drug Inspectors directly to her in both an official and an unofficial capacity. The Home Office nearly took her to tribunal; this was prevented only by her promise to change her treatment policies and to gradually retire altogether within three months, a promise she did not keep.[72] However, the fact that Dally's behaviour was hardly irreproachable does not negate the significance of the case. It does seem likely that there was a concerted effort, in her words, to 'get' Dally and other independent doctors who were treating addicts contrary to DDU policy. Moreover, regardless of whether or not there was a 'conspiracy' surrounding the case, it clearly had wider political implications.

These implications were obvious to all those involved in the GMC PCC hearing from the outset. The case began on 9 December 1986 and was chaired by Professor Duthie, professor of surgery at the University of Wales.[73] In both his opening and closing statements, Timothy Preston, QC (appearing on behalf of the GMC), commented on the significance of the case. At the beginning of the hearing he noted, 'there may be more than one school of thought as to whether it is medically . . . or socially, advisable to prescribe long term maintenance doses to addicts' and he would 'deprecate any attempt to turn this inquiry into a political debate'.[74] However, Preston's presentation of the GMC's case was itself 'political' and took a clear stance within this debate. In his final words to the committee, Preston stated that while he accepted that long-term maintenance might be necessary for some patients, it was, 'very much a second best solution to an individual patient's problem'.[75] The 'best' solution, presumably, was short-term withdrawal.

Just as Preston tried to deny the political elements of the case, Dally's defence was contingent on proving that she was not at fault but was instead the victim of a conflict over the treatment of addiction. Dally's barrister, William Gage, QC, argued in his closing statement: 'Dr Dally has had the misfortune to get caught up in the backwash of a medical dispute in the particular field in which she practices. It is our submission that that dispute lies at the heart of the charge against her'.[76] Dally's case was based around the assertion that there was not one correct way of treating addicts: there were a number of different ways. Gage stated, 'Nobody can be dogmatic as to precisely what is right for the individual. It is our case that there is a place for her [Dally's] type of treatment in the spectrum'.[77] Indeed, he found there to be a substantial body of opinion that supported Dally's methods, the existence of which demonstrated that she was not guilty of irresponsible prescription.[78]

Considering how both the specific and the more general charges in the Dally case were dealt with allows for an assessment to be made as to the relationship between the factors that were instrumental in bringing the case and deciding its outcome: Dally's apparent failings and the wider campaign against maintenance. Khalid stated that when he was first referred to Dally, she did not conduct a physical examination of him, nor did she conduct blood or urine tests for the presence of drugs; but she did examine his arms for needle marks.[79] He asserted that though he saw her for half an hour initially, most of his consultations lasted 'for ten minutes, give or take five minutes'.[80] These meetings were weekly, until the last six months of his treatment when he could no longer afford to see her so regularly, so he asked to come fortnightly instead. Khalid told the GMC that Dally prescribed injectable methadone for him and admitted under cross-examination that she did achieve a reduction in his dose over the time he was in her care. But the 'prosecution' raised serious questions about the nature of the treatment Dally provided. Preston asked Khalid: 'During the two and a half years or so that you were seeing Dr Dally, did you ever receive from her anything that could be described as treatment, other than being handed a prescription for methadone?' Khalid replied: 'Not really, no'. Dally's treatment of Khalid also appeared unsuccessful when compared to the apparent success of the clinic he was attending at the time of the hearing in getting him off drugs. Khalid told the committee that he had been going to a DDU for five weeks and was completely abstinent.[81]

Serious questions were also raised about how Khalid could afford to pay for private treatment. He admitted that though he had been in work when he first went to see Dally, he had been unemployed and drawing benefit since 1983. Sessions with Dally cost £30 each, and

Khalid told the PCC that his prescription charges could be as much as £33 and averaged £25. As he was only receiving £72 a week in unemployment benefit, Khalid said he was forced to sell some of his ampoules of methadone for around £5 each.[82] Dally, it seemed, was unwittingly supplying the 'grey' market with drugs, something that was of great concern to many DDU doctors. It was hardly surprising, therefore, that the PCC judged the second charge levelled against Dally, irresponsible prescription to Khalid, to have been proven. Indeed, the impression that Khalid was something of a 'dodgy' patient was confirmed by the fact that since he had left Dally's care, he had been arrested and was to stand trial for attempted possession of heroin.[83]

Yet the eight-day hearing was about more than Dally's failings with respect to one individual patient. Through the examination of the other, more general charge, the case brought many of the key issues in the treatment debate into sharp focus. To help them decide the extent to which Dally's treatment of addicts could be described as irresponsible (and therefore constituting serious professional misconduct), Preston repeatedly suggested that the PCC look to the *Guidelines of Good Clinical Practice in the Treatment of Drug Misuse* (the *Guidelines*) published in 1984.[84] The *Guidelines* had been devised by a medical working group comprised of DDU doctors, GPs and private practitioners involved in the treatment of addiction, including Dally herself. The production of the *Guidelines* was a highly contentious process, and despite their supposed embodiment of a consensus view, no such thing existed.[85] The *Guidelines* recommended that while generalists could have a role to play in the treatment of addiction, specialists were required in many cases. The *Guidelines* were also heavily biased towards rapid withdrawal and counselled against long-term prescription, unless this was carried out under specialist supervision.[86] The real purpose of the *Guidelines*, according to historian Sarah Mars, was to 'secure the ascendancy of one particular treatment model and impose this on doctors'. Furthermore, the *Guidelines* 'were originally intended to be used for disciplining doctors, particularly private prescribers who did not follow them, and were employed to this effect'.[87]

Throughout the GMC hearing, the *Guidelines* were used by the 'prosecution' to argue that Dally's methods were unorthodox. Preston asserted that Dally 'breached, or at any rate ignored' many of the recommendations made in the *Guidelines*. Dally claimed that she conformed to the *Guidelines* as far as possible but that they did not provide for the type of patient she saw: the long-term addict.[88] Other doctors who gave evidence to the PCC were also critical of the *Guidelines*. Dally's friend and supporter Dr Marjot told the committee that he did not agree with every word of the *Guidelines* and felt that they were of use to some GPs but of less value to those working within the field of addiction treatment. He too felt they did not address the problem of the long-term addict.[89] Beckett also thought the *Guidelines* were intended for those without experience of treating addiction and was in agreement with Marjot and Dally that they failed to deal with the chronically addicted patient.[90] However, it was John Marks who presented the most damning condemnation of the *Guidelines*. He told the committee that he referred to them as the 'misguidelines'. He argued they deserved this sobriquet because while they claimed to present guidance on good clinical practice, they did not deal with maintenance—the implication being that maintenance was not good practice. He strongly disagreed with this, branding it a 'false inference'.[91]

Marks's evidence on the subject of maintenance was crucial for Dally and the wider debate as he helped establish that this was an accepted method of treatment, albeit practised by a minority of doctors treating addicts. Marks freely admitted to prescribing to addicts on a maintenance basis. He asserted that addicts who were determined to take drugs would continue to do so. The choice was not, he said, 'between getting those drugs [on prescription] and not getting drugs at all; it is between not getting these injections or injecting street rubbish'. Marks believed that maintenance itself was not 'treatment'; it was a way of keeping the patient healthy and in contact with the appropriate services until the patient was prepared to stop taking drugs altogether.[92] Dally's defence team presented other doctors who agreed with maintenance and criticised rapid withdrawal. Dale Beckett stated that there was nothing wrong with prescribing to an addict over a long period of time; he argued, 'in fact it might be thought wrong not to.' Short-term withdrawal might result in abstinence, but the addict too often returned to drugs. He believed that addicts could lead perfectly 'normal' lives while being prescribed opioid drugs.[93] Beckett also argued that there was no one method that could be applied to the treatment of addiction, as did Marjot.[94] Marjot asserted that while the aim in treating addicts was for them to eventually be drug-free, prescription was sometimes 'the least worst option'.[95]

Dally presented her treatment of addicts to the PCC in this light, defending her own practices through a defence of maintenance. She asserted that her philosophy was 'To improve their [the addict's] general health and social situation and to help them reduce their drug need, with the hope that they would eventually become drug free.' This treatment was designed to help the addict-patient hold down a job and maintain a normal family life. She argued that the patients she treated were older, long-term addicts who 'had been addicted for so long that there was not any question of getting them off quickly'. Dally felt that there was not one single method available for treating addict-patients. Rather, 'one has to deal with the patient according to that patient; it is a very individual matter'.[96] This meant trying to 'assess each person as an individual and to decide the right treatment for that particular person and to carry it out, modifying it as circumstances change, aiming always at being drug-free in the end'.[97] Dally's general treatment philosophy and methodology thus fitted into a pattern of individual-centred maintenance designed to improve social functioning, with the ultimate goal of abstinence but not necessarily in a short, fixed period of time.

In contrast to this view, the drug addiction experts presented by the 'prosecution' were largely advocates of short-term withdrawal. Dr Farrington, consultant psychiatrist at Lady Chichester Hospital, Hove, told the committee about the practices adopted in his clinic. The goal of treatment, he asserted, was for the patient to become abstinent from drugs. He did not believe that any addict had a long-term need for opiate drugs. Most patients were offered a 'prescription contract' aimed at getting them off methadone in between four and six months; however, Farrington did admit to prescribing to a small number of addicts (ten out of 112) on a long-term basis.[98] These were what he termed 'stable' addicts, older and less problematic than the rest of the patients he saw. Dr Fleming, director of Wessex regional drug dependence services, also prescribed on a long-term basis to a handful of patients. He treated between five and ten stable addicts who were employed, in good relationships and mostly in their late thirties or early forties. He conceded that for these patients, there might be a case for allowing them to continue to take injectable drugs on prescription; however, he also stated that he had not prescribed injectable drugs to an addict in eleven years. He estimated that he had prescribed drugs in any form to only a third of his patients; the remainder received counselling. Prescription, he believed, was a minor part of treatment.[99] So despite the tacit admission that there might be a case for long-term prescription to a small number of addict-patients, the evidence of both Fleming and Farrington was broadly supportive of rapid withdrawal. It is intriguing to note that they were the only medical witnesses called by the 'prosecution'. None of the London DDU doctors gave evidence. This is surprising, as they were widely recognised to be the leading experts in the field and were the strongest advocates of short-term prescription. Dally actually wanted Connell and Bewley to appear as witnesses so that they would be forced to justify their policies. She believed under cross-examination the fallacy of their methods would be exposed.[100] It is unclear why they, or any of the other London DDU consultants, were not asked by the GMC to give evidence. It is appealing to suggest that perhaps they were too close to the case. While they may not have deliberately orchestrated the hearing, it was obvious that they had much to gain by forcing a doctor like Dally out of practice. Being seen to be so directly involved in its outcome would have exposed the political motives of this group of clinicians. Nonetheless, these political dimensions were widely recognised as being vital in determining the course of the case and particularly its outcome.

The hearing finally concluded on 30 January 1987. The committee found that the second charge against Dally (her treatment of Khalid) had been proven to their satisfaction, but there was insufficient evidence to support the first, more general charge.[101] The PCC believed that the second charge alone constituted serious professional miscon- duct. The Chairman stated that, as a result of this finding and Dally's 'blatant failure to heed the warning issued' at her 'previous appearance before the Committee in 1983 in relation to similar matters', her con- tinued registration was made conditional on her not prescribing or pos- sessing any controlled drugs for a period of 14 months.[102] Given the PCC's findings in other similar cases, this could be considered a fairly le- nient punishment. Between 1983 and 1989, 47 cases of non bona-fide prescription of controlled drugs came before the PCC. Of these, 42 were found to be guilty of serious professional misconduct: in 15 cases the doctor's name was erased from the register; in 11 cases the doctor was admonished; in 8 cases the doctor was suspended for a fixed period; 4 cases were adjourned; and in 4 cases the doctor's registration, like Dally's, was subjected to future conditions.[103] Whether this was a 'fair' verdict is another matter. Diana Brahams, barrister and legal correspon- dent for *The Lancet*, produced a detailed analysis of the case. She noted that Home Office inspectors were convinced that Dally was well moti- vated and believed she was acting in the best interest of her patients. Brahams conceded that while Dally may not have been vigilant enough in respect of a single patient (Khalid), 'and for this she can be criticised', it was 'difficult to see what will be gained by forbidding her from pre- scribing in the area if the alternatives (supplies of impure drugs, dirty needles and the wave of crime committed to pay for supplies of street heroin) are worse'. The 'street addict', she argued, was a danger to 'him- self' and to the 'community at large'. Had the 'medical establishment', Brahams concluded, 'got its priorities right?'[104]

Questions were raised by both Brahams and legal scholar Russell Smith about the way in which the treatment Dally offered had been in- terpreted as being 'irresponsible' and, therefore, constituting serious professional misconduct. Brahams argued, 'treatment which is med- ically respectable cannot at the same time be irresponsible'. As a 're- spectable body of medical opinion' approved of Dally's treatment meth- ods, she could not be considered to be guilty of irresponsible practice.[105] Smith was of a similar opinion. He argued that a doctor should not face a misconduct hearing merely because he or she had adopted a 'practice of medicine which, while having its opponents, is none the less justifi- able as one manner of treatment'.[106] In the Dally case he felt that 'one was left with the unhappy situation of a doctor having her conduct ad- judicated and its undesirability declared, presumably for the benefit of the whole medical community in knowing what was acceptable con- duct in the eyes of the GMC, when she had merely been following one school of thought which had its own substantial body of advocates.'[107] The PCC were clearly not only judging one doctor's conduct but also the suit- ability of maintenance as a form of treatment for heroin addiction.

In this sense, the conviction of Dally on the lesser of the two charges represented a partial failure for those who wished to see maintenance utterly discredited. Dally believed that the GMC had 'been unable to condemn my method of treatment' although they 'ensured that no one would be tempted to follow it'.[108] This was a broadly accurate assessment. While Dally's treatment of Khalid was exposed as being somewhat slipshod, she was able to demonstrate that her general methods and philosophy were acceptable as a form of treatment by offering a successful defence of maintenance. The GMC were able to denounce the practitioner but not the practice. Even those doctors who had appeared for the 'prosecution' conceded that some addict-patients might require long-term prescription. John Marks's powerful testimony on the benefits of this was particularly important, both as an endorsement of Dally's methods and maintenance treatment more generally. Though the verdict effectively compelled Dally to retire from the treatment of addiction and other doctors mindful of their careers may well have followed suit, maintenance treatment persisted and was even strengthened as a result.

The Dally case was important not just because it polarised many of the issues in the treatment debate but also because it brought these issues into the centre-field. Media coverage of the case helped expose its political significance, highlighting the medical dispute at its core and raising questions about the most appropriate way to handle the burgeoning drug 'problem'. Letters in support of Dally and denouncing the PCC's verdict appeared in the medical press, and pieces in broadsheet newspapers, particularly *The Guardian* and the *Observer*, also commented on the wider significance of the case.[109] The Dally case was widely reported, receiving coverage from sources as diverse as the BBC's *Panorama* to *Cosmopolitan* magazine.[110] Through exposure of the Dally case in a wide range of media, the issues at the heart of the treatment debate were brought to a non-medical audience, but within medicine there was also a gradual reconsideration of the role of maintenance in the treatment of heroin addiction. This reconsideration was partly as a result of the Dally case and the publicity it generated. In a commentary on the case, the legal correspondent for the *British Medical Journal*, Clare Dyer, observed, 'the move to curb Dr Dally's prescribing comes at a time when the threat of acquired immune deficiency syndrome [AIDS] is giving new fuel to the debate over prescribing policy for drug addicts'. Dyer noted that an argument was being made that flexible prescription would bring more addicts into clinics, and through this contact the risk of HIV infection and its transmission to the 'general population' could be reduced.[111]

Concern about incidences of HIV and AIDS among heroin addicts was growing in the immediate aftermath of the Dally case. This prompted a re-examination of the position of long-term prescription of opioid drugs to addicts. While it is impossible to quantify the impact of the Dally case on this shifting of attitudes, it did help create a climate in which a reconsideration of the long-term prescription of opioids to addicts was possible. The case had been brought by advocates of short-term withdrawal and the clinical method in order to discredit maintenance and the more 'social' approach to disease this represented. Given the power of both clinical medicine at a general level and the supporters of rapid withdrawal within the medical establishment, it is all the more surprising that a wholesale condemnation of maintenance was not produced. The Dally case represented something of a minor victory for the supporters of the long-term prescription of opioids to addicts. This was part of, and in a small way helped cause, a rapprochement towards maintenance as a form of treatment for heroin addiction.

To assess why maintenance 'won', it is necessary to return to the fluctuating relationship between the medical and the social in determining the response to heroin addiction. Changes taking place in broader drugs policy fed into the specific approach to heroin. Initiatives such as *Tackling Drug Misuse* placed greater emphasis on crime and the social problems caused by drug use. The range of agencies involved in drug issues expanded still further, representing a move away from purely medically dominated approaches to what Berridge has called the 'new policy community'.[112] Within this, clinicians needed to prove that they retained a distinct and crucial role. This could be achieved by addressing the primary concerns of this policy community, such as the social problems arising from drug use. Maintenance appeared to offer, if not a solution, at least a potential way to alleviate some of these social problems by placing individuals rather than their disease at the centre of treatment. The 'victory' of maintenance in the dispute over drug addiction treatment does not, therefore, necessarily represent the triumph of community-based biographical medicine over hospital-based clinical medicine but is more indicative of the continued adaptability of medicine in applying itself to 'social problems'. The conflict between competing styles of medicine was less significant than medicine's conflicts with outside forces. It is ironic then that to retain its role in addiction, as in other areas, 'medicine' became ever more 'social'. This was to become even more evident as those involved in the treatment of addiction faced another challenge: that of HIV and AIDS.

CHAPTER SEVEN

The Impact of HIV/AIDS on Heroin Addiction Treatment, 1984–1994

In October 1985 a team of researchers began using the newly developed HIV test on stored blood samples taken from intravenous drug users in Edinburgh. What the researchers found was deeply alarming: 51 per cent of those sampled were HIV positive.[1] If the Edinburgh findings were replicated throughout the country, it was possible there were as many as 50,000 HIV positive drug addicts throughout the country, raising 'huge consequent personal and institutional costs'.[2] Fortunately, this nightmare scenario was not realised. A WHO study of HIV prevalence among injecting drug users in cities throughout the world conducted between 1989 and 1990 found that British HIV rates were comparatively low: 12.8 per cent of injecting drug users tested were HIV positive in London, compared to 47.8 per cent in New York and 60 per cent in Madrid.[3] However, even though HIV rates were less than initially anticipated, the appearance of the virus among injecting drug users in Britain posed very real challenges to heroin addiction treatment policy and practice. Crucial tenets of pre-existing policy, such as the prioritisation of abstinence as the sole goal of treatment, were re-evaluated as HIV and AIDS came to be understood as representing a 'greater threat to public and individual health than drug misuse'.[4]

This reconfiguration had the potential to bring drug addicts and certain kinds of treatment 'in from the cold'.[5] As the Dally case indicated, attitudes towards maintenance already showed signs of a thaw. Those who had previously been staunchly opposed to the long-term prescription of drugs to addicts, such as John Strang, reconsidered their position. Prescribing drugs to addicts could, Strang argued, act as 'bait' to 'capture' the drug taker, drawing him or her into treatment and away from spreading HIV.[6] A consensus appeared to form around the idea that policy and practice should focus on attempting to reduce the dangers associated with drug use. This notion of 'harm reduction' or 'harm minimisation' led to the development of some new initiatives, such as needle exchange, as well as the re-appraisal of old ones. Yet even within these seemingly novel departures from existing practices, the tensions that had been apparent in drug addiction treatment throughout earlier decades could be detected. The dispute over what type of treatment should be offered drug addicts and which kind of doctor should administer this continued. The prescription of drugs to addicts, particularly on a maintenance basis, remained contentious. Interprofessional conflicts also persisted, and to some extent deepened, as AIDS brought new groups and individuals into the 'policy community' around drugs. Non-medical actors, particularly voluntary organisations and even drug users themselves, became more involved in responding to some of the problems presented by heroin and AIDS. But this should not necessarily be read as the emergence of an increasingly 'social' view of heroin addiction. It has been argued that AIDS resulted in a partial re-medicalisation of the drug problem as HIV and AIDS brought with it tangible, medical conditions.[7]

The apparent replacement of a socially infectious disease (drug addiction) with one that was literally infectious (HIV/AIDS) as the great public health emergency facing Britain in this period engendered an often paradoxical response. The re-medicalisation of heroin addiction treatment took place alongside de-medicalisation in other areas, and new initiatives were introduced just as many old practices were left untouched. The impact of AIDS on the treatment of heroin addiction is analyzed by focussing on three key areas. Firstly, how HIV/AIDS came to be recognised as a greater threat to public health than drug use will be discussed, as well as the immediate response offered to this. Secondly, the notion of harm reduction will be examined in more detail. Harm reduction was not an entirely new philosophy but one that was applied with new effect in the era of AIDS. Finally, the effect of AIDS on clinical practice in the treatment of addiction will be considered. It is argued that while some significant changes did take place in the wake of HIV/AIDS, these were far from revolutionary. AIDS did not so much bring heroin addiction out of the cold as to add heat to existing debates.

A GREATER THREAT? AIDS, DRUGS AND PUBLIC HEALTH

The identification of AIDS as a disease in its own right is usually dated to a report published by the Centers for Disease Control in June 1981 that noted the deaths of five young, previously healthy, homosexual men in Los Angeles from pneumocystis pneumonia, a condition found almost exclusively in people with defective immune systems.[8]

The Lancet reported the first British case in the same year, in which another previously healthy homosexual male succumbed to pneumocystis pneumonia.[9] As these early cases were all gay men, it was thought there was a link between male homosexual activity and immunodeficiency, and the condition became known as GRID (Gay-Related Immuno-Deficiency).[10] But in the subsequent months there were reports of immunodeficiency related diseases in heterosexuals too, particularly in haemophiliacs, those who had recently received blood transfusions and injecting drug users. GRID no longer seemed an appropriate label, and the condition was renamed AIDS (Acquired Immune Deficiency Syndrome) at a conference in Washington D.C. in 1982.[11] In 1983 and 1984 the virus HIV (Human Immunodeficiency Virus) was identified as the putative agent responsible for causing AIDS.[12] HIV was passed on through blood and blood products, through sexual intercourse or from mother to child during pregnancy. Though there was evidence from as early as 1983 that the virus could spread through heterosexual as well as homosexual sex, the issue of HIV/AIDS in heterosexuals was largely ignored in Britain until 1985, when the possibility of the spread of AIDS among injecting drug users was first seriously considered.[13] The first confirmed case of AIDS in an injecting drug user was reported in March 1985, although this was later reassigned to 1984.[14]

But it was the Edinburgh epidemic of 1985/6 that first brought the issue of AIDS and intravenous drug use in Britain into sharp focus. The blood samples tested for HIV had all come from the drug-using patients of GP Roy Robertson. Robertson attributed the high rates of HIV in his patients to the widespread practice of sharing syringes and injecting equipment. This was particularly common in Scotland as pharmacists there were prevented from selling syringes to addicts. There were even reports of police confiscating syringes from patients as they left Robertson's surgery.[15] Robertson reached the conclusion that 'health workers must intervene somehow either to stop needle and syringe sharing or, preferably, to stop individuals injecting heroin at all'.[16] One solution was to make syringes more widely available, but Robertson's pleas, and those of others, fell initially on stony ground. Ministers at the Scottish Home and Health Department felt that needle exchanges would condone and even encourage drug use, as well as being prohibitively expensive.[17] They did, however, concede that the problem required further investigation, and a committee was convened to provide advice on HIV and drug use. The committee, chaired by the regional director of the Blood Transfusion Service, Dr D.B. McClelland, reported in 1986.[18] McClelland's central recommendation was that the threat of the spread of HIV to the general population from injecting drug users justified a 'harm minimisation' approach, i.e. those addicts who could not or would not abstain from intravenous drug use should be brought into contact with treatment services in order to prevent them from spreading HIV.

The origins of the notion of harm minimisation and its implications for drug policy will be discussed in greater detail below, but it is important to note that the McClelland report led to some practical developments, most notably the establishment of pilot schemes to test the value of needle exchanges. Syringe distribution had already been trialled in Amsterdam, and in 1986 a handful of voluntary organisations had begun handing out syringes to addicts in regional towns and cities across Britain.[19] In 1987 the DHSS and the Scottish Home and Health Department launched experimental syringe exchange projects at 15 different agencies throughout the country. These provided injecting equipment on an exchange basis in order to both protect the public from used needles and discourage the re-use of syringes within the drug-injecting population. The project was evaluated by a team of researchers, including Stimson, from Goldsmiths College, University of London. They found that injecting equipment could be distributed on an exchange basis and that needle exchanges were reasonably successful in attracting clients, although they were less successful in retaining them.[20]

The McClelland report and the syringe exchange pilot project helped raise the profile of AIDS and drug use so that by 1987 AIDS among heroin addicts showed all the signs of becoming a major political issue. In February the *British Medical Journal* led with an editorial entitled 'AIDS and intravenous drug use: the real heterosexual epidemic'. Presenting European and American data on HIV prevalence in injecting drug users alongside that from Edinburgh, the *BMJ* asserted that while 'There is no magic bullet for controlling the spread of HIV in drug users . . . local authorities should take charge of this second AIDS epidemic now.'[21] At the national level there were also developments. In May the ACMD decided that a working group should be set up to consider the implications of HIV and AIDS for drug services.[22] The working group were to report on measures that should be taken to 'help combat the spread of HIV infection', concentrating particularly on how 'drug misusers' could be brought into contact with treatment services 'with a view to preventing or minimising unsafe injecting and other harmful behaviour'.[23] The group, chaired by Ruth Runciman of the Citizens Advice Bureau, met for four months, hearing evidence from those in the drug 'misuse' and AIDS fields and were ready to report in the autumn of 1987, but government reticence meant the final report was not published until March 1988.[24] The Runciman Committee's most important and often repeated conclusion was, 'HIV is a greater threat to public and individual health than drug misuse.'[25] This led them to recommend, as had the McClelland Committee, that services concentrating on harm minimisation should take precedence. Because not all intravenous drug users would stop injecting, the Runciman Committe commented: 'We must therefore be prepared to work with those who continue to misuse drugs to help them reduce the risks involved in doing so, above all the risk of acquiring or spreading HIV.'[26]

It has been argued that this outlook reflected a 'new public health paradigm of drug problems'. Stimson contended that 'HIV has simplified the debate. Rather than seeing drug use as a metaphorical disease, there is now a real medical problem associated with drug use.'[27] HIV and AIDS did reiterate the potential danger posed by drug use to collective health, but it is misleading to refer to the public health paradigm as a 'new' way to view drug addiction. By describing heroin addiction as a 'socially infectious condition', the second Brain report (published in 1965) was drawing on contemporary notions of public health—of the social as well as the individual body.[28] Notions of public health and drug use clearly pre-dated the Runciman report. Parallels between the 1960s and the post-AIDS era were drawn by, among others, Alan Glanz of the ARU in 1988.[29] Glanz asserted that 'Drugs policy in Britain has entered a new phase and returned to an old phase. The public health imperative has re-asserted itself in the face of the AIDS emergency.'[30] Berridge has also pointed to the public health aspects of the Brain report, noting that 'The remedies suggested by Brain—including notification and compulsory treatment—were classic public health responses.'[31] Public health has, she argues, formed a dimension of drug policy since the nineteenth century. This approach can be seen in the earlier attention paid to perceived threats to collective health such as opium adulteration, infant doping and working-class opiate use.[32] There was clearly nothing 'new' about a public health understanding of drug use in the late 1980s.

Examining the nature of this response in more detail does, however, suggest some differences with past understandings, even if the framework in which these were located was not entirely novel. Public health was not a static collection of concepts and approaches, and this is exemplified in its interaction with drug policy. The public health of the 1960s focused on sickness within the social body, on the relationship between individuals as a source of disease. Epidemiology came to the fore as a way of observing the pattern of disease and predicting where this might occur next. This was reflected in Brain's understanding of addiction as a 'socially infectious condition' that required 'epidemiological assessment and control'.[33] By the late 1980s, understandings of public health had moved away from relationships between individuals and began to centre on the behaviour of the individual. In this 'new public health', according to Alan Petersen and Deborah Lupton, 'Individuals are expected to take responsibility for the care of their bodies and to limit their potential harm to others through taking up various preventive actions.'[34] Here the concept of risk is central; 'risky' activities such as smoking, drinking and taking drugs must be prevented to preserve the health of the individual and the community. If risky behaviours cannot be altered, then the damage they cause must be controlled and reduced. This is clearly the philosophy that underpinned the recommendations of the McClelland and Runciman reports: if intravenous drug use could not be halted, then the danger it posed should be minimised. Harm minimisation was a rationale rooted in the 'new public health'.

Changes in the public health paradigm allowed for the creation of the concept of harm minimisation, but there were specific reasons as to why this was applied to drug 'misuse' in the late 1980s. Recognition of the potential damage that addiction could cause to society was also nothing new; this had been documented by Brain in the 1960s and recognised to a greater or lesser extent by those involved in the treatment of addiction from this point on. The discovery of HIV and AIDS among intravenous drug users did, however, add another important dimension to this danger. AIDS was unquestionably a killer: of the 671 British cases reported in 1987, 605 died before April 1995. Of the total 10,693 people diagnosed with AIDS between 1982 and 1994, 7,346 are known to have died before April 1995.[35] The threat AIDS posed to individual and collective health seemed to far outweigh that of drug addiction.

This facilitated the introduction of a number of previously controversial schemes, such as needle exchange. The McClelland report went on to recommend that further syringe exchange projects be established and that community pharmacists be encouraged to sell injecting equipment to drug users.[36] Information about cleaning syringes using bleach was also distributed by voluntary organisations and in DHSS-produced leaflets.[37] By 1990 there were 200 needle exchange schemes in operation, and a survey of community pharmacists conducted in 1995 found that 35 per cent sold injecting equipment, including syringes, to drug users.[38] Those who had argued that providing addicts with clean needles encouraged injecting, and that this was morally unacceptable, were increasingly drowned out by a 'new consensus on harm reduction'.[39] Britain's adoption of needle exchange was startling, for example, when compared to the difficulties faced by drug workers trying to implement similar schemes in the USA. Jon Parker, a public health student at Yale who began distributing needles to injecting drug users in New Haven and Boston in 1986, was later arrested in eight states for attempting similar programmes. Although needle exchanges did appear in American cities such as New York, San Francisco and Chicago, some of these schemes operated outside the law.[40] The federal government refused to fund needle exchange projects and, until 1992, withheld support from organisations that distributed bleach to sterilise injecting equipment.[41] But, even in Britain, concerns about syringe exchange and the rationale behind this remained. Stimson and his team found that some syringe exchange employees had 'personal doubts about the desirability of syringe exchange', and 'not all workers are able to engage in harm minimisation'.[42] This would suggest that harm reduction had a more ambivalent impact than at first might be supposed. The meaning and application of this philosophy clearly requires further investigation.

HARM REDUCTION AND HEROIN ADDICTION

According to Ernst Buning, a Dutch psychologist involved in harm reduction programmes in Amsterdam, harm minimisation was based on the rationale that 'If it is not possible to cure drug users, one should at least try to minimise the harm that is being done both to them and the wider social environment.'[43] Buning's definition of harm minimisation is significant, because the Dutch example was particularly important both in terms of needle exchange and the adoption of harm minimisation itself. Syringe exchange had started in Amsterdam in the early 1980s in response to concerns about the spread of Hepatitis B among injecting drug users. Although the programme was initially run by community pharmacies, it was taken over by groups of drug users themselves, the Junkiebonds, or Junkie Unions.[44] This programme of needle exchange and harm reduction measures attracted significant international interest. The House of Commons Social Services Committee tasked with investigating AIDS visited Amsterdam in 1987.[45] So too did Bill Nelles, a former drug user and NHS worker, who went on to establish the Methadone Alliance, a British drug user group.[46]

The Dutch experiment with harm reduction was not the only one. Although international influences were important for the adoption of harm reduction in the UK, domestic examples also played a role. Peter McDermott, a drug user activist and freelance writer, has described the introduction of a number of harm reduction initiatives in Merseyside during the late 1980s as the 'birth of harm reduction'.[47] Although the adoption of harm reduction was a much wider process, regional programmes, and particularly the one carried out in Merseyside, were important. The Mersey Drug Training and Information Centre opened one of the first needle exchanges in Britain in 1986, and McDermott also saw the willingness of James Willis, and later John Marks, at the Liverpool DDU to consider maintenance prescription as part of the harm reduction 'experiment'.[48] Although the 'Mersey experiment' came to an end, partly due to negative publicity drawn to some of its more radical elements, it did help spawn a national, and even international, movement around harm reduction: the *Mersey Drugs Journal* became the *International Journal of Drug Policy*; Liverpool played host to the first International Conference on the Reduction of Drug Related Harm in 1991; and individuals involved in the Mersey Drug Training and Information Centre, such as Pat O'Hare, were instrumental in the establishment of the International Harm Reduction Association (IHRA) in 1996.

While these were clearly important developments, questions can be raised about the extent to which the philosophy behind these was entirely 'new'. The concept of harm minimisation clearly predated HIV and AIDS. Stimson has argued that British drug policies have contained elements of harm minimisation since the publication of the Rolleston report in 1926.[49] By suggesting that the addict could be prescribed the drug of his or her addiction when all other attempts to remove the drug had failed, the Rolleston report was recommending a course of action that reduced harm to the addict.[50] In fact, the old British System was often invoked as being representative of a harm reduction strategy that needed to be re-instigated. McDermott argued that 'for some of the architects of the policy [of harm reduction]' there was 'a conscious and explicit attempt to roll back the current paradigm for dealing with drug problems to the classic principles that underpinned the original British System'.[51] Another source of ideas about harm minimisation, according to Stimson, was the drug 'underground' of the late 1960s and 1970s. He notes that the drug-using subculture of this period produced numerous books and manuals on how to use and enjoy drugs while limiting their potentially damaging effects.[52] This was the philosophy of many voluntary organisations interested in drug issues, such as Release. Release was set up in 1967 initially to provide legal advice to young people arrested for drug offences, but its work rapidly widened to deal with a range of drug-related problems.[53] Their approach, disseminated through numerous publications, talks and active casework was to encourage those using drugs to do so in a manner that reduced the possible dangers. This was epitomised in the establishment of a telephone drug information service in 1975, designed to 'prevent physical and psychological damage resulting from the use and abuse of licit and illicit drugs, adulterated or otherwise' by providing 'objective, non-hysterical information' to drug users.[54] Moreover, voluntary organisations were not the only place where harm minimisation objectives were practised. The stated purpose of the DDUs in 1968 was to treat the addict while at the same time preventing the development of the black market, a clear attempt to reduce the potential damage resulting from heroin use.

Though there was nothing 'new' about harm minimisation, there was much that was different about its adoption in the post-AIDS era. Crucially, harm reduction resulted in a shift in the way the drug user as patient was regarded. Harm reduction was not something done to drug users but done for, and increasingly by, drug users themselves. In order to reduce the spread of HIV, it was argued that services needed to be made more 'attractive' to drug users.[55] For some, this could mean the adoption of a more explicitly consumer-oriented approach. Strang and Stimson noted that 'Planners might benefit from considering drug services as if they were a business. Although it is important to ensure that established customers continue to use the service as before, is there scope for capturing more customers from the out-of-contact population?'[56] For some commentators AIDS resulted in a reconfiguration of the drug user. The anthropologist Jon E. Zibbell argues that the impact of HIV/AIDS led to the 'appearance of a new subject of government: the actively responsible drug user who could be integrated into a nexus of education and behavioural change within drug services'.[57] Harm reduction re-conceptualised the drug user as an individual who could be involved in his or her own treatment and that of others.

This had implications not just on an individual level, on the relationship between service user and service provider, but on a collective level too. As Berridge has demonstrated, AIDS was important for the formation of gay men's patient groups. There was often a strong degree of patient participation in HIV treatment; many HIV positive gay men acquired significant amounts of knowledge about their condition and demanded particular drug therapies. Other groups tried to influence the way trials of drugs such as Azidothymidine (AZT) were conducted.[58] To some extent, AIDS also acted as a motivating factor for the establishment of drug user activist groups. Needle exchanges, in particular, were sites where drug users could come together to form campaign organisations. Voluntary bodies, such as Mainliners, where drug users aimed to educate service providers about the needs of HIV positive clients, were established.[59] Yet, as was the case with gay AIDS patient groups, the political impact of these organisations, and the subsequent power of the patient 'voice', was rather limited.[60] The focus on the needs of the drug user was, to some extent, undermined by the public health imperative surrounding HIV/AIDS. Harm minimisation was intended to protect the community from the spread of HIV, suggesting that the safety of the community could be prioritised over the treatment of the individual.

CLINICAL PRACTICE AND THE TREATMENT OF ADDICTION IN THE ERA OF AIDS

This tension between the safety of the community and the perceived needs of the individual was powerfully felt in the provision of drug addiction treatment following AIDS. Examining the impact of harm reduction on clinical practice in the treatment of heroin addiction suggests that this had a more ambiguous legacy than might at first be supposed. Although treatment methods and goals were re-appraised, this did not necessarily translate into real change on the ground. A key area was the prescription of drugs to addicts. The prioritisation of harm reduction strongly implied the need for a re-evaluation of the role of prescription in drug treatment. The Runicman report identified two 'wider purposes' for the prescription of drugs to addicts to assist in the containment of the spread of HIV: firstly, 'attracting more drug users to services and keeping them in contact', and, secondly, 'facilitating change away from HIV risk practices'.[61] The working group noted there was evidence to suggest that 'a prescribing function in a drug service can be successful in attracting some drug misusers who would not otherwise approach services'. This was important because 'drug misusers in contact with prescribing agencies are less likely to share injecting equipment'. The group concluded that 'prescribing can be a useful tool in helping to change the behaviour of some drug misusers either towards abstinence or towards intermediate goals such as a reduction in injecting or sharing'.[62] A more flexible approach to prescribing was thus legitimated.

There was some evidence to show that attitudes towards prescription in general and maintenance in particular were beginning to shift. The inability of the GMC to wholly condemn maintenance in the Dally case of 1986/7 was followed by a number of other signs that there might be more flexibility around the issue of prescription. At a conference of the Royal College of Psychiatrists in 1987, John Marks proposed a motion in support of the long-term prescription of opioid drugs to addicts. Although the vote went against the motion (38 opposed, 29 in favour and 9 abstentions) it was indicative of a gradual change of opinion.[63] Even some of the strongest advocates for short-term withdrawal were forced to alter their stance. In a televised debate on the treatment of addiction in March 1987, Connell agreed that maintenance should be re-examined as a possible form of treatment for addiction.[64] In May he announced that the *Guidelines* would be revised to reconsider the position of long-term prescription to addicts, especially in the light of the problems presented by HIV and AIDS.[65] An editorial in *The Lancet* that same month came out staunchly in favour of the long-term prescription of opioids to addicts. A number of arguments were made for maintenance, including the futility of expecting a rapid 'cure' for addiction and the problems arising from the illicit trade in drugs, such as rising crime. According to *The Lancet,* 'all the arguments for a review would hold even if AIDS had never existed . . . a return to some form of controlled availability, which exercises control over inevitable use by rendering alternative methods uneconomic, is not a retrograde step—on the contrary . . . it is the only feasible way forward.'[66] *Drug Scenes*, a special report on drugs and drug dependence by the Royal College of Psychiatrists also published in 1987, discussed maintenance as a method of treatment in an even-handed manner. The report asserted: 'it is not a question of whether methadone maintenance is in some intrinsic sense "good" or "bad" but whether it is likely to be the best option for a particular patient in particular circumstances.'[67]

Examining the response of a leading DDU consultant to AIDS and the prescribing issue does, however, highlight tensions between this and existing ideas and debates. John Strang, a DDU consultant psychiatrist who had been opposed to the long-term prescription of drugs to addicts, pointed to a number of roles for prescribing in the light of HIV. Strang stated that prescribing could be used for 'relief of withdrawal', as 'bait to capture the drug taker', as 'adhesive to improve retention' or as a 'promoter of change'.[68] This could be seen as a retreat from the abstinence-orientated policies he had pursued in his Manchester DDU.[69] Yet allusions to more negative consequences of prescription suggest the extent of change was limited. Strang also noted that prescription might 'obstruct change', and there was a danger of prescription becoming the 'end state', whereby the user would be indefinitely maintained on an opioid drug.[70] Strang's position was that prescribing might have its uses, but it must not lead to maintenance. Maintenance should be replaced with 'a more active approach which sought to identify a series of intermediate goals . . . so as to encourage appropriate changes in behaviour'.[71]

Long-term prescription, it seems, did not become the widespread method of treatment offered by DDUs, despite its perceived benefits in terms of preventing the spread of HIV. Stimson found that while the total amount of methadone being prescribed seemed to have increased, this did not necessarily mean it was being administered on a maintenance basis. He stated that the amount of methadone distributed to pharmacies from wholesalers increased from 93,166 grams in 1988 to 338,458 grams in 1992, a four-fold increase. Yet 'methadone was mostly prescribed on a reducing basis, though many patients were maintained by default (i.e. after failing to reduce and become abstinent).' Stimson went on to note that there were no structured methadone programmes in Britain in this period like those found in the USA, and 'Prescriptions for heroin were rare, and mainly confined to older addicts who had received prescriptions since the 1960s.'[72]

Other researchers also found that actual DDU practices seemed to have changed surprisingly little. A study of the DDU at St Mary's Hospital, London, revealed that 'Harm reduction was not seen as the foremost treatment priority.' Instead, achieving abstinence remained 'the main treatment goal'.[73] This finding was replicated in another study of DDUs in the wake of AIDS. A group of researchers, led by Steve Cranfield, from a range of backgrounds, including clinical psychiatry, argued that the DDUs were largely resistant to change. AIDS forced a re-evaluation of maintenance, but this remained 'highly controversial and difficult for established centres to accept'.[74] Cranfield and his colleagues asserted that there were few changes in DDU prescription policies in the wake of AIDS, with the only exceptions being those patients who were HIV positive. Moreover, they noted that the traditional autonomy of the DDUs was threatened by the apparent need to collaborate with a range of services as a result of the threat posed by AIDS. Cranfield and his colleagues observed the drug treatment services in one District Health Authority and found that there was open hostility and rivalry between staff at the DDU and those running the needle exchange, such that needle exchange staff stopped referring patients to the DDU, sending them to local GPs instead.[75] This led the researchers to argue that though DDUs remain central to the response to drugs in the wake of AIDS, 'Like other psychiatric institutions, they sometimes resist attempts to move towards a community-based approach.'[76]

The reason for this resistance can be related to the central divide between hospital and community, between clinical and biographical and between the medical and the social at the heart of debates about the treatment of addiction. Clinical psychiatrists working at DDUs often saw and responded to disease in a particular way. As a result of their location within hospitals and their adoption of clinical methods, DDU doctors largely emphasised the cure of addiction. Maintenance was seen as merely perpetuating the disease. Though there might be benefits to society by prescribing to the addict in order to prevent him or her from spreading HIV, this did nothing to cure the addict of addiction. As Strang noted: 'If the drug addict is on a slippery slope from which the only escape route is complete abstinence, then discussions of reducing dose, cutting back on injecting or moderating the extent of use will merely encourage the drug taker to consider unrealistic options.'[77] This contrasted with the view of many community-based physicians involved in the treatment of addiction. As a result of paying greater attention to the patient rather than the disease, these doctors frequently placed more emphasis on intermediate goals of improving the patient's social functioning before working towards abstinence. For this reason, community-based practitioners frequently offered long-term prescription to addict-patients. This brought them into conflict with the DDUs because they offered an alternative view of addiction and subsequently an alternative way of treating this.

Far from closing the divide between the hospital and the community, HIV and AIDS may actually have served to separate the two spheres even further. The relative danger of HIV compared to drug addiction suggested that a community-based approach, stressing intermediate goals and in tune with harm minimisation, was a more appropriate response than the abstinence-orientated, hospital-based, clinical method. In order to retain a role in the treatment of addiction, DDUs needed to adopt elements of the community-based, harm-minimisation approach, at least in principle. As Cranfield and his colleagues indicate, however, the extent to which this effected real change in clinical practice is more questionable. What is more, AIDS complicated matters still further by widening the range of actors, medical and non-medical, involved in dealing with the drug problem.

But even before AIDS, there seem to have been moves to widen the 'policy community' around drugs. The role of non-medical agencies in drug policy had gradually increased since the 1960s, when Brain's definition of addiction as a social disease brought a wider range of actors into the arena. In the 1980s, this trend appeared to pick up speed, as the drug taker became 'normalised'. The ACMD, in *Treatment and Rehabilitation*, called for the 'development of a range of services to help those with problems arising from the misuse of drugs', and this was partially realised through the Central Funding Initiative (CFI). The CFI pumped £17.5 million into community-based services between 1983 and 1987 in a direct attempt to shift focus from hospital-based treatment provision and civil servants actively encouraged a more 'bottom-up' approach, bringing voluntary agencies, former drug users and even current drug users into the 'policy community'.[78] This can clearly be seen in the pattern of grants awarded under the CFI. Just 18 per cent of funds went to the DDUs, with almost half (46 per cent) going to community-based walk-in centres.[79]

This could be interpreted as a move away from a specialist medical response to heroin addiction. Stimson asserted in 1987 that 'medicine is being displaced from a central role and being replaced by a more extensive and diffuse response involving a broader range of agencies and ideas about drug problems.'[80] American drug and alcohol expert Jerome Jaffe, in his 1986 lecture to the Institute of Psychiatry, appeared to confirm this when he said that medicine no longer sat 'at the top of the table.'[81] On one level, AIDS seemed to reinforce this drift away from the medical. Emphasis was placed less on curing the addict of their addiction and more on reducing the harm that this could pose to the individual and society. As harm minimisation became the orthodoxy, those who had often existed outside the mainstream 'policy community', such as voluntary organisations and drug user groups, were admitted to the fold.

Yet, on another level, medicine's position in dealing with drugs was reconfirmed by AIDS. AIDS and HIV presented a number of clearly 'medical' problems for infected drug users and those treating them. AIDS could result in a range of other diseases: respiratory conditions such as pneumonia and tuberculosis, neurological disorders and dementia, gastrointestinal diseases and bacterial infections, problems with liver functioning and skin conditions.[82] Almost arguing against himself in his earlier work, Stimson suggested that AIDS resulted in a partial 're-medicalisation' of drug addiction treatment, as psychiatrists had to relearn physical medicine in order to conduct examinations for signs of HIV and AIDS related conditions.[83] Berridge also notes the revival of 'medical' involvement in drug addiction as a result of AIDS, pointing to the greater emphasis placed on the general health of the drug user.[84] This might have threatened the position of the psychiatrist as the leading expert on drug addiction as other kinds of specialists, most notably in genitourinary medicine, accumulated knowledge and expertise on AIDS.[85] This can be seen, for example, in some of the early editorials on AIDS and drug use: these were written by genitourinary specialists, not addiction psychiatrists.[86]

Despite the emergence of other kinds of expertise in drugs, psychiatrists seem to have retained their dominant position. The complications to the treatment of addiction presented by HIV and AIDS did not prevent psychiatrists from continuing to take a leading role in the drug 'policy community'. Of the thirteen members of the ACMD working group on AIDS and drug 'misuse', only six were from a non-medical background. Of the remaining seven doctors, four were psychiatrists, the largest single group.[87] A parallel can clearly be drawn here with the earlier ACMD report *Treatment and Rehabilitation*, when four of the seven doctors on the working group were psychiatrists.[88] Further evidence to suggest that psychiatry remained central to the formulation of the response to drug addiction can be found by examining the nature of this response more closely. The Runicman report stressed that GPs and 'other generic professions' should play a greater role in the treatment of addiction.[89] The working group argued that the advent of HIV made it 'essential that all GPs should provide care and advice for drug misusing patients to help them move away from behaviour which may result in them acquiring and spreading the virus'.[90] However, the part GPs were expected to play in the treatment of addiction was constrained. It was recommended that GPs should be equipped to deal with short-term detoxifications and medium-term withdrawal regimes. Furthermore, it was suggested that these be undertaken in cooperation with the Community Drug Teams (usually headed by a psychiatrist), and specialists, at either the district or regional level, were to deal with more 'difficult' cases, that is those involving non-reducing, long-term prescriptions or the use of injectable drugs.[91] Once more, there were echoes of the recent past. *Treatment and Rehabilitation* (1982) and the *Guidelines* (1984) similarly suggested a limited role for the generalist: supervision of GPs treating addicts by specialists and limitations to their prescription of drugs to addicts.[92]

Indeed, a brief analysis of the revised *Guidelines* on the treatment of drug addiction (published in 1991) indicates that the two central debates in the field, on maintenance and on the involvement of generalists, were very much still alive despite the appearance of AIDS. The *Guidelines* accepted the principle of harm reduction, stating that 'the doctor should always look for ways to reduce the harm from continued drug use.'[93] Adapting advice first distributed by the drug users' voluntary organisation Mainliners, they also offered guidance on how to clean syringes with bleach. But at the same time, abstinence remained the goal of treatment. A schematic diagram illustrating the 'management of a drug problem' had 'drug free' as its expected end state. And, on the more contentious issues, such as maintenance, the advice offered was much more ambiguous. The *Guidelines* noted that 'Prescribing a substitute drug where appropriate can be a useful tool in helping to change the behaviour of some drug misusers either towards abstinence or towards intermediate goals', but it was clear that the kind of prescription envisaged was not expected to continue for any length of time.[94] Though the *Guidelines* conceded that 'There is at least a small proportion of patients for whom this [maintenance] is a helpful approach', this was 'a specialised form of treatment best provided by, or in consultation with, a specialist drug misuse service'.[95] It would appear that AIDS had done little to diminish the importance of the clinical psychiatrist in drug policy.

CONCLUSION—ASSESSING THE IMPACT OF HIV/AIDS ON HEROIN ADDICTION TREATMENT

The continued dominance of psychiatry in the treatment of addiction following AIDS is just one of a number of continuities with the past response to heroin. The involvement of generalists was still seen as problematic, as something to be controlled and directed by specialists. Tensions around prescription, and particularly maintenance, also failed to dissipate. Public health concerns were once more brought to the fore, albeit in a different form. This has led many observers to question the impact of HIV/AIDS on heroin addiction treatment. Berridge notes, 'despite the apparent revolution in the rhetoric of drug policy achieved by AIDS, many aspects of post AIDS policy were inherent in drug policy in the 1980s.'[96] Stimson asserts that 'new' ideas about how to deal with heroin addiction in the wake of AIDS had their roots in earlier work, that change was 'perhaps a matter of emphasis and direction, rather than abrupt rupture with the recent past'.[97] Susanne MacGregor has also expressed doubts as to whether AIDS prompted the development of a distinct phase of drug policy, suggesting there was more of a modification of existing practices.[98]

That is not to say, however, that AIDS had no impact whatsoever. Prioritising the limitation of the spread of HIV and AIDS over the treatment of drug addiction had important consequences. Harm reduction opened up the possibility that addiction treatment could be more flexible, allowing for a wider range of options in treatment. AIDS also facilitated the involvement of a greater range of bodies and individuals in the drugs field, not least the drug user him or herself. Yet the continuities between the pre and post AIDS periods would seem to be unavoidable, for the conflicts pointed to throughout this book persist into the present.[99]

CHAPTER EIGHT

Treatment Works?

Drug Policy and Addiction Treatment Since 1994

In his first online broadcast to the nation in February 2000, the Labour Prime Minister Tony Blair addressed Britain's drug problem. He stated, 'Being Prime Minister is a difficult job but nothing's more difficult than being a parent. And there are few bigger worries when you are a parent than drugs.' According to Blair, what was needed to tackle this 'modern menace' was 'tougher punishment, better education, better treatment' and 'better coordination across government'.[1] New laws, including the power to test criminals and prisoners for drugs, referral of convicted drug offenders to treatment and a seven-year-minimum sentence for drug dealers were to be introduced.

This tough talk on drugs was indicative of two key changes in British drug policy since the 1990s. Firstly, Blair's choice of the 'drug problem' as the topic of his broadcast represented a much greater level of political involvement in the drug issue. Central government, in the form of politicians, civil servants from various departments and new 'special advisors', became involved in the making of drug policy and practice on an unprecedented scale. At the same time, the policy community around drugs away from central government expanded still further, as new actors, such as the pharmaceutical industry, became involved. Secondly, as a further extract from the Prime Minister's speech illustrates, the tenor of drug policy appeared to have changed. Drugs, Blair asserted, 'fuel . . . so much of our crime'. As a result, drug policy has increasingly focused on the relationship between drug use and crime. A whole raft of initiatives aimed at breaking the link between drugs and crime have been introduced, involving the criminal justice system much more closely in drug policy and practice.

This apparent shift has led some commentators, such as the sociologist-turned-activist Gerry Stimson, to argue that drug policy has moved away from treatment and towards control. A concern for public health and harm reduction, has, he contends, been replaced with a 'punitive and coercive ethos'.[2] Yet, while drugs and crime have undoubtedly become a much more prominent issue since the mid-1990s, the treatment and criminal justice agendas on drugs are not necessarily oppositional or even, in some instances, distinct. As has been the case since the 1920s, medical, treatment-oriented approaches are often combined with penal measures directed towards the control of drugs and those who use them. The introduction, in 1998, of Drug Treatment and Testing Orders (DTTOs), which place drug-using offenders in treatment as an alternative to prison, would seem to typify such a process.[3] Moreover, the effect of the drugs-crime agenda on addiction treatment has not been to reduce the importance of treatment within drug policy as a whole. In fact, treatment services have rapidly expanded over the last ten years. A study conducted by the voluntary organisation DrugScope, cited in the 2002 updated drug strategy, found that the number of drug treatment services had increased by a third since 1997.[4]

Much of this growth has been underpinned by the frequently repeated statement that 'treatment works'. Research into addiction treatment has produced evidence indicating its effectiveness when measured against a number of goals, particularly a reduction in drug-related crime. The National Treatment Outcome Research Study (NTORS) followed a cohort of drug users through various forms of treatment and found that one year later involvement in crime had been reduced by half.[5] This finding has been widely cited as supporting the new emphasis on drugs and crime, but the use of research in drug policy and practice is part of a much wider move towards evidence-based medicine and evidence-based policy.

The use of evidence to determine effectiveness within addiction treatment raises a number of issues. Interpretations differ as to what is 'treatment' and what can be said to 'work'. Old debates about the appropriateness of maintenance appear to have returned, if indeed they ever went away. Other conflicts between specialists and generalists, and between private practitioners and NHS doctors, also seem to have resurfaced. In 2006, the GMC struck Dr Colin Brewer (director of the private drug clinic the Stapleford Centre) off the medical register for serious professional misconduct. In a case strongly reminiscent of aspects of the Dally case twenty years previously, Brewer and his colleagues were criticised for their unorthodox methods within the context of a wider debate about the treatment of addiction.[6] It would seem that while significant changes within addiction policy and practice have taken place, long-running disputes remain unresolved. An examination of the key developments in drug policy since the mid-1990s will reveal significant continuities within the recent, and not so recent, past.

'A MULTI-MILLION POUND INDUSTRY'—
THE EXPANSION OF THE DRUG FIELD

The treatment of drug addiction has become big business. Meeting the needs of over 300,000 drug users is now a multi-million pound 'industry' involving the public, private and voluntary sectors.[7] In 2006/7 annual spending on all drug treatment services was estimated to be in excess of £500 million.[8] DrugScope's database of treatment services recorded the existence of 1,071 treatment services in 2007, a significantly higher number than the 323 dedicated drug services identified by MacGregor and her colleagues in 1989.[9] Yet what can now be described as the 'drug field' has not just increased in size; it has also increased in scope. The expansion of the policy community around drugs seen in the late 1980s has continued apace. A far greater range of groups and individuals are now involved in different aspects of drug treatment policy and practice than ever before.

The programme of the third National Drug Treatment Conference (NDTC), held in Glasgow in March 2006, provides a useful snapshot of the current state of the drug field.[10] This conference was organised by Exchange Supplies, a company that provides injecting paraphernalia such as citric acid, sterile cups and water to needle exchanges, as well as general information and advice to drug users and practitioners on harm reduction.[11] Exchange Supplies describe themselves as a 'social enterprise,' defined by the Department of Trade and Industry as 'businesses with primarily social objectives whose surpluses are principally reinvested for that purpose in the business or in the community, rather than being driven by the need to maximise profit for shareholders and owners'.[12] The involvement of this sort of hybrid organisation is indicative of wider changes in the voluntary sector in Britain but also of the increasing diversification of the drug addiction field.[13] Medical professionals and statutory services are no longer the only interested groups: the NDTC conference was attended by at least 650 delegates representing voluntary organisations, universities, private companies, drug action teams, primary care trusts, specialist treatment services, general practices, nursing teams, mental health groups, prisons, probation services and drug user groups.[14] Conference presentations were on subjects as diverse as 'discrimination: the user's view', 'management of physical illness in drug users' and 'developing drug and alcohol treatment in the prison setting'.[15]

Those attending the conference were not only exposed to a range of views on different aspects of drug treatment but also to representatives of private (for-profit) companies and businesses. The conference was sponsored by Schering-Plough, a global pharmaceutical company that produces Subutex (Buphrenorphine) and Suboxone (Buphrenorphine and Naltrexone), two drugs that are used in the treatment of opiate addiction.[16] Schering-Plough was joined at the NDTC by a range of other businesses offering services to treatment providers, such as Altrix, which conducts screening for the presence of drugs and blood-borne viruses.[17] The presence of these companies clearly suggests there is money to be made in heroin addiction treatment. This potential for profit is a further indication of the size and scale of the current drug problem but also of the redefinition of addiction as a chronic, relapsing condition requiring long-term treatment.[18] Changing definitions of addiction and its treatment will be discussed in greater detail in the Conclusion, but the long-term treatment of a large, chronically ill population obviously provides long-term opportunities for pharmaceutical companies and other ancillary businesses. The implications of industry involvement in the treatment of addiction have yet to be fully analysed, but more general critiques of the pharmaceutical industry suggest that its influence on medical research and practice is significant. Pharmaceutical companies, it is argued, have helped construct new illnesses that require medications and continually produce expensive 'new' drugs that are variations on 'old' drugs simply to make more money.[19] In the drugs field, a number of new drugs have appeared in recent years. Subutex (buprenorphine) was licensed for use in the treatment of addiction in Britain in 1999.[20] Subutex is a longer-acting opiate substitute drug than methadone, and it is a partial opioid agonist. This means that it prevents the user from going into withdrawal but also reduces the effect of heroin if this is taken at the same time.[21] The use of full opioid agonists, like Naltrexone, which block the effect of heroin on the addict's brain altogether, is also becoming more widespread. While Naltrexone has been available for thirty years or so, it has recently been developed as an implant and is currently being considered by the National Institute for Health and Clinical Excellence (NICE) for approval for use within the NHS.[22]

Whatever the precise ramifications of pharmaceutical industry involvement in the treatment of addiction, its presence is representative of the increasing diversification of the drug field. One of the most striking 'new' voices in heroin addiction treatment is that of the addict him or herself. As seen throughout this book, the views of addicts were largely ignored in the development of addiction treatment in Britain. Although drug users did play a role in the drugs field, particularly in the therapeutic communities and in voluntary organisations, they were not a large force within policy and practice; however, since the mid-1990s, the drug user has become much more visible.[23] This can be seen in two main areas. Firstly, drug users are increasingly having an input in the development and delivery of treatment services at a local and national level. Users are represented within statutory groups involved in the delivery of drug treatment, such as the National Treatment Agency (NTA).[24] They have also formed their own groups, such as the Alliance (formerly the Methadone Alliance) to campaign for better service provision and act as advocates for individual addicts seeking change in their own drug treatment.[25] User-produced publications such as *Black Poppy* and *The Users'*

Voice give peer-led harm reduction advice as well as providing addicts with an opportunity to voice their own opinions. Secondly, a politically active user movement seems to be developing. Users are increasingly campaigning for not only their right to appropriate treatment but also the right to use drugs. This has led some drug user groups to challenge what they see as a global system of prohibition of illegal drugs. It is here that British groups are also linking into a nascent international user movement that has sprung up in recent years, particularly around harm reduction.[26]

The development of harm reduction and the impact of HIV/AIDS on drug addiction treatment goes some way towards explaining the emergence of the drug user as a force within drug policy. As seen in Chapter Seven, the public health danger posed by AIDS required treatment providers to listen to the views of drug addicts more closely so that they could be brought into treatment and encouraged to adopt safer practices to prevent the spread of HIV. This undoubtedly played a role in giving drug users a voice, but in the domestic context other policy influences have also been important. Since the late 1980s, increasing attention has been paid to the 'consumer' of health care services.[27] This can be seen in developments such as the introduction of the internal market within the NHS in 1989 and the creation of the Patient's Charter in 1991.[28] The New Labour government has pushed this trend even further, and in its desire to create a 'patient centred NHS' has introduced a range of new measures that add weight to the views of the 'patient consumer'.[29] All statutory health service providers are now obliged to involve patients in decisions about their own treatment and the delivery of services more generally.[30] This applies to drug addiction treatment as it does to any other area of medicine. Although the impact of these reforms on the drugs field can be questioned, as many limitations to 'user power' seem to remain, this is nonetheless an important development.[31] Heroin addiction treatment is no longer solely about publicly funded DDUs run by NHS consultant psychiatrists; they have been joined by a wide range of groups and individuals with widely differing views on drugs, addiction and its treatment.

Some attempt has been made to manage this diversification and direct it towards agreed objectives through moves to coordinate drug policy and practice from the centre. Since the introduction of the first national strategy on drugs, *Tackling Drug Misuse* in 1985, there have been two more efforts to outline drug policy on a national scale.[32] In 1995, John Major's Conservative government produced *Tackling Drugs Together*, which placed equal importance on reducing drug-related crime, limiting the availability of drugs and reducing the health risks associated with drug use. *Tackling Drugs Together* also established Drug Action Teams (DATs) in each health authority area, which were designed to tackle drug-related problems at a local level and were made up of representatives from the police, probation and prison services and local authorities.[33] In 1998, the New Labour government under Tony

Blair introduced *Tackling Drugs to Build a Better Britain: The Government's 10-year Strategy for Tackling Drug Misuse.* This document outlined a number of key developments in drug policy.[34] The 1998 drug strategy has been seen as representative of a move towards a criminal justice agenda on drugs, and the measures it introduced to deal with a link between drugs and crime will be discussed in greater detail below, but *Tackling Drugs to Build a Better Britain* also had important implications for the way drug policy was made and delivered.[35] DATs were given more authority at the local level and have since taken on the responsibility of commissioning treatment services from NHS and voluntary sector service providers for drug users in their region.[36]

Yet control was not totally devolved to the regions. A potentially powerful central force was introduced with the creation of the role of the UK Anti-Drugs Coordinator, popularly known as the 'Drugs Tsar', in 1998. The first (and only) Drugs Tsar was Keith Hellawell, a former police chief constable. In a development that had some parallels with George Bush Sr's appointment of a cabinet-level Drug Tsar (William Bennett) to run the Office of National Drug Control Policy in 1988, Hellawell was given control of the UK Anti-Drugs Coordination Unit.[37] Hellawell and his deputy, Mike Trace, were tasked with implementing the drugs strategy and providing 'day-to-day' leadership on the drugs issue; however, Hellawell quickly ran into problems with politicians, civil servants and the media. Hellawell argued that his difficulties stemmed from having responsibility for dealing with the drug problem but little power to do so effectively. Civil servants, he maintained, were obstructive, and the different departments involved in the drug issue, principally the Home Office, the Department of Health and the Department for Education and Skills, were impossible to coordinate.[38] At the same time, his opinions differed from those of key politicians such as the Cabinet Minister Mo Mowlam and the Home Secretary, David Blunkett. In a process Hellawell describes as 'death by a thousand cuts' his credibility was undermined through a number of newspaper articles questioning his abilities.[39] Hellawell resigned in June 2002, partly as a result of these ongoing issues and also because of a public disagreement with Blunkett over the reclassification of cannabis as a Class C drug, a move Hellawell says he always opposed.[40] The Drug Tsar was not replaced, and his departure was followed by a revamped drugs strategy in 2002.[41]

This brief experiment in central coordination of the drugs issue by one individual illustrates some of the new dynamics that now surround drug policy making. As the drug field has grown, so too have the range of government departments and other interested parties involved. This has made the field more complex, bringing in actors with widely differing agendas. Such a situation would appear to contrast sharply with the 1960s and 1970s, when drug policy was made by a handful of London-based DDU doctors who largely agreed with one another on the correct course of action to take. The expansion of the drug field, and the series of attempts made to coordinate it centrally, has put specialist drug addiction psychiatrists into a paradoxical position. On the one hand, clinical psychiatrists have clearly been displaced from their single-handed role in drug policy making. Their monopoly has been replaced by a diverse collection of groups and individuals approaching drugs from a variety of angles. Yet, on the other hand, specialists retain a major responsibility in the delivery of drug addiction treatment and in the key areas of policy that surrounds this, such as the prescription of drugs to addicts. Even the growing emphasis on the relationship between drug use and crime has not necessarily undermined their importance. Treatment has become enmeshed within seemingly criminal justice orientated measures, as a further consideration of these programmes demonstrates.

DRUGS, CRIME AND TREATMENT

Since 1995, drug policy has become increasingly concerned with a supposed link between drug use and crime. For Karen Duke, there has been a 'criminalisation' of drug policy seen in 'a retreat away from the harm-reduction principles of the previous phase of policy . . . and a move towards the discourses of "crime", "enforcement" and "punishment" and greater involvement of the criminal justice system in drug issues'.[42] As Mike Hough notes, 'drug-related crime has largely usurped HIV/AIDS as a stimulus in Britain not only for research investment, but also for the expansion of drug services.'[43] Drug users, it is argued, commit crime in order to support their habit. NTORS recorded in 1995 that just over 1,000 drug 'misusers' reported more than 27,000 acquisitive criminal offences in a 90-day period before starting treatment.[44] This finding attracted considerable political and public attention and has frequently been used to support the focus on drugs and crime. The preface to *Tackling Drugs to Build a Better Britain*, for example, stated that the intention was to 'break once and for all the vicious cycle of drugs and crime which wrecks lives and threatens communities.'[45]

This enhanced focus on reducing drug-related crime has resulted in the criminal justice system (the police, courts, prisons and probation service) becoming much more involved in drug policy and practice than was previously the case.[46] For some commentators, such as Stimson, this development is indicative of a 'reorientation of policy away from health and to[wards] drugs and crime'. He argues that a 'healthy' drug policy (in existence from 1987 until 1997) based around tolerance, pragmatism, concern for human rights and 'a consensus between government and those working in the field' has been replaced by an 'unhealthy' policy concentrating on the link between drugs and crime.[47] This case can, however, be overstated. Firstly, there has rarely been a universally acknowledged consensus on the treatment of heroin addiction or on drug policy more widely. Even in the era of AIDS, dissenting voices against harm reduction could be found. Secondly, while the new attention being directed towards drugs and crime is indisputable, the consequences of this development are less certain. The introduction of more punitive measures has not necessarily resulted in a move away from the traditional emphasis on treatment within British drug policy.

In fact, the main criminal justice response to drug-related crime has been to refer more drug users to treatment services rather than to lock them up. This is because it is widely believed that treatment can reduce drug-related crime. Again, research from the NTORS study has played a crucial role in justifying policy change. NTORS reported that one year after treatment, involvement in crime within the study population was shown to have reduced by half and acquisitive crime by one third.[48] Partly as a result of this finding, a series of initiatives have been introduced since the end of the 1990s that bind treatment and crime reduction objectives much more closely together. Many of these schemes attempt to control drug users through treatment, but this, of course, is not a new development, as the early experiences of the DDUs discussed in Chapter Three indicated. What is new is the level of cooperation between the treatment and criminal justice systems. As Duke suggests, 'there has been a sea change in terms of the willingness of treatment providers to work within the criminal justice system.'[49]

This partnership between the treatment and criminal justice systems can be seen particularly clearly in the development of the Drug Intervention Programme (DIP). DIP was introduced in 2003 to develop 'interventions' for getting drug users 'out of crime, and into treatment'.[50] DIP coordinates a number of other pre-existing programmes that operate at different levels of the criminal justice system, beginning with arrest and ending with prison. Under DIP, individuals charged with a so-called 'trigger offence', such as property crime, robbery, begging and drug offences, can be required to be tested for the presence of an illegal drug.[51] Following the introduction of the Drugs Act in 2005, individuals can also be tested for the presence of illegal drugs on arrest, rather than after being charged.[52] Those who test positive undergo an assessment by a drugs worker. For individuals convicted of a first offence, this is usually followed by a 'conditional caution', and he or she is referred to treatment without further punishment, although the addict can be prosecuted if he or she fails to attend treatment.[53] More serious and repeat offenders can be dealt with by Drug Treatment and Testing Orders (DTTOs). DTTOs were brought in through the Crime and Disorder Bill in 1998. A DTTO is a community sentence, administered by the probation service, which compels drug users to enter treatment as an alternative to other types of sentence, usually prison.[54] The DTTO model has been further developed with the introduction of Drug Abstinence Orders (DAOs). These give the courts the power to order an individual to abstain from using heroin, cocaine or any other Class A drug for a period of between six months and three years, with regular drug tests. Failing to obey the conditions of the order can result in further penalties, such as imprisonment.[55] Taken together, DTTOs and DAOs appear to be something like the US drug court system, where individuals are sent into mandatory treatment instead of jail, and dedicated drug courts are being trialled in London and in Leeds with the possibility of these being rolled out across the country.[56]

Encouraging addicts into treatment as an alternative to prison does represent the introduction of a greater degree of coercion into drug treatment. This has had significant implications for the nature of addiction treatment and the way it is provided. Using coercion and compulsion has always been a controversial issue within drug treatment. The Rolleston Committee and both the Brain committees flirted with the idea of compulsory treatment. Compelling addicts to enter treatment was rejected, however, as 'compulsory treatment seems to meet with little success.'[57] More recently, the effectiveness of coercion (although not compulsion) has been reassessed. There is evidence to suggest that coerced patients do no worse than those who enter treatment voluntarily; some studies even suggest coerced individuals remain in treatment longer. However, there are clearly practical and political issues surrounding the greater use of coercion in treatment. Some treatment providers find coerced treatment ethically unacceptable.[58] Moreover, coercing patients into a form of treatment that they may not find acceptable would seem to run counter to broader policies that promote increased levels of consumer choice within health services. For treatment providers, there is also an obligation that coercive treatment must be effective treatment. It would be unethical and undesirable, as psychiatrist Emily Finch and editor of *Drug and Alcohol Findings* Mike Ashton point out, to coerce individuals to enter into treatment that would be unlikely to produce good results.[59]

Judging the effectiveness of treatment depends very much on what the desired outcome is thought to be. It is here that the drugs-crime agenda would seem to have had a significant impact, as the reduction of drug-related crime is regarded not just as an overall policy objective but as a key treatment outcome. In recent years, as psychologist Michael Gossop states, 'there has been an increasing emphasis upon crime reduction as an appropriate *clinical goal* for drug misuse treatment services.'[60] The adoption of crime-reduction as a treatment objective has evidently had a considerable effect on the type of treatment offered to drug users and heroin addicts in particular. Oral methadone maintenance has appeared to become the main method of treatment. In 2003/4, 63 per cent of patients in structured drug treatment were receiving substitute prescriptions, and 75 per cent of these were receiving oral methadone on a maintenance basis.[61]

This striking departure from past treatment policy (which prioritised abstinence and short-term withdrawal over maintenance) can be explained by three key factors. Firstly, as seen in Chapter Six, the climate of opinion about methadone maintenance had already begun to change as a result of HIV/AIDS. Maintenance had been shown to play an important part in reducing the harm associated with drug use, particularly the spread of HIV. This created a situation within which treatment goals other than just abstinence could be considered, as well as providing support for maintenance itself. Secondly, methadone maintenance has been shown to be cost-effective. As Susanne MacGregor has demonstrated, the cost-effectiveness of drug treatment has become increasingly important.[62] This is not just because of limited resources but also as a result of the introduction of performance management and performance indicators: treatment must demonstrate its value for money by meeting certain targets. Here, methadone maintenance is seen as a success. The authors of NTORS calculated that for every £1 spent on treatment, £3 was saved on the cost of criminal justice interventions and on the cost to the economy of drug-related crime.[63] This figure has recently been adjusted so that it is now estimated that the ratio is £1 spent on treatment to £9.50 saved on crime.[64] Finally, and perhaps most importantly, methadone maintenance is widely regarded as reducing drug-related crime. NTORS found that acquisitive crime among methadone patients fell by one third after one year in treatment, compared to a fall of one quarter for those in drug-free residential rehabilitation.[65] Crucially, as Gossop pointed out, 'less crime is committed by patients on methadone maintenance than by comparable groups of addicts out of treatment.'[66]

Although this finding was novel in a British context, the notion that methadone could be used to reduce crime was not itself new. Methadone maintenance programmes were introduced in the USA thirty years previously with this specific aim in mind. Jerome Jaffe's experimentation with methadone maintenance in Illinois during the 1970s had resulted in a 40 per cent reduction in crime among programme attenders. Results such as these convinced the Nixon administration to allocate $105 million dollars to treatment and rehabilitation programmes in a bid to reduce overall crime figures.[67] But methadone maintenance was not viewed in the same way in Britain. Methadone maintenance became increasingly rare during the 1970s, with DDUs preferring to prescribe methadone on a withdrawal basis. Where methadone maintenance was offered, often in private or general practice, this was aimed more at improving the social functioning of the patient than at reducing crime; however, as the drug-crime link has risen up the agenda, methadone maintenance has been reappraised.

The apparent effectiveness of methadone maintenance in reducing crime, and its relative cost-effectiveness has meant that resources have been poured into drug treatment. Since 2002, financial support for drug treatment services has come from the Pooled Treatment Budget (PTB), which combines funds from the Home Office with those from the Department of Health. Resources from the PTB are then allocated to DATs, which are also supplemented by mainstream funding from the NHS. The PTB has steadily increased, from £253 million to £385 million in 2006/7.[68] To oversee the allocation of this funding and the resulting expansion in treatment services, the government established the National Treatment Agency for Substance Misuse (NTA) in 2001. The NTA is a special health authority tasked to 'improve the availability, capacity and effectiveness of drug treatment for drug misuse in England'.[69] The NTA set itself two key objectives. Firstly, the NTA wanted to double the number of people in treatment from approximately 100,000 in 1998 to 200,000 by 2008. In September 2006, the NTA claimed to have met this target, two years ahead of schedule. Secondly, the NTA aimed to 'increase the proportion of people who successfully complete or, if appropriate, continue treatment.'[70] The wording of this objective is crucial, as an increase in methadone maintenance by its very nature means that more patients will remain in treatment for longer periods of time. This objective, therefore, hints at a deeper shift in determining the goals of drug treatment. The apparent increase in methadone maintenance suggests that the purpose of addiction treatment has moved away from helping addicts achieve abstinence and towards other goals, principally the reduction of crime. Abstinence does not feature in either the 1998 or 2002 drug strategies, although it was still deemed to be the 'ultimate goal' of drug services by the 1995 strategy.[71] And it is not just politicians who seem to have moved away from abstinence. In 1999, the Medical Working Group that created the revised clinical guidelines on drug treatment agreed that 'the primary role of the doctor is *not* to ensure that individuals become drug free—that is a moral issue—but to reduce the harm to individuals'.[72]

'TREATMENT WORKS'—EVIDENCE AND EFFECTIVENESS

This apparent abandonment of abstinence amounts not only to a significant change in drug policy but also to a paradigm shift in defining what is 'treatment' and also what 'works'. Treatment works because it is seen to reduce crime, not because it helps individuals withdraw from drugs. Yet a series of important questions can be raised about how evidence is used to define effectiveness and also how far such a change has taken place in practice. Evidence became a central feature of drug policy during the mid-1990s. Concerned about the effectiveness of existing drug treatment services, in 1994 the Conservative government set up a Task Force to review treatment provision. From the outset, the Chairman of the Task Force, the Reverend Dr John Polkinghorne, was clear that 'the conclusions and recommendations of the report needed to be evidentially based.'[73] However, the Task Force found there was little suitable evidence available, so they commissioned nine research projects. The most significant of these was NTORS, a long-term prospective follow-up study that tracked the progress of over 1,000 drug users who entered four different types of drug treatment in 1995. NTORS was modelled on American studies such as the Drug Abuse Reporting Programme (DARP), the Treatment Outcome Prospective Study (TOPS) and the Drug Abuse Treatment Outcome Study (DATOS).[74] Interestingly, the US programmes pre-dated NTORS by a number of years: DARP, the first study, was conducted in 1968.[75] Once again, this probably reflects the earlier emphasis on using treatment to reduce crime in the USA. In the British context, it is difficult to disentangle which came first: did the evidence indicate treatment could reduce drug-related crime, or was policy already moving in that direction?

As discussed above, some of the data from NTORS has been used extensively in justifying policy change and in shaping policy documents, like the 1998 drug strategy. But NTORS is not the only study made use of by policy makers; there has been a more general trend towards using evidence to shape drug policy. The 2002 revised drug strategy contains a five-page appendix listing 'improvements in the evidence base' from 1998 to 2002 for various aspects of the strategy such as the reduction of drug supply and drug treatment.[76] In the treatment field itself, there has also been an increased use of evidence. In her doctoral thesis, Sarah Mars compared the various sets of guidelines on good practice in the treatment of drug addiction issued in 1984, 1991 and 1999. She found that the 1984 guidelines made no reference to the published literature on the treatment of addiction, the 1991 guidelines contained five references and the 1999 edition listed almost 100.[77] Mars attributes this to other changes within the health service, including the growth of evidence-based medicine.

Evidence was also at the heart of the Task Force review. Polkinghorne may have attributed his original emphasis on commissioning research to his scientific background, which he stated, 'had accustomed me to the assessments of evidence-based beliefs', but the collection of evidence and its application to policy and practice was symptomatic of the emergence of evidence-based medicine and also evidence-based policy.[78] Although some analysts trace the history of evidence-based medicine back to Hippocrates and Galen, evidence-based, as opposed to scientific, medicine is a recent development.[79] The drive towards evidence-based medicine began in the 1990s, fuelled by a desire to bring research into a closer relationship with clinical practice.[80] It was believed that the increased use of research findings would improve the effectiveness and efficiency of treatment interventions. As Rob Baggott notes, doctors saw evidence-based medicine as a way of preserving the scientific credibility (and, one could add, the power) of medicine, but for politicians and health service managers, evidence-based medicine was also a way of making limited resources go further and giving them a greater influence over how these resources were utilised.[81] Evidence-based medicine thus led to evidence-based policy. In 2001 Professor of Health Services Research Nick Black asserted, 'The need to be seen to be making evidence based decisions has permeated all areas of British public life.' Although Black states that 'it seems difficult to argue with the idea that scientific research should drive policy' he does highlight several problems with evidence-based policy.[82] Firstly, policy makers may have goals other than maximising clinical effectiveness. Policy, Black argues, can be driven by ideology, value judgements, financial stringency, economic theory, political expediency and intellectual fashion. Secondly, evidence may be dismissed when it conflicts with tacit knowledge or accepted clinical practice. Thirdly, there may be a lack of consensus about research evidence leading to different interpretations and, therefore, different possible policies or to evidence being used selectively. Finally, research evidence may conflict with other kinds of evidence that are equally or more highly valued, such as clinical experience and expert opinion.[83]

Many of the issues Black raises concerning evidence-based medicine and policy can be detected in the drug field. The evidence produced by NTORS, for example, has been used selectively to support the drugs-crime agenda, when the actual data produced was much more equivocal about the link between drug use and crime. The study's authors reported that only half of drug users committed acquisitive crime and the majority of those fairly infrequently. Most crime was committed by a small number of users, with 10 per cent committing 75 per cent of all acquisitive crime. Gossop concluded, 'crime and drug misuse do not inevitably go together' but that this finding was often overlooked.[84] Polkinghorne, Gossop and Strang noted that NTORS had the 'possibly unfortunate side-effect' of encouraging a 'greater focus upon reduced crime as a goal of drug misuse treatment.'[85] Evidence from NTORS could actually be used to support a critique of the drugs-crime agenda, as this would appear to focus on the minority of drug users who commit crime, rather than the majority who do not. Indeed, there is other evidence from around the world that has called the strength of the drugs-crime link into question. Duke argues that the relationship between drugs and crime is complex, and much of the available research on this issue is inconclusive.[86] Other commentators have expressed concern about the use of the phrase 'treatment works'. MacGregor argues that 'treatment works' was primarily created as a counter-point to the notion that 'prison works'.[87] Polkinghorne, Gossop and Strang were also cautious about the idea that 'treatment works'. As they remarked: 'No "magic bullet" has been identified that would lead simply and straightforwardly to the attainment of abstinence.'[88] Indeed, if abstinence is still a goal, although perhaps not the *only* goal of treatment, there is other evidence to suggest that treatment rarely works at all. Statistics from the National Drug Treatment Monitoring System show that just 6 per cent of patients discharged from all forms of treatment in 2003/4 were drug-free.[89] '

Of course, the selective use of research evidence to support change within drug policy is nothing new. As seen in Chapter Three, evidence from the Hartnoll and Mitcheson trial comparing oral methadone with injectable heroin was used to justify the move to methadone in the 1970s, although the study also demonstrated there were some advantages to prescribing heroin over methadone. Clinical experience played a significant role in determining the switch to methadone, and it continues to do so today. As Black suggested, the type of evidence used to make policy is not always derived from research. Mars has demonstrated that though the 1999 guidelines on the treatment of drug addiction were based on 'evidence', they were heavily reliant on a specific type of 'evidence', mainly expert committee reports and clinical experience, despite the existence of a growing body of published research on drug treatment. She concluded, 'Once again, it seemed, treatment policy was to be determined by "respected authorities" albeit with some extra research backing.'[90]

The continued power of clinicians is also manifest in the way other evidence is ignored, or down-played, even when it appears to be in line with a broader policy goal. Currently, there would seem to be political support for the increased prescription of injectable heroin to addicts. In 2001, the Home Secretary, David Blunkett, called for a five-fold increase in the prescription of injectable heroin.[91] The wider availability of heroin prescription became a policy objective in 2002, when the revised drug strategy asserted that heroin prescription should be available to those patients who have a clinical need for the drug.[92] A number of prominent public figures have spoken out in favour of heroin prescription, including Ken Jones, president of the Association of Chief Police Officers (ACPO).[93] What is more, evidence can be found to justify such a move. Trials of injectable heroin conducted in Switzerland and the Netherlands during the late 1990s both pointed to the benefits of heroin prescription in terms of improving the health and social functioning of those participating, as well as reducing their criminal activity.[94] British trials of heroin prescription are currently underway at the Maudsley Hospital in south London and in Darlington, County Durham.[95]

Yet neither the policy imperative nor the evidence base seems to have resulted in a significant increase in the prescription of heroin to British addicts. It is difficult to find comparable figures, but the number of individuals being prescribed heroin may actually have decreased. Nicky Metrebian and her colleagues at Imperial College London found that 448 users were receiving prescriptions for injectable heroin in 2000, and this figure continues to be repeated in NTA policy documents and in other more recent reports on heroin prescription.[96] However, the NTAs prescribing audit, published in 2006, found that diamorphine (heroin) was prescribed in 19 different services to just 151 clients.[97] There are two possible reasons why heroin prescription has not become more widespread. Firstly, heroin maintenance is more expensive than methadone, costing between £10,000 and £15,000 per year per patient, compared to around £2,000 a year for methadone.[98] Secondly, doctors continue to find the prescription of heroin to addicts a contentious issue and remain concerned about the long-standing question as to whether injectable opiate prescription can be considered to be treatment.[99]

Clinical reserve about heroin prescription can be found in the NTA's guidance report on the 'potential role' injectable heroin and injectable methadone might play in drug treatment. The NTA guidance report, published in 2003, supports the view that injectable opioid prescription may be beneficial but inserts a number of caveats. The NTA guidance, based on a 'majority consensus approach', published evidence and the 'experience of expert practitioners', is clear that heroin prescription may be beneficial for a 'minority' of patients.[100] Furthermore, the guidance recommends that injectable prescription should only be considered in line with eight principles determined by the expert group. Essentially, these principles advise that: heroin prescription should only be used as a last resort when other treatments have failed; it should form part of a 'package' of other psycho-social interventions; the consumption of injectable drugs must be supervised and the prescription of injectable substitute drugs requires 'specialist levels of clinical competence'.[101] The NTA's guidance on the prescription of heroin to addicts therefore places clear limits on the expansion and application of this treatment method and, at the same time, re-iterates the importance of expert opinion and specialist experience.

A RETURN TO OLD DEBATES?

The content of the NTA prescribing guidance and the general failure to expand heroin prescription despite the available evidence base and a policy imperative to do so raises two important issues. Firstly, specialist psychiatrists are evidently still a powerful force with drug policy and practice, and, secondly, there has been a return to old debates about the nature of addiction, its proper treatment, and what kind of doctor is best placed to offer this treatment if, indeed, these tensions ever really disappeared. It is possible to question the extent to which methadone maintenance has actually become the main method of addiction treatment and, furthermore, whether abstinence has entirely disappeared as a treatment goal. For methadone maintenance to work effectively, a series of components have been identified, making up what is called 'optimised oral methadone maintenance'.[102] The most crucial component of optimised oral methadone maintenance is the size of the dose prescribed. If the user is prescribed too little methadone, he or she may continue to use street drugs in addition to the methadone prescription, reducing the benefit of methadone treatment to the user, and to society in terms of reduced crime. The NTA's guidance on prescription states that daily doses of between 60mg and 120mg have been shown to be most effective, yet the NTA's prescribing audit found that the daily mean methadone maintenance dose was 56.7mg, with doses ranging from 6.5mg to 127mg.[103] The possibility that some services might be prescribing too little methadone for effective maintenance is also born out by a recent joint NTA and Health Care Commission report on the quality of drug services. The report found that while the majority of services had good policies on methadone prescribing, some services were still prescribing insufficient doses to maintain users and prevent the use of illicit drugs. The NTA and the Health Commission recommended that there should be a move away from standard policies, which prescribe the same amount for each user, and instead for prescribing to be linked more closely to individual need.[104] Methadone maintenance, at least in its most effective and individualised form, is perhaps not as widespread as at first appears.

At the same time, it would seem that abstinence remains a goal for many drug users in treatment and also for many treatment providers. Professor Neil McKeganey and his colleagues from the Centre for Drug Misuse Research at the University of Glasgow found that 56.6 per cent of drug users entering treatment stated that abstinence was the only change they hoped to achieve by entering treatment.[105] The NTA's first annual user satisfaction survey would appear to be even more unequivocal about the continued importance of abstinence: 81.2 per cent of heroin users taking part in the survey stated that they would like to stop using the drug completely.[106] There are, of course, problems with such findings. As McKeganey himself recognised, by stating that they wanted to become abstinent from drugs it is possible that users were providing what they thought to be the most socially acceptable response, not the one that actually reflected their reasons for entering treatment.[107] Furthermore, neither study indicates how quickly drug users wanted to become abstinent: it is not clear whether abstinence is a long- or short-term aim. It may be that abstinence is the ultimate goal for many addicts entering treatment, but not the most immediate one. However, while there are clearly limitations to the findings of these studies, both do point to the continued significance of abstinence for drug users entering treatment.

It is possible that the intense policy focus on methadone maintenance as a way of reducing crime has obscured the growth of other, drug-free forms of treatment. Methadone maintenance may be the main form of treatment for drug users, but it is by no means the only one. Abstinence-oriented treatment remains a significant part of the overall pattern of drug treatment provision, especially when treatment outside the NHS is considered. Self-help groups based on the 12-step philosophy, like Narcotics Anonymous (NA), have become widespread. In 1991 there were approximately 223 weekly NA meetings in Britain; by 2004 there were well over 500.[108] In addition to community-based programmes, there are also a plethora of residential facilities, the majority of which insist on patients being drug-free on entry. There has been a concerted effort by the government to provide more places in residential rehabilitation, precisely because it has been shown to be the most successful treatment in terms of getting users to achieve sustained periods of abstinence.[109] This would suggest that abstinence remains a policy objective, too, despite the lack of public attention drawn to this aim.

Moreover, methadone maintenance itself has recently come in for substantial criticism. Delegates at the NDTC conference in 2006 debated the motion 'This house believes that we are plainly failing to reduce harms with current policies, and that we should place more emphasis on getting addicts drug free than on prescribing methadone maintenance.'[110] The motion was proposed by Neil McKeganey and seconded by David Bryce, an ex-user and founder of the Calton Athletic Recovery Group. McKeganey based his arguments against methadone maintenance on two points. Firstly, HIV/AIDS had not materialised as the significant threat to public health envisaged in the late 1980s and early 1990s, therefore removing some of the impetus for harm reduction and methadone maintenance. Secondly, a majority of users contacting drug treatment services wanted treatment that would result in them being abstinent, not in reducing the harm associated with their drug use. McKeganey's arguments were reinforced by Bryce's personal testimony, as he asserted that his addiction to heroin had simply been replaced by addiction to methadone, and the widespread use of maintenance was denying users the opportunity to come off drugs. For Pat O'Hare, Honorary President of the International Harm Reduction Association, and Bill Nelles, founder of the drug user group Alliance, who were opposing the motion, these arguments amounted to an attack not just on methadone maintenance but also on harm reduction. Nelles, himself a former drug user, contended that abstinence was simply not an achievable goal for all patients.

The debate prompted a heated response from the audience, with delegates speaking in favour of and against the motion. In the final vote, the motion was overwhelmingly defeated, but this did not prevent some participants from seeing the debate as part of a potential 'backlash' against methadone maintenance. The psychiatrist Tom Carnwarth and GP Chris Ford wrote a comment piece on the debate in the journal *Drink and Drug News*, entitled 'Methadone challenged on its home turf: is there a worrying methadone backlash about?'[111] Carnwarth and Ford detected a possible shift away from methadone maintenance and towards 12-step programmes and drug-free residential rehabilitation. Their article prompted a stream of letters to subsequent editions of the journal. Rowdy Yates, senior research fellow in addiction studies at the University of Stirling, argued, 'The truth is, far from being under threat, substitute prescribing . . . has become the undoubted cuckoo in the treatment nest.'[112] Dr David McCartney, an Edinburgh GP with a self-declared 'special interest in addictions', repeated McKeganey's arguments about the majority of drug-addicted patients actually wanting abstinence rather than harm reduction. 'Are we', he contended, 'to drown out their voices with a tidal wave of methadone?'[113]

This debate indicates that methadone maintenance remains a contentious issue despite the outward appearance of consensus, and supposed dominance, of this form of treatment. Other recent events would suggest that this is not the only conflict within drug addiction treatment to persist. In February 2004 a case came before the GMC that appeared to place maintenance prescription and the treatment of addiction in private practice on 'trial' once again. Seven doctors working at the private drug addiction treatment clinic the Stapleford Centre were accused of serious professional misconduct in relation to the irresponsible prescription of drugs to addict-patients. The doctors were alleged to have failed to assess patients properly and acted irresponsibly with respect to the type, quantity and combination of drugs prescribed.[114] One addict treated by the centre's founder, Dr Colin Brewer, died in September 2001 after being sent home with a 'DIY home detox' kit. The patient choked on his own vomit after taking a combination of drugs prescribed by Brewer. It was suggested that the patient's mother was not told that additional drugs prescribed were to be taken instead of, not as well as, the original prescription.[115]

This case demonstrates that conflict between the private and public sectors over the treatment of heroin addiction, and between those who support maintenance and those who advocate withdrawal, has not disappeared. The Stapleford Centre was reported to have offered maintenance prescriptions of both heroin and methadone to addicts who felt unable to come off drugs.[116] Owen Dyer, writing in the *British Medical Journal*, noted that 'Heroin maintenance programmes have frequently been rejected by NHS clinics, who prefer to wean patients off the drug'.[117] The significance of the Stapleford case was widely recognised. *The Guardian* reported that the enquiry was to 'centre on conflicting schools of opinion regarding the prescription of drugs to recovering addicts'.[118] *The Independent* noted that the outcome of the case 'may determine the future direction of drug addiction treatment' and that it would 'ask profound questions of the liberal school of heroin treatment'.[119] *The Times* stated that the hearing is 'seen as a test case for the treatment of addiction in Britain' and that it represented 'a showdown between rival schools of thought on the treatment of drug addicts'.[120]

It has been suggested that the Stapleford case was being used to remove the private practitioner from the treatment of addiction. Nick Davies, the journalist who assisted Dally during her disciplinary hearing in 1986/7, quoted a source close to the Home Office as saying, '"They have been talking about getting rid of every private doctor who prescribes for heroin users."'[121] This was also the argument made about the Dally hearings in 1983 and 1986/7. Parallels between the two cases abound. There is even a direct link between them: Brewer was asked to take on Dally's patients by the Home Office in 1987 when she was no longer able to prescribe to addicts.[122] Also like Dally, Brewer had drawn attention to himself and his practice by a very public disagreement with the recognised leading drug addiction experts in Britain. In a series of editorials and letters, Brewer argued with Professor John Strang over addiction treatment, particularly over Brewer's use of Naltrexone.[123] As with the Dally case, there were also suggestions that the case had dubious origins. Although the family of the patient who died did eventually complain about his treatment to the GMC, this was reportedly after the GMC had begun proceedings against two other doctors at the Stapleford Centre, although not against Brewer himself.[124] Davies maintained that Home Office inspectors had combed through records of chemists dispensing to Stapleford patients, looking for breaches in the rules in order to bring a case against doctors at the clinic.[125] Though the *British Medical Journal* reported that the charges 'seem to have originated after routine monitoring by the Home Office Drugs Inspectorate', the suspicion remained that the case had been deliberately brought in order to make a statement about maintenance prescription and the private treatment of heroin addiction.[126]

In November 2006, after the longest case in the GMC's history, the professional conduct committee finally reached a decision. Brewer was found guilty of serious professional misconduct, as were two other doctors working at the clinic, Dr Tovay and Dr Kindness. Brewer was struck off the medical register, conditions were placed on Tovay's ability to prescribe drugs and Kindness was admonished for his behaviour. In delivering their judgement, the GMC praised Brewer for his 'pioneering' role in both the use of methadone maintenance and Naltrexone, but found that he had been 'dismissive of views that did not accord with your own' and that he was 'over confident in your treatment of patients'. Although the panel asserted that they were 'not required to judge the validity of your opinions as contrasted with the opinions of others', the panel further stated that 'even now, in some instances, you do not accept the criticisms which were levelled at your practice by the medical experts'.[127]

It may be that Brewer's behaviour was a departure from 'good medical practice', but as was seen in the Dally case twenty years previously, defining what is good medical practice in the treatment of heroin addiction is a highly politicised process. Carnwarth, in an article in *Druglink* about the Brewer case, argued, 'In a field where moral opinion often weighs as heavily as clinical evidence, the GMC relies on clinical consensus to assess those who transgress.'[128] Carnwarth's article was entitled 'Doctors at war', but whether this was a deliberate attempt to recall the article of the same name, in the same publication, about the Dally case twenty years previously, or whether it was a coincidence, it is unclear.[129] Nonetheless, the article does recall some of the tensions that surrounded the treatment of addiction during the mid-1980s. Since the verdict, Brewer himself has accepted that mistakes were made but said his treatment, 'could not be any worse than what is happening in the NHS'.[130] He contended that many doctors were still nervous about prescribing methadone, and the small doses prescribed forced addicts to continue to buy street drugs.

Again, as with the Dally case, it is the wider ramifications of the Stapleford hearing that are of significance. The treatment of addiction in private practice obviously remains controversial, and while the treatment of addiction in general practice has become more widespread, here, too, are tensions. Home Office proposals in 2000 and again in 2005 to extend the licensing system for the prescription of heroin to addict-patients to all controlled drugs (except oral methadone) provoked a resurgence of conflict over licensing and the wider issue of who should be involved in the treatment of addiction.[131] Some GPs and consultant psychiatrists felt these proposals were being introduced to curb the prescribing habits of a few private doctors practising in London. In a letter to *Druglink* in January 2001, a group of GPs asserted that licensing would 'deter doctors from working in this area. This was exactly why a similar licensing proposal was rejected in 1984.'[132] An editorial written by some of the same authors also appeared in the *British Medical Journal*. Again arguments similar to those twenty years previously were made. It was suggested that 'The proposals . . . convey a negative message about drug misuse treatment, reinforcing the disinclination of generalists to prescribe for drug misusers.'[133]

Tension between specialists and generalists over the treatment of addiction can also be seen in the 1999 treatment guidelines. Mars, in her analysis of the discussions of the working group that wrote the guidelines, has shown that although they agreed that maintenance prescription was suitable for primary care, some specialist members of the group were less keen on the idea that GPs could do so unsupervised.[134] Consequently, the guidelines recommended that GPs should not prescribe for drug users in 'isolation,' but should participate in 'shared care agreements' with specialists or a new category of doctor, the 'specialised generalist'.[135] 'Specialised generalists' were defined as either specialists whose work was not primarily concerned with the treatment of addiction or as GPs with a special interest in treating drug users.[136] To some extent this can be seen as a compromise solution to the problem of increasing treatment provision for drug users by allowing GPs a greater role and at the same time maintaining the treatment of addiction as a specialist area of medicine. But the creation of specialised generalists was also concomitant with other changes in primary care, particularly the creation of 'General Practitioners with a Special Interest'. There have been more general attempts to develop an intermediate layer of doctors between GPs and specialists both as a way of modernising the NHS and also providing more career opportunities for GPs.[137] In the treatment of drug addiction, this has chiefly manifested itself in the creation of the Substance Misuse Management in General Practice group in 1995 to support GPs treating addicts and the introduction of a Royal College of General Practitioners certificate in the management of drug use in primary care in 2004.[138]

Yet it is questionable that these changes have led to a substantial power shift in the actual treatment of addiction. Data from the National Drug Treatment Monitoring System (NDTMS) on the type of treatment received by drug users indicates that specialists retain a central role. NDTMS reported that 54 per cent of patients in drug treatment were given specialist prescribing; 21 per cent had structured counselling; 9 per cent were prescribed drugs by a GP; 6 per cent received structured day care; 5 per cent were given another structured intervention and 2 per cent went into residential rehabilitation.[139] It would seem that the treatment of addiction remains very much a specialist preserve.

CONCLUSION

The continued authority of specialist psychiatrists in the treatment of addiction, despite the significant developments in the drug field pointed to at the beginning of this chapter, raises questions about the extent to which things have really changed. There have been significant developments in drug policy and the treatment of addiction, particularly in the last ten years. The rise of the drugs-crime agenda has made maintenance treatment acceptable once more, even if it continues to provoke heated debate. The seemingly ever-increasing number of drug users has necessitated that the policy community around drugs expand dramatically, and new actors have been brought into what can now best be described as the 'drug field'. Yet, underneath the surface, conflict persists. Disagreements about what the proper treatment of addiction should be and who is best placed to deliver this treatment continue to thrive. Furthermore, the maintenance vs. withdrawal debate, in evidence since at least the 1920s, shows little sign of disappearing. Here to stay, too, so it seems, are tensions between private doctors and those working in the NHS, and between specialists and generalists.

Echoes of the past resonate in drug policy and practice more widely. Drug policy currently seems to be in a situation in which criminal justice measures to deal with drug use appear to be overpowering treatment approaches, but like the 1920s, these different modes are actually working together. Plus ça change? Maybe, but it is not enough simply to state that nothing changes. There is a need at least to attempt to understand why. The Conclusion of this book will, therefore, pick up the theme of continuity and change in an overview of the development of ideas about the treatment of addiction from 1920 to the present.

Conclusion

The Treatment of Heroin Addiction—
Past, Present and Future

In the future, according to Sir David King, Chief Scientific Advisor to the government and head of the Office of Science and Technology, we will see 'much improved treatments for addictions and other mental health disorders, and the development of new "recreational" drugs some of which might lead to fewer harms and lower risks of addiction than the substances in use today'.[1] New developments in our understanding of the brain and of addiction could see the condition completely disappear. Neuroscientists involved in the Foresight project, an initiative that brought together scientists, social scientists and historians to consider the management of psychoactive substances in the future, suggested a number of likely developments. 'Cognition enhancers' might become available to 'reactivate control and break the drug-seeking cycle'. New drugs will help addicts 'unlearn' their addiction. In the future, 'drugs that have abuse potential' may only be administered when 'combined with a "forgetting" drug to reduce the risks of addiction'. Furthermore, vaccines will prevent individuals, especially those deemed genetically susceptible, from developing an addiction in the first place.[2]

Although this vision of the future is strongly reminiscent of Aldous Huxley's *Brave New World*, it is seemingly based on science fact, not science fiction. According to Alan Leshner, former director of the American National Institute on Drug Abuse, 'addiction is a brain disease, and it matters.' He argues that 'scientific advances' over the last twenty years have demonstrated that drug addiction is a 'chronic relapsing brain disorder'. Prolonged use of certain psychoactive substances leads to changes in the brain's chemical structure and activity such that the 'addicted brain is distinctly different from the non-addicted brain'.[3] Psychoactive drugs have been found to act on neurotransmitters in the brain, and these are understood to drive behaviour.[4] This view is further supported by neuroimaging studies that demonstrate what happens inside an addict's brain when a drug is administered.[5] Other scientific research has attempted to uncover the aetiology of addiction. Genetic makeup is thought to be crucial: studies have shown that the genetic contribution to susceptibility to addiction is between 25 and 60 per cent across a range of substances including alcohol, nicotine and illegal drugs.[6] Science, according to Leshner, is 'rapidly dispelling both popular and clinical myths about drug abuse and addiction and what to do about them'.[7]

This scientific view of addiction has the potential to revolutionise addiction treatment, drug policy and even drug history. Howard Kushner, in a recent review article in the *Bulletin of the History of Medicine*, called upon historians to 'take biology seriously' when examining addiction. Kushner notes that historians have long been interested in the cultural construction of addiction and that 'although scepticism about medical and scientific claims is merited, ignoring them may not be.'[8] In a similar vein, David Courtwright, in his keynote lecture at the International Conference on Drugs and Alcohol History in 2004, asserted that neuroscientific, genetic and epidemiological evidence has unified a range of previously differentiated substances within the addiction paradigm.[9] In a response to critiques of this lecture, he contended that historians have become 'too comfortable in [their] social-constructivist ways' that 'there *is* progress in science and that progress can be liberating.' Courtwright recommends breaking 'history's last taboo. Take a hit of neuroscience. Just don't get addicted.'[10]

Historians are increasingly engaging with science and with policy makers, as the involvement of Virginia Berridge and Tim Hickman in the Foresight project demonstrates.[11] This relationship can clearly work both ways: there is much that scientists and policy makers might gain from history. This comes not in the form of 'lessons from history', but, rather, historical analysis offers an insight into how and why particular occurrences happened as they did. Some of these insights may be far from palatable. What this book has shown is that science, in the sense of an objective, rational form of knowledge, has actually played little role in determining drug policy and heroin addiction treatment. Where scientific evidence was used, as in the 1970s with the Hartnoll-Mitcheson heroin trial, it was shaped to fit pre-existing agendas. The response to heroin addiction in Britain over the course of the twentieth century was instead governed by a range of other factors. Much importance can be attached to who was found to be addicted. The middle-aged, middle-class, therapeutic addicts of the Rolleston era were treated differently than the young, 'recreational' addicts of the 1960s and beyond. The significance of who is seen to be addicted in determining the response to addiction seems to be a common theme in most drug histories, in Britain and elsewhere.[12] The 'who' of addiction was as influential as how addiction was defined and how addiction was treated. Understandings of addiction shifted according to the addict population but also moved in line with broader changes in the conception of disease and of public health. The late 1960s interpretation of addiction as a socially infectious condition fit with the then-current understandings of social diseases and the threat these posed to public health. The reconfiguration of addiction as a risky behaviour in the late 1980s and early 1990s corresponded with a new focus on lifestyle as a source of disease. These conceptual shifts were important in determining the overall shape of the response to heroin addiction, but professional disputes (within medicine and outside it) were crucial to the practical delivery of treatment. In a sense, these disputes were also about concepts, as community-based generalists came to see addiction in a different way from hospital-based specialists. These differing views of addiction and the addict engendered contrasting approaches, leading to conflict. At key moments throughout the period under consideration, other policy imperatives intruded into the drugs field. The heroin explosion of the 1980s, AIDS and the recent focus on drug-related crime all helped shape drug policy, but treatment practice changed only very slowly and unevenly. Nothing, it seemed, could obliterate the long-running tensions over treatment methods and between the different types of practitioner.

Despite the newfound confidence in the scientific view of addiction, contradictions persist. Upon closer examination, it would appear that current ideas about addiction are far from united. The causation of addiction, for example, remains contentious. In 1998, the ACMD published their report *Drug Misuse and the Environment*. They found that 'the environment affects the choices which individuals can and do make' about drugs. A number of environmental factors influencing drug use were highlighted, the most notable of which was social deprivation. The ACMD asserted that 'on [the] strong balance of probability, deprivation is today in Britain likely often to make a significant causal contribution to the cause, complications and intractability of damaging kinds of drug misuse.' A successful drug policy, they argued, should address the causes and consequences of deprivation, as well as drug use itself.[13] Griffith Edwards, at the forefront of addiction research in Britain for over forty years, has also recently argued that social deprivation influences patterns of drug use. Surveying evidence from the UK and the USA, Edwards noted: 'It is unusual to find a relationship between deprivation and occasional, non-destructive drug taking.' In affluent areas he found that heroin addiction was extremely rare, whereas in less well-off areas there could be as much as a one in six chance of an individual becoming addicted to heroin. Edwards concluded: 'The ability to exercise self-responsibility is empowered or impaired by conditions for which the young person is in no way responsible.'[14]

Stressing the role played by the social environment in producing addiction could undermine some scientific views of addiction. Yet, when taken together, recent scientific understandings of the causation of addiction and the links made to social deprivation have something in common. Both interpretations would seem to liberate the individual from responsibility for his or her drug problem. Leshner asserts: 'Scientific data are slowly but clearly eroding such stigmatising distinctions as "no-fault" versus "fault" illnesses and what to do about them.'[15] Despite this, the notion of addiction as an immoral behaviour retains popular and political credence. Following the death of a two-year-old boy from drinking methadone belonging to his parents in 2005, Duncan McNeil, a Labour member of the Scottish Parliament, called for contraception to be added to methadone to prevent addicts from having further children. He commented: 'I don't think it's a good idea that when you're addicted to drugs, you should start a family', the implication being that addicts inherently make bad parents.[16] In 2006, the Home Office's decision to award compensation to former prisoners for failing to provide them with adequate treatment and forcing them to withdraw from drugs while in custody provoked a stream of media controversy. Although legal advice to the Prisons Minister had pointed to an 'appalling' record of clinical negligence in the treatment of drug-dependent inmates, this was not how the tabloid press saw the matter. Headlines such as 'Even behind bars the junkies get to mug taxpayers yet again' and 'Cash for addicts has driven me out of the country' indicate that even if the scientific view of addiction is changing, fear and moral panic continue to exert their power over public opinion.[17]

Addiction, it seems, remains a condition at war with itself. The apparent impact of the social environment on patterns of drug use and the persistence of moral concerns about drugs complicates and confounds a neat scientific view of addiction as a brain disease. Even those who extol the biological interpretation of addiction, like Leshner, see addiction as a 'bio-behavioural' disorder.[18] Addiction, he concedes, 'is not just a brain disease. It is a brain disease for which the social contexts in which it has both developed and is expressed are critically important.'[19] Professor of Public Health Wayne Hall, of the University of Queensland, Australia, argues in a survey of recent scientific research on addiction that this condition is likely to be the result of a complex interaction between genes, the social environment and brain chemistry. The challenge for addiction researchers, he contends, 'will be to give biology its due while recognizing that drug use and addiction are affected by individual and social choices'. This has many implications, not least for treatment policy and practice. As Hall points out, even if new treatments for drug addiction are more effective than those used in the past, 'Addicts are often ambivalent about quitting and often comply only modestly with pharmacological treatments.' 'Disappointment' with poor patient compliance with these treatments could result in wider calls for coercive or even compulsory treatment, a development that, as Hall notes, has serious ethical implications.[20]

Clearly the tensions between the treatment and control of drug addiction that have been present throughout the past have not abated. Indeed, many of the conflicts highlighted by this book remain. While there have been changes in heroin addiction treatment and drug policy over the last eighty years, key underlying issues persist. This is most clearly demonstrated in the fate of maintenance treatment. As a treatment method for addiction, maintenance has gone in and out of favour. At times, as in the period after the Rolleston report, and since HIV/AIDS, maintenance appears to enjoy clinical respectability, and yet in other periods, such as from the 1970s to the mid-1980s, maintenance was largely rejected by the medical mainstream. But, at each time, a minority group of doctors who opposed the apparent consensus can be detected. Supporters of maintenance could be found in the 1970s and 1980s, just as advocates of withdrawal could be found in the 1920s and today. This would indicate that there has rarely, if ever, been agreement on the most appropriate method to treat addiction.

To explain this, it is necessary to look to a deeper conflict and to a deeper ambiguity. As the continued existence of competing social, scientific, medical and moral understandings of addiction demonstrates, there has been little agreement about what addiction is, and therefore there can be no consensus on how to deal with it. This is as true today as it was at the beginning of the twentieth century. Whatever else happens in the treatment of addiction—and there have been some notable changes—disagreement about what addiction is and what the right response to it should be remain. It is this persisting sense of doubt about addiction that underpins all the other continuities pointed to by this book and explains why the treatment of addiction has been so riddled with conflict.

The presence of these conflicts could mean that the concept of addiction collapses under the weight of its own contradictions. Addiction might disappear, although not for the reasons that neuroscientists believe. Addiction could cease to seem like a useful way of describing some of the problems associated with the use of certain psychoactive substances. As the sociologist Robin Room notes, 'addiction/dependence is rather irrelevant to the content and application of most policies concerning psychoactive substances.'[21] There are some signs that addiction is being rejected. Emphasis seems to be moving away from the addictiveness of various drugs and towards the harm that these cause. In 2005/6 the House of Commons Science and Technology committee investigated the British system of drug classification, which places drugs in categories A, B and C. They noted that 'the weakness of the evidence base on addiction and drug abuse is a severe hindrance to effective policy making.' The committee also concluded that the classification system was 'not fit for purpose' and should be replaced 'with a more scien-tifically based scale of harm, decoupled from penalties for possession and trafficking'.[22] In 2007, the psycho-pharmacologist David Nutt, Leslie King from the Forensic Science Service, William Saulsbury from the Police Foun-dation and Colin Blakemore, the Chief Executive of the Medical Research Council, published an article in *The Lancet* that proposed a 'rational scale to assess the harm of potential drugs of misuse'. Nutt and his colleagues posited that there are three main categories of harm that drugs (including alcohol and tobacco) can cause. These were: physical harm, dependence, and social harm. Based on these categories, the researchers ranked twenty substances according to the harm they caused. Heroin was ranked first, but alcohol was ranked fifth, tobacco ninth and cannabis eleventh.[23]

It is increasingly common to see legal drugs, like alcohol and to-bacco, considered alongside illegal drugs. A recent report produced for the Royal Society of Arts on drug policy contended that 'in their differ-ent ways, alcohol and tobacco cause far more harm than illegal drugs.' For this reason, they recommended that drug policy should bring all psychoactive substances, including alcohol and tobacco, into a single regulatory framework. This appears to be an international trend as well as a domestic one. The 2006 United Nations Office of Drug Control (UNODC) annual report on world drug trends makes reference to 'licit' drugs, such as tobacco, as well as illicit ones.[24] It is arguable that such a development has been facilitated by further changes in the addiction paradigm. In recent years, a number of observers have pointed to a drawing together of legal and illegal drugs under headings such as ATOD (Alcohol, Tobacco and Other Drugs) and 'psychoactive sub-stances'.[25] Policy responses do still differ and, as Room has suggested, may in some cases be moving in different directions: just as tobacco be-comes more tightly regulated, alcohol policy in many countries, includ-ing the UK, is becoming more liberal.[26] But ideas about different psy-choactive substances are becoming more alike, and one way in which this is happening is through the wider application of the concept of ad-diction. Addiction was, until recently, not a term used in relation to to-bacco. Nineteenth-century doctors and polemists believed smoking to-bacco was merely 'habit-forming' in contrast to the 'addictions' of drinking alcohol and drug-taking.[27] Some research on smoking in the 1970s pointed to the possibility of nicotine 'dependence', but the 'ad-dictive' properties of the drug were not discussed until the late 1980s and early 1990s. The report on smoking produced by the American Surgeon-General in 1988, for example, focused on nicotine 'addiction'.[28]

Another trend appears to be the application of the term 'addic-tion' to a whole range of behaviours that do not involve ingesting a psychoactive substance of any kind. Gambling addiction is perhaps the best known of these 'behavioural addictions' and the one for which there is the largest literature, but there are many others.[29] There has been a proliferation of addictions in recent years: type 'addiction' into an Internet search engine and literally millions of pages pop up. Treatment can be found for addictions to sex, shopping, overeating, undereating, exercise, chocolate, co-dependency, computer games, e-mail and, of course, the Internet itself. It is clearly not time to write addiction's obituary just yet. A future without addiction of any kind, and heroin addiction in particular, seems unlikely. It is estimated that there are 11 million heroin users worldwide, with around 2–4 million in Western Europe and North America alone.[30] Opium production in Afghanistan (which accounts for around 89 per cent of global opium production) had fallen in recent years, but since the overthrow of the Taliban, poppy cultivation has increased once more.[31] There are signs that heroin use has stabilised in Western Europe and North America, but it is rising significantly in Russia and the former states of the Soviet Union, on the Indian sub-continent, throughout the Middle East and in many countries in East Africa.[32] Meanwhile, studies from Australia, Europe and North America have shown that while illegal opiate use might have stabilised, the use of legal opiate analgesics such as fentanyl, morphine and oxycodone (known as 'hillbilly heroin') has risen. Yearly incidences of opiate analgesic use in the USA have increased from 600,000 in 1990 to more than 2.4 million by 2001, a figure that is more than double the number of known heroin users. This could be, according to Benedikt Fischer and Jurgen Rehm of the Centre for Addictions Research of British Columbia, representative of a 'paradigm shift' in illicit opiate use. They assert that 'the role of heroin use as the perceived dominant core of the street drug use problem in Australia, Europe and North America may have come to an end or at least become substantially diminished, and that instead the opiate abuse phenomenon may be in the process of shifting into a landscape dominated by the illicit use of a great variety of prescription opioids'.[33]

Of course, we've been here before. Legally prescribed but illegally distributed medications have been part of the drug scene for decades. Overprescription by GPs in the 1960s was cited as one of the main reasons for introducing the DDUs, as were restrictions on the prescription of heroin to specialists. In the 1980s, perceived overprescription by private doctors and GPs was the pretext on which a campaign against their involvement in the treatment of addiction was launched. The supposed existence of a 'grey market' in pharmaceutical drugs was also another way to undermine the value of maintenance treatment and intensify calls for greater restrictions on prescription to addicts. The current putative consensus on the value of methadone maintenance may yet be under threat. Are substitute prescribing programmes, Fischer and Rehm ask, 'aiming at the right target?'[34] It is impossible to say if history will repeat itself, but what is clear is that the same debates, conflicts and tensions that have beset drug addiction treatment since the beginning of the twentieth century endure. And, for as long as these inconsistencies in our understanding of heroin addiction continue, our response to it is likely to remain just as confused.

List of Abbreviations

ACDD   Advisory Committee on Drug Dependence

ACMD   Advisory Council on the Misuse of Drugs

AIDA   Association of Independent Doctors in Addiction

AIDS   Acquired Immune Deficiency Syndrome

APA   American Psychiatric Association

ARU   Addiction Research Unit

BMA   British Medical Association

BMJ   British Medical Journal

CFI   Central Funding Initiative

CMAC   Contemporary Medical Archives Centre

DARP   Drug Abuse Reporting Programme

DAT   Drug Action Team

DATOS   Drug Abuse Treatment Outcome Study

DDU   Drug Dependence Unit

DHSS   Department of Health and Social Security

DIP   Drug Intervention Programme

DTI   Department of Trade and Industry

DTTOS   Drug Treatment and Testing Orders

EMCDDA   European Monitoring Centre for Drugs and Drug Addiction

GMC   General Medical Council

HIV   Human Immunodeficiency Virus

ISDD   Institute for the Study of Drug Dependence

MRC	Medical Research Council
NA	Narcotics Anonymous
NDTMS	National Drug Treatment Monitoring System
NHS	National Health Service
NTA	National Treatment Agency for Substance Misuse
NTORS	National Treatment Outcome Research Study
PCC	Professional Conduct Committee
PTB	Pooled Treatment Budget
RCGP	Royal College of General Practitioners
RMPA	Royal Medico-Psychological Association
SCODA	Standing Conference on Drug Abuse
SSOT	Society for the Suppression of the Opium Trade
TNA	The National Archives
TOPS	Treatment Outcome Prospective Study
UNODC	United Nations Office of Drug Control
WHO	World Health Organisation

Notes

INTRODUCTION

1. The National Archives (hereafter TNA) MH 58/275 Memorandum from Dr E.W. Adams to Dr George McCleary, Deputy Senior Medical Officer, Ministry of Health, 17 February 1923.

2. David Courtwright, *Dark Paradise: A History of Opiate Addiction in America* (Cambridge, Mass.: Harvard University Press, 2001), 4.

3. John Kaplan, *The Hardest Drug: Heroin and Public Policy* (Chicago: Chicago University Press, 1983); David E. Smith and George R. Gay (eds), *'It's So Good, Don't Even Try It Once': Heroin in Perspective* (Hemel Hempstead: Prentice Hall, 1972).

4. This situation is changing; more and more substances are being considered to be addictive. See discussion in the Conclusion.

5. Jordan Goodman, Paul Lovejoy and Andrew Sherratt (eds), *Consuming Habits: Drugs in History and Anthropology* (London: Routledge, 1995); Roy Porter and Mikas Teich (eds), *Drugs and Narcotics in History* (Cambridge: Cambridge University Press, 1995).

6. David T. Courtwright, *Forces of Habit: Drugs and the Making of the Modern World* (Cambridge, Mass.: Harvard University Press, 2001): 31–33, 9.

7. Florence Ayscough (trans.), *Tu Fu: The Autobiography of a Chinese Poet AD 712–770* (Boston: Houghton Mifflin Co., 1929), cited in Julia Lee, "Alcohol in Chinese poems: references to drunkenness, flushing and drinking," *Contemporary Drug Problems,* 13 (1986): 303–38.

8. Jessica Warner, "'Resolv'd to drink no more': addiction as a pre-industrial construct," *Journal of Studies on Alcohol,* 55 (1994): 687.

9. Roy Porter, "The drinking man's disease: the 'pre-history' of alcoholism in Georgian Britain," *British Journal of Addiction,* 80 (1985): 385–96.

10. Ibid. See also William L. White, *Slaying the Dragon: The History of Addiction Treatment and Recovery in America* (Bloomington, Illinois: Chestnut Health Systems, 1998), 1–4.

11. Harry G. Levine, "The discovery of addiction: changing conceptions of habitual drunkenness in America," *Journal of Studies on Alcohol,* 39 (1978): 143–74.

12. Virginia Berridge, *Opium and the People: Opiate Use and Drug Control Policy in Nineteenth and Early Twentieth Century England* (London: Free Association Books, 1999), 135–36.

13. Griffith Edwards, *Matters of Substance: Drugs—And Why Everyone's A User* (London: Allen Lane, 2004), 79; Tom Carnwarth and Ian Smith, *Heroin Century* (London and New York: Routledge, 2002), 15–16.

14. Terry Parssinen and Karen Kerner, "Development of the disease model of drug addiction in Britain, 1870–1926," *Medical History,* 24 (1980): 291.

15. Virginia Berridge, "Morality and medical science: concepts of narcotic addiction in Britain, 1820–1926," *Annals of Science,* 36 (1979): 73.

16. Parssinen and Kerner, "Development of the disease model of addiction in Britain," 291.

17. Levine, "The discovery of addiction," 152–53.

18. William L. White, "The lessons of language: historical perspectives on

the rhetoric of addiction," in Sarah W. Tracy and Caroline Jean Acker (eds), *Altering American Consciousness: The History of Alcohol and Drug Use in the United States, 1800–2000* (Amherst & Boston, Mass.: University of Massachusetts Press, 2004), 34–35.

19. Geoffrey Harding, *Opiate Addiction, Morality and Medicine: From Moral Illness to Pathological Disease* (Basingstoke: Macmillan, 1988).

20. Parssinen and Kerner, "Development of the disease model of drug addiction in Britain," 283.

21. Berridge, "Morality and medical science," 72, 77.

22. Michel Foucault, *The History of Sexuality, Volume One: An Introduction* (Middlesex: Penguin, 1990); Michel Foucault, *Madness and Civilisation: A History of Insanity in the Age of Reason* (London and New York: Routledge, 2001).

23. See, for example, Michael Mason, *The Making of Victorian Sexuality* (Oxford: Oxford University Press, 1994); Frank Mort, *Dangerous Sexualities: Medico-Moral Politics in Great Britain Since 1830* (London and New York: Routledge, 1987). For a more recent overview of developments in the history of sexuality, see Harry G. Cocks and Matt Houlbrook (eds), *Palgrave Advances in the Modern History of Sexuality* (Palgrave: Basingstoke, 2005).

24. Janet Farrell Brodie and Marc Redfield, "Introduction," in Janet Farrell Brodie and Marc Redfield (eds), *High Anxieties: Cultural Studies in Addiction* (Berkeley, Los Angeles and London: University of California Press, 2002), 2.

25. Mariana Valverde, "'Slavery from within': the invention of alcoholism and the question of free will," *Social History*, 22 (1997): 257. See also Mariana Valverde, *Diseases of the Will: Alcohol and the Dilemmas of Freedom* (Cambridge: Cambridge University Press, 1998), 24–28, 59–67, 68–75.

26. Carol Smart, "Social policy and drug addiction: a critical study of policy development," *British Journal of Addiction*, 79 (1984): 31–39.

27. Ibid., 35–36.

28. Ministry of Health, *Departmental Committee Report on Morphine and Heroin Addiction* (London: HMSO, 1926), 11.

29. Ministry of Health, *Drug Addiction: The Second Report of the Interdepartmental Committee on Heroin Addiction* (London: HMSO, 1965), 8.

30. Ministry of Health, *Drug Addiction: The Report of the Interdepartmental Committee on Heroin Addiction* (London: HMSO, 1961), 9.

31. Virginia Berridge, "Opium and the doctors: disease theory and policy," in R.M. Murray and T.H. Turner (eds), *Lectures on the History of Psychiatry: The Squibb Series* (London: Royal College of Psychiatrists, 1990), 101.

32. American Psychiatric Association, *Diagnostic and Statistical Manual of Mental Disorders (DSM-IV)*, "Substance Dependence," available from http://allpsych.com/disorders/substance/substancedependence.html and World Health Organization (WHO), *ICD-10* "Mental and behavioural disorders due to psychoactive substance use," available from http://www.who.int/classifications/apps/icd/icd10online/gF10.htm.

33. See William B. McAllister, *Drug Diplomacy in the Twentieth Century: An International History* (London and New York: Routledge, 2000); David R. Bewley-Taylor, *The United States and International Drug Control, 1909–1997* (London: Continuum, 1999).

34. Henry B. Spear, *Heroin Addiction Care and Control: The British System 1916–84* (London: DrugScope, 2002), 1.

35. Ibid. On Lindesmith and his views on the treatment of heroin addiction, see Caroline Jean Acker, *Creating the American Junkie: Addiction Research in the Classic Era of Narcotic Control* (Baltimore, Maryland: Johns Hopkins Press, 2002), 201–4.

36. Edwin M. Schur, *Narcotic Addiction in Britain and America: The Impact of Public Policy* (Bloomington & London: Indiana University Press, 4th ed., 1968); Alfred Lindesmith, *The Heroin Addict and the Law* (Bloomington: Indiana University

Press, 1965); Horace F. Judson, *Heroin Addiction in Britain* (New York: Harcourt, Brace & Jovanovich, 1973); Arnold Trebach, *The Heroin Solution* (New Haven & London: Yale University Press, 1982).

37. Courtwright, *Dark Paradise*; David Musto, *The American Disease: Origins of Narcotic Control* (Oxford and New York: Oxford University Press, 3rd ed., 1999).

38. Virginia Berridge, "The 'British System' and its history: myth and reality," in John Strang and Michael Gossop (eds), *Heroin and the British System: Volume One—Origins and Evolution* (London and New York: Routledge, 2005), 15.

39. John Strang and Michael Gossop, "The 'British System': visionary anticipation or masterly inactivity?" in John Strang and Michael Gossop (eds), *Heroin Addiction and British Drug Policy: The British System* (Oxford: Oxford University Press, 1994), 343–51.

40. Griffith Edwards, "Some years on: evolutions in the 'British System,'" in West, *Problems of Drug Abuse in Britain*, 1–51. Henry B. Spear, "The early years of the 'British System' in practice," in Strang and Gossop (eds), *Heroin Addiction and British Drug Policy: The British System* (Oxford: Oxford University Press, 1994), 6–27.

41. John Witton, Francis Keaney and John Strang, "Opiate addiction and the 'British System': looking back on the twentieth century and trying to see its shape in the future," in Janie Sheridan and John Strang (eds), *Drug Misuse and Community Pharmacy* (London: Taylor & Francis, 2003), 5–16, 7.

42. Berridge, "Myth and reality," 7.

43. Trevor Bennett, "The British experience with heroin regulation," *Law and Contemporary Problems*, 51 (1988): 300.

44. David Downes, *Contrasts in Tolerance: Post War Penal Policy in the Netherlands and in England and Wales* (Oxford: Clarendon Press, 1988).

45. Berridge, "Myth and reality," 15.

46. See, for example, Shane Blackman, *Chilling Out: The Cultural Politics of Substance Consumption, Youth and Drug Policy* (Maidenhead: Open University Press, 2004), 22–24, 26–27; Carnwarth and Smith, *Heroin Century*, 63–64, 25–26; Edwards, *Matters of Substance*, 111, 114–17.

47. Transform, *After the War on Drugs: Options for Control* (Transform: Bristol, 2006).

48. See Alex Mold and Virginia Berridge, *Voluntarism, Health and Society Since the 1960s: Voluntary Action and Illegal Drugs* (Basingstoke: Palgrave, forthcoming).

49. Precise figures are 1977, 2,016; 1987, 10,389. Home Office, *Statistics of Drug Addicts Notified to the Home Office, 1988* (London: HMSO, 1989).

50. Virginia Berridge, "AIDS and British drug policy: continuity or change?" in Virginia Berridge and Philip Strong (eds), *AIDS and Contemporary History* (Cambridge: Cambridge University Press, 1993), 141.

1—TREATMENT AND CONTROL

1. *The Times*, 11 February 1916, 3.

2. This case is also discussed by Marek Kohn, *Dope Girls: The Birth of the British Drug Underground* (London: Granta, 1992, this ed. 2001), 34–35.

3. Berridge, *Opium and the People*, 253.

4. TNA MH 58/275, Report and attached statement from Thomas Henderson regarding his addiction to morphia, 20 November 1922.

5. Ministry of Health, *Departmental Committee on Morphine and Heroin Addiction*, 11.

6. Kohn, *Dope Girls*.

7. Bewley-Taylor, *The United States and International Drug Control*.

8. Courtwright, *Dark Paradise*; Musto, *The American Disease*.

9. Berridge, *Opium and the People*; Terry Parssinen, *Secret Passions, Secret Remedies: Narcotic Drugs in British Society 1820–1930* (Manchester: Manchester University Press, 1983).

10. Berridge, *Opium and the People*, 105–9.

11. Ibid., 113–22.

12. Ibid., 239–46; Bewley-Taylor, *The United States and International Drug Control*, 16–27.

13. Virginia Berridge and Sarah Mars, "Glossary: history of addictions," *Journal of Epidemiology and Community Health*, 58 (2004): 749.

14. Berridge, *Opium and the People*, 258–60.

15. James Mills, *Cannabis Britannica: Empire, Trade and Prohibition* (Oxford: Oxford University Press, 2003), 152–87.

16. *The Times*, 14 December 1918, 5.

17. Kohn, *Dope Girls*, 2.

18. On the concept of 'folk devils' and their role in moral panics, see Stanley Cohen, *Folk Devils and Moral Panics* (London: MacGibbon & Kee, 1972).

19. Kohn, *Dope Girls*, 7–8, 108–9, 134–39.

20. *The Times*, 12 May 1922, 17.

21. TNA MH 58/275, Minute from ST [?] at the Home Office to Dr Smith-Whitaker, Ministry of Health, 13 March 1923.

22. TNA MH 58/277, Home Office memorandum submitted to the Rolleston Committee, 14 October 1924.

23. Ibid.

24. TNA MH 58/275, Minute from Sir Malcolm Delevingne, Home Office, to Dr G. McCleary, Ministry of Health, 9 March 1923.

25. Ministry of Health, *Departmental Committee on Morphine and Heroin Addiction*, 2.

26. Virginia Berridge, "'Stamping out addiction': the work of the Rolleston Committee, 1924–1926," in Hugh Freeman and German E. Berrios (eds), *150 Years of British Psychiatry, Volume Two—The Aftermath* (London: Athlone Press, 1996), 44–60.

27. TNA MH 58/276, Minutes of the Departmental Committee, 4th meeting, 14 November 1924.

28. TNA MH 58/275, Minute from ST [?] at the Home Office to Dr Smith-Whitaker, Ministry of Health, 13 March 1923.

29. TNA MH 58/277, Evidence of the Rolleston Committee, further note by Dr FSD Hogg, no date [1924].

30. TNA MH 58/276, Minutes of the Departmental Committee, 3rd meeting, 1 November 1924.

31. TNA MH 58/277, Evidence of Dr Ivy Mackenzie, 1924.

32. *Ministry of Health, Departmental Committee on Morphine and Heroin Addiction*, 32; 18.

33. Ibid., 10.

34. On the origins of the Addicts Index, see Rachel Lart, "Changing images of the addict and addiction," *International Journal of Drug Policy*, 1 (1992): 118–25. Spear, *Heroin Addiction Care and Control*, 41–2.

35. Henry B. Spear, "The growth of heroin addiction in the United Kingdom," *British Journal of Addiction*, 64 (1969): 245–55.

36. Seven cases, including that of Henderson, are detailed in a letter from the Ministry of Health to Delevingne in 1922. See TNA MH 58/275.

37. Ministry of Health, *Departmental Committee Report on Morphine and Heroin Addiction*, 30.

38. Ibid., 9.

39. Ministry of Health, *Report of the Interdepartmental Committee on Heroin Addiction*, 20.

40. Alan Block, "European drug traffic and traffickers between the wars: the policy of suppression and its consequences," *Journal of Social History* (1989): 315–37.

41. Bewley-Taylor, *The United States and International Drug Control*, 56, 59.

42. Berridge, *Opium and the People*, 282.

43. See, for example, *The Times*, 20 May 1955, 7; *The Times*, 4 June 1955, 3; *The Times*, 14 June 1955, 4. The dispute is also covered by Spear in *Heroin Addiction Care and Control*, 71–89.

44. *The Times*, 19 November 1955, 5.

45. TNA MH 58/564, Draft submission on the appointment of the advisory committee, 1957.

46. TNA MH 58/564, Letter from Mr Green (Home Office) to Mrs Hauff (Ministry of Health), 16 November 1956.

47. The Home Office's concerns are set out in Ibid.

48. Ibid.

49. Ministry of Health, *Interdepartmental Committee on Drug Addiction*.

50. TNA MH 58/564, Letter from the National Council of Women of Great Britain to Minister of Health, Derek Walker-Smith, 10 July 1958.

51. TNA MH 58/564, Reply to the National Council of Women of Great Britain from Woodlock (Walker-Smith's private secretary), 28 July 1958.

52. TNA MH 58/564, Letter from Clark at the Ministry of Health to Sir Russell Brain, 21 November 1957.

53. TNA MH 58/564, Letter from Honnor to Clark, 25 October 1957.

54. TNA MH 58/565, Memorandum from Home Office, Ministry of Health and Department of Health for Scotland, presented to the Brain Committee, 1960.

55. TNA MH 58/566, Evidence from other organisations, 1958; TNA MH 58/571, Minutes of the 3rd meeting, 7 May 1959.

56. TNA MH 58/571, Minutes of the 2nd meeting, 22 October 1958.

57. Ministry of Health, *Interdepartmental Committee on Heroin Addiction*, 9.

58. TNA MH 58/568, Minutes of the 1st meeting, 16 July 1958.

59. Ministry of Health, *Interdepartmental Committee on Drug Addiction*, 22.

60. Reference to the WHO's definition in the Seventh Report of the Expert Committee on Addiction Producing Drugs (1957) is made in the minutes of the 3rd meeting, 7 May 1959. Definition quoted from Ministry of Health, *Interdepartmental Committee on Drug Addiction*, 8.

61. Ibid., 8–9.

62. TNA MH 58/566, Evidence of the British Medical Association (BMA), no date [1958/9].

63. Ministry of Health, *Interdepartmental Committee on Heroin Addiction*, 9.

64. TNA MH 58/566, Evidence of the Royal Faculty of Physicians and Surgeons, no date [1958/9].

65. TNA MH 58/566, Evidence of the BMA, no date [1958/9].

66. TNA MH 58/566, Evidence of the Royal Medico-Psychological Association (RMPA), no date [1958/9].

67. Ministry of Health, *Interdepartmental Committee on Heroin Addiction*, 11.

68. Ibid., 12–16.

69. This episode is described in Judson, *Heroin Addiction in Britain*, 35–38.

70. Spear, *Heroin Addiction Care and Control*, 111.

71. Ibid., 110.

72. Henry B. Spear, "The early years of Britain's drug situation in practice up to the 1960s," in Strang and Gossop (eds), *Heroin Addiction and the British System: Vol 1*, 17–42.

73. For a full list of witnesses, see Ministry of Health, *Interdepartmental Committee on Drug Addiction*, 19.

74. TNA MH 58/566, Letter from Michael Cullen to the Secretaries of the Interdepartmental Committee, 26 September 1959.

75. Ministry of Health, *Interdepartmental Committee on Heroin Addiction*, 12.

76. Ministry of Health, *Second Report of the Interdepartmental Committee on Heroin Addiction*, 14.

2—THE NEW ADDICTS AND THE ESTABLISHMENT OF THE DRUG DEPENDENCE UNITS, 1962–1968

1. Isabella M. Frankau and Patricia M. Stanwell, "The treatment of drug addiction," *Lancet* (24 December 1960): 1377–79.

2. Figures taken from Ministry of Health, *Second Report of the Interdepartmental Committee on Heroin Addiction*, 6. The doctor responsible for this prescription is not actually named in the report, but Spear asserts that the doctor cited was Frankau. See Spear, *Heroin Addiction Care and Control*, 144.

3. Brain quoted both in Spear, *Heroin Addiction Care and Control*, 136, and in Marek Kohn, *Narcomania* (London: Faber and Faber, 1987), 100.

4. TNA MH 149/164, Letter from Godber to Dr Brotherson, Scottish Home and Health Department, 22 May 1964.

5. Ministry of Health, *Second Report of the Interdepartmental Committee on Heroin Addiction*, 4.

6. Ibid., 8.

7. Ibid., 5.

8. TNA MH 149/166, quoted in Home Office Memorandum presented to the Interdepartmental Committee on Drug Addiction, 1964.

9. Arnold Trebach, *The Heroin Solution* (New Haven & London: Yale University Press, 1982), 174.

10. Ibid., 110; Gerry Stimson and Edna Oppenheimer, *Heroin Addiction: Treatment and Control in Britain* (London: Tavistock, 1982), 61, 94–113; Gerry Stimson, "Treatment or control? Dilemmas for staff in drug dependency clinics," in D.J. West (ed.), *Problems of Drug Abuse in Britain: Papers Presented to The Cropwood Round-Table Conference* (Cambridge: Institute of Criminology, 1978), 52–73.

11. Interview with Griffith Edwards quoted in Judson, *Heroin Addiction in Britain*, 145; David K. Whynes, "Drug problems, drug policies" in David K. Whynes and Philip T. Bean (eds), *Policing and Prescribing: The British System of Drug Control* (Basingstoke: Macmillan, 1991), 3.

12. Ministry of Health, *Second Report of the Interdepartmental Committee on Heroin Addiction*, 14.

13. Spear, *Heroin Addiction Care and Control*, 126–27.

14. TNA MH 149/166, Memorandum by the Home Office, no date [1964].

15. Spear, *Heroin Addiction Care and Control*, 133.

16. TNA MH 149/164, Letter from Sir George Godber to Dr M.A. Partridge, St George's Hospital, 22 May 1964.

17. TNA MH 149/165, Minutes of the 1st meeting of the Brain Committee, 18 August 1964.

18. TNA MH 149/166, Memorandum by the Home Office, no date [1964].

19. Ministry of Health, *Second Report of the Interdepartmental Committee on Heroin Addiction*, 5; TNA MH 149/165, minutes of meetings.

20. TNA MH 149/165, Minutes of the 3rd meeting, 4 December 1964.

21. TNA MH 149/165, Minutes of the 2nd meeting, 29 October 1964.

22. TNA MH 149/165, Minutes of the 4th meeting, 3 February 1965.

23. Ministry of Health, *Second Report of the Interdepartmental Committee on Heroin Addiction*, 8.

24. Ibid., 8.

25. Matthew Hilton, *Smoking in British Popular Culture 1880–2000: Perfect Pleasures* (Manchester: Manchester University Press, 2000), 179–80, 189–90.

26. On the use of epidemiology in defining the response to heroin addiction, see Alex Mold, "Illicit drugs and the rise of epidemiology during the 1960s," *Journal of Epidemiology and Community Health,* 61 (2007): 278–81.

27. Ministry of Health, *Second Report of the Interdepartmental Committee on Heroin Addiction,* 9.

28. Stimson and Oppenheimer, *Heroin Addiction,* 54.

29. David Armstrong, *The Political Anatomy of the Body* (Cambridge: Cambridge University Press, 1983).

30. Michel Foucault, *The Birth of the Clinic: An Archaeology of Medical Perception* (London: Tavistock Publications, 1973).

31. Lart, "Changing Images of the Addict and Addiction," 1–8. Lart elaborates on these themes in her Ph.D dissertation "HIV and English Drugs Policy," PhD diss., University of London, 1996, 40, 51–55.

32. Ibid. Here Lart is clearly drawing on notions of surveillance and discipline in Foucault, *Discipline and Punish.*

33. Virginia Berridge, *Health and Society in Britain Since 1939* (Cambridge: Cambridge University Press, 1999), 48–54. See also Dorothy Porter, *Health, Civilisation and the State: A History of Public Health From Ancient to Modern Times* (London and New York: Routledge, 1999) and John Welshman, *Municipal Medicine: Public Health in Twentieth-Century Britain* (Oxford and Bern: Peter Lang, 2000).

34. Ministry of Health, *Second Report of the Interdepartmental Committee on Heroin Addiction,* 8.

35. Smart, "Social policy and drug addiction," 35–36.

36. Stimson and Oppenheimer, *Heroin Addiction,* 94, 205–19; Stimson, "Treatment or control?" 52–73.

37. *British Medical Journal,* 27 November 1965, 1259–60.

38. Ibid.

39. *The Times,* 21 December 1965, 5; Stimson and Oppenheimer, *Heroin Addiction,* 54.

40. *Lancet,* 27 November 1965, 1113–14.

41. TNA MH 149/170, Letter from the Scottish BMA to Sharp, 6 December 1966.

42. Dangerous Drugs Act, 1967; Dangerous Drugs (Notification of Addicts) Regulations, 1968.

43. Trebach, *The Heroin Solution,* 183.

44. *The Times,* 26 July 1967, 3.

45. TNA MH 149/170, Meeting between representatives of the Ministry of Health and Dr Goulding, 10 May 1966.

46. Ibid.

47. H. Dale Beckett, "Society at Work: Maintaining Heroin Addicts," *New Society* (14 September 1967): 360–61; H. Dale Beckett, "The Salter Unit—an experimental in-patient treatment centre for narcotic addiction in men," *British Journal of Addiction,* 63 (1968): 51–53.

48. See Thomas H. Bewley, "Conversation with Thomas Bewley," *Addiction,* 90 (1995): 887; Thomas H. Bewley, "Advantages of special centres," *British Medical Journal* (1967): 498–99; Thomas H. Bewley, "Heroin and cocaine addiction," *Lancet* (10 April 1965): 808–10; TNA MH 149/172, Meeting between representatives of the Ministry of Health and Dr Bewley and Dr Monro, 1966.

49. TNA MH 149/172, Meeting between representatives of the Ministry of Health and Dr Bewley and Dr Monro, 1966.

50. TNA MH 150/369, HM 67 (16), "Treatment and Supervision of Heroin Addiction," (March 1967).

51. Ministry of Health, *Second Report of the Interdepartmental Committee on Heroin Addiction,* 8.

52. TNA MH 149/172, Outline scheme for implementing the recommendations of the Brain Committee, 31 October 1966.

53. Betsy Thom, *Dealing With Drink: Alcohol and Social Policy From Treatment to Management* (London: Free Association Books, 1999), 45–66; Betsy Thom and Virginia Berridge, "'Special units for common problems:' the birth of alcohol treatment units in England," *Social History of Medicine,* 8 (1995): 75–93.

54. Douglas Bennett, "The drive towards the community," in German E. Berrios and Hugh Freeman (eds), *150 Years of British Psychiatry, 1841–1991* (London: Royal College of Psychiatrists, 1991), 321–32; Kathryn Jones, *Asylums and After: A Revised History of the Mental Health Services From the Early Eighteenth Century to the 1990s* (London: Athlone Press, 1993), 181–93; Edward Shorter, *A History of Psychiatry From the Era of the Asylum to the Age of Prozac* (New York: John Wiley & Sons Inc., 1997), 277–81; Berridge, *Health and Society,* 30–32.

55. See David Evans, "Tackling the 'hideous scourge': the creation of the venereal disease treatment centres in early twentieth-century Britain," *Social History of Medicine,* 5 (1992): 413–33. For a discussion of the dispensaries established to treat tuberculosis, see Armstrong, *Political Anatomy of the Body,* 7–18.

56. TNA MH 160/709, Memorandum from Moyes (Ministry of Health) to Slater, 9 February 1967.

57. TNA MH 160/709.

58. TNA MH 160/709, Note of meeting between Winner (Ministry of Health) and Clark (Guy's Hospital), 15 December 1966.

59. TNA MH 160/709, Note of meeting between Moyes, Tooth, (Principal Medical Officer, Ministry of Health) and Powditch (St. Mary's Hospital), 7 February 1967.

60. TNA MH 160/709, Note of meeting between Winner and Clark, 15 December 1966.

61. TNA MH 149/170, Letter to Hodges from Adams, 18 November 1965.

62. TNA MH 160/709, Memorandum from Moyes to Slater, 9 February 1967.

63. TNA MH 160/710, Letter from Driscoll at St Thomas' Hospital to Moyes, 26 September 1967; Estimate of Costs of Unit for the Treatment of Addiction, no date.

64. TNA MH 160/709, Letter to Hauff from the House Governor of the Westminster Hospital, 7 June 1967.

65. London Metropolitan Archive (hereafter LMA) H1/ST/A128/13, Letter to the Ministry of Health from the Chairman of the Medical Committee, St Thomas' Hospital, 3 April 1967.

66. TNA MH 160/710, Slater to Tooth and Shore, 28 July 1967.

67. Beckett, "Society at work: maintaining heroin addicts," 360–61.

68. *The Hansard Journal of Parliamentary Debates: House of Commons,* vol. 732, 21 July 1966, 865; question by William Deedes, 24 May 1966, vol. 729, 283–84; question by Renee Short, 21 July 1966, vol. 732, 865–66.

69. See, for example, William Deedes, *The Drugs Epidemic* (London: Tom Stacey, 1970); *Hansard: Commons,* 30 January 1967, vol. 740, 121–74.

70. Ibid.

71. *The Sunday Times,* 20 August 1967, 3.

72. *Guardian,* 16 November 1967, 4.

73. *The Times,* 8 July 1967, 1.

74. TNA MH 160/709, Letter from Dr A. Hawes to K. Robinson, 31 May 1967.

75. TNA MH 160/709, Moyes to Slater on the options of how to deal with Hawes, 15 June 1967.

76. TNA MH 160/709, Reply to Hawes, 22 June 1967. The teaching hospitals' replies to Hawes' letters are also reproduced in an appendix to an article by Kenneth Leech, then a curate in Hoxton and later a drug voluntary organisation leader. See: Kenneth Leech, "The junkies' doctors and the London drug

scene in the 1960s: some remembered fragments," in David Whynes and Philip Bean (eds), *Policing and Prescribing: The British System of Drug Control* (Basingstoke: Macmillan, 1991), 58–59.

77. *The Times,* 8 July 1967, 1.

78. See, for example, *The Times,* 14 July 1967, 7, *The Times,* 18 July 1967, 8 and *The Sunday Times,* 20 August 1967. The debacle is also outlined by Leech, "The junkies' doctors," 47–50.

79. A. Hawes, *Lancet,* (22 July 1967), 208.

80. *British Medical Journal,* (11 February 1967), 319–20; *British Medical Journal,* (2 March 1968), 719.

81. TNA MH 160/709, Organisation of the Treatment and Supervision of Heroin Addiction, no date.

82. TNA MH 150/369, HM 67 (16) "Treatment and Supervision of Heroin Addiction," March 1967.

83. Figures from Stimson and Oppenheimer, *Heroin Addiction,* 81.

84. Ibid., 81–82.

85. TNA MH 150/369, Letter from County Medical Officer of Health, Cambridgeshire to the Ministry of Health, 4 March 1968.

86. TNA MH 160/709, Report of visit to Charing Cross Hospital.

87. Interview with Margaret Tripp quoted in Judson, *Heroin Addiction in Britain,* 93. Interview with Dale Beckett quoted in Richard Davenport-Hines, *The Pursuit of Oblivion: A Global History of Narcotics 1500–2000* (London: Weinfield & Nicholson, 2001), 321–22.

88. Interview with Martin Mitcheson quoted in Judson, *Heroin Addiction in Britain,* 87.

89. Voluntary organisations around drugs are discussed in more detail in Mold and Berridge, *Voluntarism, Health and Society Since the 1960s.*

90. Alex Mold, "The 'welfare branch of the alternative society'? The work of drug voluntary organisation Release, 1967–1978," *Twentieth Century British History,* 17:1 (2006): 50–73.

91. Nigel South and Nicholas Dorn, *Helping Drug Users: Social Work, Advice Giving, Referral and Training Services of Three London Street Agencies* (Aldershot: Gower, 1985).

92. Interview between author and David Turner, February 2005.

93. Advisory Committee on Drug Dependence, *The Rehabilitation of Drug Addicts* (London: HMSO, 1968), 3.

94. Penelope Campling, "Therapeutic communities," *Advances in Psychiatric Treatment* 7 (2001): 366. For an overview of the history of therapeutic communities, see David Kennard, *An Introduction to Therapeutic Communities* (London: Jessica Kingsley, 1998).

95. Barbara Rawlings and Rowdy Yates, "Introduction," in Barbara Rawlings and Rowdy Yates (eds), *Therapeutic Communities for the Treatment of Drug Users* (London: Jessica Kingsley, 2001), 9–25. Rod Janzen, *The Rise and Fall of Synanon: A California Utopia* (Baltimore and London: Johns Hopkins Press, 2001).

96. Mitchell Rosenthal "Therapeutic communities," in Ilana Belle Glass (ed.), *The International Handbook of Addiction Behaviour* (London and New York: Routledge, 1991), 259.

97. Interview between author and Griffith Edwards, October 2004, and Griffith Edwards, "Relevance of American experience of narcotic addiction to the British scene," *British Medical Journal* (12 August 1967): 425–29.

98. David Warren Holland, "The development of concept houses in Great Britain and Southern Ireland, 1967–1976," in D.J. West (ed.), *Problems of Drug Abuse in Britain: Papers Presented to the Cropwood Round Table Conference* (Cambridge: Institute of Criminology, 1978), 125.

99. *Phoenix House: The Featherstone Lodge Project Annual Report, 1970–71.*

3—PSYCHIATRY AND THE TREATMENT OF HEROIN ADDICTION, 1969-1979

1. Philip H. Connell, "Drug dependence in Britain: A challenge to the practice of medicine," in H. Steinberg (ed.), *Scientific Basis of Drug Dependence* (London: J & A Churchill, 1969), 294–95.

2. Henry B. Spear, "The early years of Britain's drug situation in practice, up to the 1960s," in John Strang and Michael Gossop (eds), *Heroin Addiction and the British System: Volume One* (London: Routledge, 2005), 38.

3. On the reorganisation of psychiatric services, see Jones, *Asylums and After,* 181–92 and Bennett, "The drive towards the community," 326–27. On the pharmacological revolution, see Shorter, *A History of Psychiatry,* 239–55.

4. Figures quoted in Stimson and Oppenheimer, *Heroin Addiction,* 102.

5. Richard Hartnoll et al., "Evaluation of heroin maintenance in controlled trial," *Archives of General Psychiatry,* 37 (1980): 877–84.

6. Bewley, "Conversation with Thomas Bewley," 885; Philip H. Connell, "Conversation with Philip Connell," *British Journal of Addiction,* 85 (1990): 16–17.

7. Spear, *Heroin Addiction: Care and Control,* 189–93.

8. Harold Perkin, *The Rise of Professional Society: England Since 1880* (London and New York: Routledge, 1990), 347.

9. Charles Webster, "Psychiatry and the early National Health Service: the role of the Mental Health Standing Committee," in German E. Berrios and Hugh Freeman (eds), *150 Years of British Psychiatry, 1841–1991* (London: Royal College of Psychiatrists, 1991), 103–4.

10. George Weisz, *Divide and Conquer: A Comparative History of Medical Specialisation* (Oxford: Oxford University Press, 2006), 227–29.

11. Roy Porter, *Madmen: A Social History of Madhouses, Mad-Doctors and Lunatics* (Stroud: Tempus, 2004), 173–227.

12. Bennett, "The drive towards the community," 326–27; Webster, "Psychiatry and the early National Health Service," 103–16.

13. On anti-psychiatry, see Nick Crossley, "R.D. Laing and the British anti-psychiatry movement: a socio-historical analysis," *Social Science and Medicine,* 47 (1998): 877–89; Digby Tantam, "The anti-psychiatry movement," in German E. Berrios and Hugh Freeman (eds), *150 Years of British Psychiatry, 1841–1991* (London: Royal College of Psychiatrists, 1991), 333–47 .

14. Roy Porter, "Two cheers for psychiatry! The social history of mental disorder in twentieth century Britain," in Hugh Freeman and German Berrios (eds), *150 Years of British Psychiatry Volume Two—The Aftermath* (London: Athlone, 1996), 399.

15. Ibid., 398. Nikolas Rose, *Governing the Soul: The Shaping of the Private Self* (London: Free Association Books, 2nd ed., 1999), vii-viii, 217–35.

16. Foucault, *The History of Sexuality,* 103–5.

17. Nikolas Rose, *Inventing Our Selves: Psychology, Power and Personhood* (Cambridge: Cambridge University Press, 1996).

18. Shorter, *A History of Psychiatry,* 255.

19. Richard DeGrandpre, *The Cult of Pharmacology: How America Became the World's Most Troubled Drug Culture* (Durham, N.C.: Duke University Press, 2006), 166–69, 193–94.

20. John G. Howells, "The establishment of the Royal College of Psychiatrists," in German E. Berrios and Hugh Freeman (eds), *150 Years of British Psychiatry, 1841–1991* (London: Royal College of Psychiatrists, 1991), 117–34.

21. Ministry of Health, *Departmental Committee on Morphine and Heroin Addiction,* 11; Ministry of Health, *Second Report of the Interdepartmental Committee on Heroin Addiction,* 9–10.

22. H. Steinberg, "Chairman's Introduction," in H. Steinberg, *Scientific Basis of Drug Dependence* (London: J & A Churchill, 1969), 286.

23. For the role of psychiatry in alcoholism, see Valverde, *Diseases of the Will,* 48–50, 99–101, 106–11. Thom and Berridge, "Special units for common problems," 80.

24. Max Glatt, "Conversation with Max Glatt," *British Journal of Addiction,* 78 (1983): 240–41.

25. Bewley, "Conversation with Thomas Bewley," 885.

26. Spear, *Heroin Addiction Care and Control,* 192–93.

27. TNA FD 7/1583, Minutes of the Medical Research Council Conference on research into drug dependence, 18 January 1968.

28. Eddy et al., "Drug dependence: its significance and characteristics," *World Health Organisation Bulletin,* 32 (1965), cited in Jock Young, *The Drugtakers: The Sociological Meaning of Drug Taking* (London: Paladin, 1971), 44.

29. Berridge, "Opium and the doctors: disease theory and policy," 101.

30. TNA FD 7/1584, Terms of reference for working party, May 1968. There were also working parties on the epidemiology of addiction and the biochemical and pharmacological aspects of drug dependence.

31. TNA FD 7/1583, Letter from Faulkner, (Medical Research Council, hereafter MRC) to Professor Dornhorst, 22 February 1968.

32. Ministry of Health, *Report of the Second Interdepartmental Committee on Heroin Addiction,* 13.

33. *Hansard: Commons,* Vol. 732, 26 July 1966, 248.

34. TNA MH 149/162, Memorandum regarding the re-appointment of the ACDD, December 1969; Misuse of Drugs Act 1971, *Public General Acts and Measures of 1971,* Part I, Chapters 1–49, Chapter 38, 639–80, 639–40.

35. Ministry of Health, *Report of the Second Interdepartmental Committee on Heroin Addiction,* 13; TNA MH 149/162, Membership of the ACDD, October 1966.

36. For a consideration of the Maudsley and the Institute of Psychiatry and its interaction with drug addiction treatment, see Judson, *Heroin Addiction in Britain,* 12; Berridge, *Health and Society in Britain Since 1939,* 32.

37. TNA MH 150/94, Letter from Sir George Godber to Sir Denis Hill, 6 January 1967.

38. TNA MH 150/94, Proposal for the establishment of a centre for drug addiction research at the Institute of Psychiatry, January 1967.

39. TNA MH 150/94, Proposal for the Consolidation of the Addiction Research Unit, August 1969.

40. Carol Smart, "Social policy and drug dependence: an historical case study," *Drug and Alcohol Dependence,* 16 (1985): 171.

41. TNA MH 150/94, Proposal for the establishment of drug addiction research at the Institute of Psychiatry, January 1967.

42. Ibid.

43. TNA MH 150/94, Report on the activities of the Addiction Research Unit, Institute of Psychiatry, September 1968.

44. TNA FD 7/878, Minutes of the Working Party meeting, 30 October 1969.

45. TNA FD 7/1591, Third draft of Working Party report, April 1970.

46. An MRC official on 9 March 1970 noted that methadone was already being widely used. See TNA FD 7/878, Note for file, N.H. Winterton, 9 March 1970.

47. TNA FD 7/1599, Working group on drug dependence: survey of research into drug dependence in progress in the UK, 1971–1972.

48. The exception was a controlled study of oral maintenance on substitute drugs for heroin users conducted by Dr Peter Chapple of the charity-run National Addiction and Research Centre, an organisation viewed with suspicion by the Ministry of Health and some drug addiction experts as a result of Chapple's unorthodox views and the fact that he operated in private practice. See TNA MH 154/431

National Addiction and Research Day Centre, Chelsea; Spear, *Heroin Addiction Care and Control,* 193, 205.

49. TNA FD 7/1599, Working group on drug dependence: survey of research into drug dependence in progress in the UK, 1971–1972.

50. Griffith Edwards, "British policies on opiate addiction: ten years working of the revised response, and options for the future," *British Journal of Psychiatry,* 134 (1979): 11.

51. Richard Hartnoll et al., "Evaluation of heroin maintenance in controlled trial," 877–84.

52. Spear, *Heroin Addiction Care and Control,* 309–10.

53. Edwards, "British policies on opiate addiction," 9.

54. Smart, "Drug Dependence Units in England and Wales: the results of a national survey," *Drug and Alcohol Dependence,* 15 (1985): 132.

55. Gerry Stimson, "British drug policies in the 1980s: a preliminary analysis and some suggestions for research," *British Journal of Addiction,* 82 (1987): 480.

56. Jayne Love and Michael Gossop, "The process of referral and disposal within a London Drug Dependence Clinic," *British Journal of Addiction,* 80 (1985): 440.

57. David Owen, "Need for a scientific strategy to curb the epidemic of drug abuse in the United Kingdom, lecture to the Society of Clinical Psychiatrists Research Fund, 15 October 1985," *Lancet* (26 October 1985): 958.

58. The emergence of evidence-based medicine and its use in addiction treatment will be discussed in greater detail in Chapter 8.

59. Philip H. Connell, "'I need heroin.' Thirty years of drug dependence and of the medical challenges at local, national, international and political level. What next?" *British Journal of Addiction,* 81 (1986): 462; Connell, "Conversation with Philip Connell," 16; Spear, *Heroin Addiction Care and Control,* 291.

60. Connell, "Conversation with Philip Connell," 16; TNA MH 154/431, Dr Baker to Miss Hedley, 12 August 1969.

61. TNA MH 154/431, Minute from Miss Hedley to Brown and Cashman, Ministry of Health, 14 August 1969.

62. Connell, "Conversation with Philip Connell," 16.

63. See, for example, Connell, "Drug dependence in Great Britain," 291–99 and Philip H. Connell, "Importance of research," *British Medical Journal* (20 May 1967): 499–500.

64. Connell, "Drug dependence in Great Britain: a challenge to the practice of medicine," 298–99.

65. Martin Mitcheson, "Drug clinics in the 1970s," in Strang and Gossop (eds), *Heroin Addiction and British Drug Policy,* 178; Stimson and Oppenheimer, *Heroin Addiction,* 94; Trebach, *The Heroin Solution,* 186; Spear, *Heroin Addiction Care and Control,* 205–11.

66. Ramon Gardner and Philip Connell, "One year's experience in a Drug-Dependence Clinic," *Lancet* (29 August 1970): 455.

67. The need for such a test was recognised by (among others) Connell in 1967. See Connell, "The importance of research," 500.

68. Stimson and Oppenheimer, *Heroin Addiction,* 84–85.

69. Ibid., 85.

70. Ibid., 90; Judson, *Heroin Addiction in Britain,* 93; Smart, "Social policy and drug dependence," 177.

71. Judson, *Heroin Addiction in Britain,* 94.

72. John C. Ball, Harold Graff and John J. Sheenan, "The heroin addicts' view of methadone maintenance," *British Journal of Addiction,* 69 (1974): 91.

73. Talcott Parsons, *The Social System* (Glencoe, Illinois: Free Press, 1951).

74. Discussion of Parsons's formulation of the sick role in Myfanwy Morgan, Michael Calan and Nick Manning, *Sociological Approaches to Health and Medicine* (London: Croom Helm, 1985), 45–52.

75. Ibid., 52–56.

76. Thomas Szasz, *Ceremonial Chemistry: The Ritual Persecution of Drugs, Addicts and Pushers* (London: Routledge & Kegan Paul, 1975), xvi.

77. Stimson & Oppenheimer, *Heroin Addiction*, 88.

78. Ibid., 85–86.

79. See Christopher J. Ham, "Power, patients and pluralism," in Keith Barnard and Kenneth Lee (eds), *Conflicts in the National Health Service* (London: Croom Helm, 1977), 99–110. Margaret Stacey, "The health service consumer: a sociological misconception," *The Sociological Review Monograph: The Sociology of the National Health Service*, 22 (1978): 194–200.

80. This will be discussed in greater detail in Chapter 8.

81. Smart, "Social policy and drug dependence," 177; Judson, *Heroin Addiction in Britain*, 107; Gerry Stimson and Rachel Lart, "The relationship between the State and local practice in the development of national policy on drugs between 1920 and 1990," in Strang and Gossop, *Heroin Addiction and Drug Policy*, 333–34.

82. Stimson and Oppenheimer, *Heroin Addiction*, 96–97.

83. Ibid., 97.

84. Ibid., 216.

85. John Strang, Sue Ruben, Michael Farrell and Michael Gossop, "Prescribing heroin and other injectable drugs," in Strang and Gossop, *Heroin Addiction and Drug Policy*, 202; Will Self, quoted in Davenport-Hines, *The Pursuit of Oblivion*, 202.

86. Stimson and Oppenheimer, *Heroin Addiction*, 216.

87. J. Glancy, "The treatment of narcotic dependence in the United Kingdom," *Bulletin on Narcotics*, 24 (1972): 1–9, cited in Spear, *Heroin Addiction Care and Control*, 235.

88. Stimson and Oppenheimer, *Heroin Addiction*, 102.

89. Glancy, cited in Spear, *Heroin Addiction Care and Control*, 235.

90. Stimson and Oppenheimer, *Heroin Addiction*, 102.

91. John Strang and Janie Sheridan, "Heroin and methadone prescriptions from a London drug clinic over the first 15 years of operation (1968–1983): old records examined," *Substance Use and Misuse*, 41 (2006): 1231–33.

92. Trebach, *The Heroin Solution*, 201.

93. Strang, Ruben, Farrell, and Gossop, "Prescribing heroin and other injectable drugs," 198.

94. Current estimates put the cost of heroin maintenance at £10,000 to £15,000 a year per addict, compared to £2,000 a year for methadone. Drugscope News, 31 January 2001, http://www.drugscope.org.uk/news_item.asp?a=1&intlD=679; *The Guardian*, 15 January 2001, http://www.guardian.co.uk/Archive/Article/0,4273,4335607,00.html. Spear argues that heroin prescription only became expensive when injectable tablets were replaced with freeze-dried ampoules, but he makes no mention of the relative cost of methadone. See Spear, *Heroin Addiction Care and Control*, 244–45.

95. Mitcheson, "Drug clinics in the 1970s," 182–88.

96. Davenport-Hines, *Pursuit of Oblivion*, 291; David F. Musto and Pamela Korsmeyer, *The Quest For Drug Control: Politics and Federal Policy in the Period of Increasing Substance Use, 1963–1981* (New Haven: Yale University Press, 2002), 30.

97. Courtwright, *Dark Paradise*, 163–66; Michael Massing, *The Fix* (Berkley and Los Angeles: University of California Press, 1998, this ed. 2000), 88–89.

98. J.W. Gerritsen, *The Control of Fuddle and Flash: A Sociological History of the Regulation of Alcohol and Opiates* (Leiden: Brill, 2000), 199.

99. Courtwright, *Dark Paradise*, 165.

100. Massing, *The Fix*, 103.

101. Ibid., 112–31; Musto and Korsmeyer, *Quest for Drug Control*, 87–105.

102. Interview between author and Griffith Edwards, 20 October 2004. For a

more detailed exploration of the introduction of therapeutic communities to the UK, see Mold and Berridge, *Voluntarism and Health,* Chapter 2.

103. TNA FD 7/1584, 'Drug dependence in the USA,' Bewley Report to the WHO on five and a half week visit to study drug dependence programmes, 1968; Thomas H. Bewley, "Drug dependence in the USA," *Bulletin on Narcotics,* 21 (1969): 13–20.

104. Bewley, "Conversation with Thomas Bewley," 887.

105. Mitcheson, "Drug clinics in the 1970s," 180.

106. Judson, *Heroin Addiction in Britain,* 88.

107. Ibid., 109–11; Spear, *Heroin Addiction Care and Control,* 237–38.

108. Mitcheson, "Drug clinics in the 1970s," 178.

109. Strang et al., "Prescribing heroin and other injectable drugs," 198.

110. Hartnoll et al., "Evaluation of heroin maintenance in controlled trial," 877–84; Mitcheson, "Drug clinics in the 1970s," 182–83.

111. Richard Hartnoll and Martin Mitcheson, "Conflicts in deciding treatment within drug dependency clinics," in D.J. West (ed.), *Problems of Drug Abuse in Britain: Papers Presented to the Cropwood Round Table Conference* (Cambridge: Institute of Criminology, 1978), 76.

112. Hartnoll et al., "Evaluation of heroin maintenance in controlled trial," 882–83.

113. Hartnoll and Mitcheson, "Conflicts in deciding treatment within drug dependency clinics," 76.

114. Ibid.

115. Hartnoll et al., "Evaluation of heroin maintenance in controlled trial," 884.

116. Mitcheson, "Drug clinics in the 1970s," 183.

117. Mitcheson states that this research was presented to staff at other clinics in 1976: see Mitcheson, "Drug clinics in the 1970s," 182. He and Hartnoll presented their findings at the Cropwood conference in 1977: see Hartnoll and Mitcheson, "Conflicts in deciding treatment within drug dependency clinics."

118. Interview with Mitcheson quoted in Trebach, *The Heroin Solution,* 193.

119. Stimson and Oppenheimer, *Heroin Addiction,* 218–19.

120. Ibid., 217.

121. Spear, *Heroin Addiction Care and Control,* 228–31.

122. Stimson and Oppenheimer, *Heroin Addiction,* 5; Spear, *Heroin Addiction Care and Control,* 247.

123. Mitcheson, "Drug clinics in the 1970s," 75; Hartnoll et al., "Evaluation of heroin maintenance in controlled trial," 883; interviews with doctors quoted in Stimson and Oppenheimer, *Heroin Addiction,* 219.

124. ACMD, *Treatment and Rehabilitation: Report of the Advisory Council on the Misuse of Drugs* (London: HMSO, 1982), 3.

125. Editorial "Drug addiction: British System failing," *Lancet* (9 January 1982): 83.

126. Mitcheson, "Drug clinics in the 1970s," 89.

127. Carol Smart, "Drug dependence units in England and Wales: the results of a national survey," *Drug and Alcohol Dependence,* 15 (1985): 139.

128. Lart, "HIV and English drugs policy," 66.

129. Philip H. Connell and John Strang, "The creation of the clinics: clinical demand and the formation of policy," in Strang and Gossop, *Heroin Addiction and Drug Policy,* 173.

130. For an account of the increasing controls placed over addicts and an example of a 'good behaviour contract,' see Stimson and Oppenheimer, *Heroin Addiction,* 101–13.

131. That is not to imply that a doctor taking on a role in social control is anything new. As Gareth Stedman Jones points out, 'social control' is a sufficiently

broad phrase to encompass all political and ideological institutions and their agents. See Gareth Stedman Jones, "Class expression versus social control? A critique of recent trends in the social history of leisure," *History Workshop Journal*, 4 (1977): 162–70. Other commentators have dealt more closely with the role medicine plays in social control. Revisiting the works of Talcott Parsons and others, Uta Gerhardt examines the relationship between sociology and medicine in the labelling of 'deviants' and the linkages this has to social control in Uta Gerhardt, "The dilemma of social pathology," in Dorothy Porter (ed.), *Social Medicine and Medical Sociology in the Twentieth Century* (Amsterdam: Rodopi, 1997), 137–64. Returning to the issue of social control and addiction, Trebach makes the point that doctors are agents of social control, and separating treatment and control in drug addiction treatment often sets up a false dichotomy. See Trebach, *The Heroin Solution*, 224.

132. On differences in early clinical practice at the DDUs, see Smart, "Social policy and drug dependence," 178.

133. Spear, *Heroin Addiction Care and Control*, 243; Mitcheson, "Drug clinics in the 1970s," 183; Bewley, "Interview with Thomas Bewley," 889.

134. Stimson and Oppenheimer, *Heroin Addiction*, 219.

135. This code of practice was drawn up by Connell and was reproduced in the *British Journal of Addiction* in 1991. See Philip H. Connell, "Document: treatment of drug dependent patients, 1968–1969," *British Journal of Addiction*, 86 (1991): 913–15. On peer pressure, see Smart, "Social policy and drug dependence," 178. Spear, *Heroin Addiction Care and Control*, 304.

136. Too much should not be read into the move from the DHSS to the Home Office; Spear claims this was simply because there were more parking spaces at the Home Office. Spear, *Heroin Addiction Care and Control*, 243.

137. Ibid., 242.

138. James Willis, Letter to the *British Medical Journal* (13 August 1983): 500.

139. Connell, "Drug dependence in Britain," 298; Connell, "Document: treatment of drug dependent patients," 914.

140. Spear, *Heroin Addiction Care and Control*, 243; Trebach, *The Heroin Solution*, 200.

141. Stimson and Oppenheimer, *Heroin Addiction*, 220.

142. ACMD, *Treatment and Rehabilitation*, 120.

143. Ibid., 51.

4—THE HEROIN EXPLOSION AND THE RE-INTERVENTION OF THE GENERALIST, 1980–1987

1. Robert Ashton, *This Is Heroin* (London: Sanctuary House, 2002), 136. The television advertisement is available to view on The National Archives website. See http://www.nationalarchives.gov.uk/films/1979to2006/filmpage_dummy.htm For copies of the print advertisements, see http://www.advertisingarchives.co.uk/

2. Ashton, *This Is Heroin*, 137; Davenport-Hines, *The Pursuit of Oblivion*, 375.

3. Ashton, *This Is Heroin*, 137.

4. Home Office, *Statistics of Drug Addicts Notified to the Home Office, United Kingdom, 1988* (London: HMSO, 1989).

5. Virginia Berridge, "AIDS and British drug policy: continuity or change?" 141.

6. *Sunday Times*, 4 May 1975, 14.

7. *Daily Telegraph*, 20 July 1979, 8.

8. *The Hansard Journal of Parliamentary Debates: Lords*, 30 October 1979, Vol. 402, 1979–1980: 353–56; *The Hansard Journal of Parliamentary Debates: Commons*, 21 December 1979, Vol. 976, 1979–1980: 1066–72.

9. *Hansard: Lords*, 30 October 1979: 353; *Hansard: Commons*, 21 December 1979: 1066.

10. ACMD, *Treatment and Rehabilitation*, 115.

11. Home Office, *Statistics of Drug Addicts, 1988*.

12. Ibid.

13. Spear, *Heroin Addiction Care and Control*, 272.

14. *Statistics of Drug Addicts Notified to the Home Office, 1988*.

15. Stimson, "British drug policies in the 1980s," 480. The ACMD also noted the inadequacy of data on drug users and suggested that the number notified to the Home Office only represented a fraction of the total, ACMD, *Treatment and Rehabilitation*, 4.

16. Ministry of Health, *Report of the Second Interdepartmental Committee on Heroin Addiction*, 8.

17. *Hansard: Lords*, 30 October 1979, 355.

18. Geoffrey Pearson, "Social deprivation, unemployment and patterns of heroin use," in Nick Dorn and Nigel South (eds), *A Land Fit For Heroin? Drug Policies, Prevention and Practice* (Basingstoke: Macmillan, 1987), 65–67; Spear, *Heroin Addiction Care and Control*, 273.

19. Geoffrey Pearson and Mark Gilman, "Local and regional variations in drug misuse: the British heroin epidemic of the 1980s," in Strang and Gossop, *Heroin Addiction and Drug Policy*, 102.

20. ACMD, *Treatment and Rehabilitation*, 25.

21. Gerry Stimson, "The war on heroin: British policy and the international trade in illicit drugs," in Dorn and South (eds), *A Land Fit for Heroin?* 39.

22. Pearson, "Social deprivation," 62–63.

23. Susanne MacGregor, "The public debate in the 1980s," in Susanne MacGregor (ed.), *Drugs in British Society: Responses to a Social Problem in the 1980s* (London: Routledge, 1989), 3.

24. Ibid., 4.

25. Kohn, *Narcomania*, 114.

26. *Yorkshire Post*, 29 June 1984, quoted in MacGregor, "The public debate in the 1980s," 4–5.

27. Pearson and Gilman, "Local and regional variations in drug misuse," 103, 106–11; Pearson, "Social deprivation, unemployment and patterns of heroin use," 62–63.

28. Edwards, *Matters of Substance*, 269.

29. Spear, *Heroin Addiction Care and Control*, 228, 271; ACMD, *Treatment and Rehabilitation*, 25.

30. Davenport-Hines, *The Pursuit of Oblivion*, 364; Robert Power, "Drug trends since 1968," in Strang and Gossop, *Heroin Addiction and Drug Policy*, 34–35.

31. ACMD, *Treatment and Rehabilitation*, 130.

32. Paul Griffiths, Michael Gossop and John Strang, "Chasing the dragon: the development of heroin smoking in the United Kingdom," in Strang and Gossop (eds), *Heroin Addiction and Drug Policy*, 124.

33. Stimson, "The war on heroin," 39–41; Roger Lewis, "Flexible hierarchies and dynamic disorder—the trading and distribution of illicit heroin in Britain and Europe, 1970–1990," in Strang and Gossop (eds), *Heroin Addiction and Drug Policy*, 42–65; Spear, *Heroin Addiction Care and Control*, 255–74.

34. Griffiths, Gossop and Strang, "Chasing the dragon," 125.

35. Ibid., 121.

36. Ibid.; Davenport-Hines, *The Pursuit of Oblivion*, 365.

37. Griffiths, Gossop and Strang, "Chasing the dragon," 128–29.

38. Power, "Drug trends since 1968," 31; Spear, *Heroin Addiction Care and Control*, 259–66.

39. Spear, *Heroin Addiction Care and Control*, 265.

40. Ibid., 255–59; Power, "Drug trends since 1968," 38–39.

41. A. Hamid Ghodse, "Casualty departments and the monitoring of drug dependence," *British Medical Journal* (1977): 1381–82.

42. Edwards, *Matters of Substance,* 36–37.

43. Anne Jamieson, Alan Glanz and Susanne MacGregor, *Dealing With Drug Misuse: Crisis Intervention in the City* (London: Tavistock, 1984), 15–19.

44. Editorial, "Drug addiction: time for reappraisal," *Lancet* (11 August 1979): 289.

45. Ghodse, "Casualty departments and the monitoring of drug dependence," 1381–82; David Turner, "The development of the voluntary sector: no further need for pioneers?" in Strang and Gossop (eds), *Heroin Addiction and Drug Policy,* 225; Mitcheson, "Drug clinics in the 1970s," 184.

46. Editorial, "Drug addiction: British System failing," *Lancet* (9 January 1982): 83.

47. MacGregor, "The public debate in the 1980s," 1–3.

48. Kohn, *Narcomania,* 119.

49. *The Times Index,* January-December 1985, 255–56.

50. *The Times Index,* January-December 1983, 301.

51. Kohn, *Narcomania,* 107. Stimson also notes that 1984 was the year that heroin became a major media issue. See Stimson, "British drug policies in the 1980s," 481.

52. Kohn, *Narcomania,* 109.

53. Cohen, *Folk Devils and Moral Panics.*

54. MacGregor, "The public debate in the 1980s," 1–5 and 8–9.

55. See Nick Dorn and Nigel South, "Introduction" in Dorn and South, *A Land Fit For Heroin?,* 2–3.

56. The Misuse of Drugs Act, 1971. *Public Acts and Measures of 1971,* Part 1, Chapters 1–49: 639–80.

57. Home Office, *Tackling Drug Misuse: A Summary of the Government's Strategy* (London: HMSO, 1985), Foreword.

58. Stimson, "The war on heroin," 43.

59. Massing, *The Fix,* 140.

60. Ibid., 174–90.

61. Davenport-Hines, *The Pursuit of Oblivion,* 46; Stimson, "The war on heroin," 43.

62. Courtwright, *Dark Paradise,* 176; Richard Hartnoll, "The international context," in Susanne MacGregor (ed.), *Drugs in British Society,* 36–51.

63. Stimson, "The war on heroin," 41–2. David Owen also gave a speech to the Society of Clinical Psychiatrists Research Fund on the need for a scientific strategy to curb the epidemic of drug 'abuse' in October 1985. See Owen, "Need for a scientific strategy."

64. MacGregor, "The public debate in the 1980s," 13.

65. House of Commons Social Services Committee, *Misuse of Drugs With Special Reference to the Treatment and Rehabilitation of Misusers of Hard Drugs, Session 1984–1985* (London: HMSO, 1984–1986); House of Commons Home Affairs Committee, *First Report From the Home Affairs Committee, Session 1985–1986: Misuse of Hard Drugs* (London: HMSO, 1985–86).

66. Social Services Committee, *Misuse of Drugs,* liii.

67. Editorial, "Drug addiction: British System failing," *Lancet* (9 January 1982): 83. *The Sunday Times* echoed these sentiments in 1983. See *The Sunday Times,* 27 February 1983, 18.

68. Rudolf Klein, *The Politics of the NHS* (Essex: Longman, 2nd ed., 1989) 201–4, 229–35.

69. Ibid., 229.

70. ACMD, *Treatment and Rehabilitation,* 26, 37.

71. DHSS, *Health Service Development: Services For Drug Misusers Health Circular*

(84) 14 and Local Authority Circular (84), 12 (London: DHSS, 1984). For an elaboration on 'Cinderella' services, see Christopher Ham, *Health Policy in Britain: The Politics and Organisation of the National Health Service* (Basingstoke: Macmillan, 3rd ed., 1992), 23–24 and Rob Baggott, *Health and Health Care in Britain* (Basingstoke: Macmillan, 2nd ed., 1998), 98.

72. Susanne MacGregor and Betsy Ettorre, "From treatment to rehabilitation —aspects of the evolution of British policy on the care of drug takers," in Dorn and South (eds), *A Land Fit For Heroin?* 145.

73. Angela Burr, "Increased sale of opiates on the blackmarket [sic.] in the Piccadilly area," *British Medical Journal* (24 September 1983): 883. Jayne Love and Michael Gossop, in their study of the workings of one London DDU between June and December 1983, found that waiting periods of approximately one month between each stage of treatment was not uncommon. See Love and Gossop, "The processes of referral and disposal," 438.

74. Social Services Committee, *Misuse of Drugs,* xxxv.

75. Editorial, "British System failing," 83.

76. John Strang, "Personal View," *British Medical Journal,* 283 (1 August 1981): 376.

77. Editorial, "British System failing," 83.

78. A.B. Robertson, letter to the *British Medical Journal,* 287 (9 July 1983): 126.

79. Ibid., 126.

80. ACMD, *Treatment and Rehabilitation,* 120.

81. Home Office, *Statistics of Drug Addicts Notified to the Home Office, 1988.*

82. Alan Glanz and Colin Taylor, "Findings of a national survey of the role of general practitioners in the treatment of opiate misuse: extent of contact with opiate misusers," *British Medical Journal,* 293 (16 August 1986): 427, 430.

83. Ibid., 430.

84. ACMD, *Treatment and Rehabilitation,* 51, 2.

85. Stimson, "Drug policies in the 1980s," 478.

86. Susanne MacGregor, "Choices for policy and practice," in *Drugs in British Society,* 173.

87. Spear, *Heroin Addiction Care and Control,* 276.

88. Rowdy Yates, "Treatment and Rehabilitation: report of the Advisory Council on the Misuse of Drugs, 1982. View from a street agency: money-shy," *British Journal of Addiction,* 78 (1983): 123–24.

89. Mike Ashton, "Doctors at war, part one," *Druglink* (May/June 1986): 13.

90. ACMD, *Treatment and Rehabilitation,* 3.

91. Ibid., 87–88.

92. Connell and Bewley are not referred to directly by Spear at this point, but as he goes on to list papers they presented as evidence for the way London DDU psychiatrists tried to preserve their monopoly on treatment, likely it is them to whom he refers. Spear, *Heroin Addiction Care and Control,* 276.

93. ACMD, *Treatment and Rehabilitation,* 3.

94. Ibid. An editorial in the *British Journal of Addiction* suggested that this report was not properly published but was available on demand from the DHSS. "Editorial: An informed and thinking basis for debate," *British Journal of Addiction,* 78 (1983): 113.

95. ACMD, *Treatment and Rehabilitation,* 5.

96. Ibid., 23–25.

97. Ibid., 26–29.

98. Ibid., 31.

99. Ibid., 34.

100. Ibid., 4, 34. For a discussion of the Kessel Committee and its findings, see Thom, *Dealing With Drink,* 120–25.

101. Thom, *Dealing With Drink,* 120.

102. ACMD, *Treatment and Rehabilitation,* 34.

103. Gerry Stimson, "Treatment and Rehabilitation: report of the Advisory Council on the Misuse of Drugs, 1982. Views of a sociologist: drug problems as an everyday part of our society," *British Journal of Addiction,* 78 (1983): 121.

104. Lart, "HIV and English Drugs Policy," 78.

105. ACMD, *Treatment and Rehabilitation,* 34, 36.

106. Stimson, "Views of a sociologist," 21.

107. ACMD, *Treatment and Rehabilitation,* 51.

108. Tony Slater, "Treatment and Rehabilitation: report of the Advisory Council on the Misuse of Drugs, 1982. View from a therapeutic community: the spirit of the thing," *British Journal of Addiction,* 78 (1983): 118.

109. Thom, *Dealing With Drink,* 123.

110. ACMD, *Treatment and Rehabilitation,* 51.

111. Ibid., 52–53.

112. Ibid., 53.

113. Ibid., 55–56.

114. Yates, "View from a street agency: money-shy," 124.

115. Anne Digby, *The Evolution of British General Practice, 1850–1948* (Oxford: Oxford University Press, 1999), 290–92.

116. Frank Honigsbaum, *The Division in British Medicine: A History of the Separation of General Practice From Hospital Care, 1911–1968* (London: Kogan Page, 1979), 2, 298–302.

117. Digby, *The Evolution of British General Practice,* 293–94.

118. Alan Glanz, "The fall and rise of the general practitioner," in Strang and Gossop, *Heroin Addiction and Drug Policy,* 154.

119. Margot Jefferys and Hessie Sachs, *Rethinking General Practice: Dilemmas in Primary Medical Care* (London: Tavistock, 1983), 46.

120. Glanz, "The fall and rise of the general practitioner," 155.

121. Jefferys and Sachs, *Rethinking General Practice,* 47.

122. Justin Tudor-Hart, *A New Kind of Doctor: The General Practitioner's Part in the Health of the Community* (London: Merlin Press, 1988), 93.

123. David Armstrong, "The emancipation of biographical medicine," *Social Science and Medicine,* 13A (1979): 5. For more information on the foundation of the RCGP, see J. Howie, "Research in general practice," in Irvine Loudon, J. Horder and Charles Webster (eds), *General Practice Under the National Health Service 1948–1997* (Oxford: Clarendon Press, 1998), 148–51.

124. For the early history of the patient-as-a-person movement, see Roy Porter, *The Greatest Benefit to Mankind: A Medical History of Humanity From Antiquity to the Present* (London: Harper Collins, 1997), 682–83; Armstrong, *The Political Anatomy of the Body,* 105–8.

125. Marshall Marinker, "'What is wrong' and 'how we know it': changing concepts of illness in General Practice," in *General Practice Under the NHS,* 74.

126. Armstrong, "The emancipation of biographical medicine," 5.

127. Marinker, "What is wrong," 73; Tudor-Hart, *A New Kind of Doctor,* 88.

128. Markiner, "What is wrong," 71.

129. Ibid., 78; Tudor-Hart, *A New Kind of Doctor,* 89.

130. Glanz, "The fall and rise of the general practitioner," 158–59.

131. John Strang, "A model service: turning the generalist on to drugs," in *Drugs in British Society,* 147.

132. Philip H. Connell and Martin Mitcheson, "Necessary safeguards when prescribing opioid drugs to addicts: experience of drug dependence clinics in London," *British Medical Journal,* 288 (10 March 1984): 767–69; Thomas H. Bewley, "Prescribing psychoactive drugs to addicts," *British Medical Journal* (16 August 1980): 497–98; Thomas H. Bewley and A. Hamid Ghodse, "Unacceptable face of private practice,"

British Medical Journal, 286 (11 June 1983): 1876–77; A. Hamid Ghodse, "Treatment of drug addiction in London," *Lancet* (19 March 1983): 636–38.

133. Connell and Mitcheson, "Necessary safeguards," 769.

134. Ann Dally, *A Doctor's Story* (Basingstoke: Macmillan, 1990), 62–69, 79–80, 83. The treatment policies of Dally are discussed in more detail in Chapter Five.

135. A.B.V. Bucknall, J. Roy Robertson and J.G. Strachan, "The use of psychiatric treatment services by heroin users from general practice," *British Medical Journal,* 292 (12 April 1986): 999.

136. Ibid., 999.

137. Ibid., 999.

138. A.B.V. Bucknall, J. Roy Robertson & K. Foster, "Medical facilities used by heroin users," *British Medical Journal,* 293 (8 November 1986): 1216.

139. Alan Glanz, "Findings of a national survey of the role of general practitioners in the treatment of opiate misuse: dealing with the opiate misuser," *British Medical Journal,* 293 (23 August 1986): 487.

140. Alan Glanz, "Findings of a national survey on the role of general practitioners in the treatment of opiate misuse: views on treatment," *British Medical Journal,* 293 (30 August 1986): 544.

141. Glanz and Taylor, "Extent of contact with opiate users," 427.

142. Glanz, "Views on treatment," 544.

143. Ibid., 544.

144. Glanz, "Dealing with the opiate misuser," 487.

5—DISPUTED TERRITORY

1. ACMD, *Treatment and Rehabilitation,* 54.

2. Editorial, "Drug addiction: British System failing," *Lancet* (9 Jan 1982): 83.

3. Strang, "Personal view," 972.

4. Dally, *A Doctor's Story,* 62. Ann Dally, "Personal view," *British Medical Journal,* 283 (26 September 1981): 857.

5. On the dispute over pay beds, see Charles Webster, *Health Services Since the War, Vol II: Government and Health Care, The National Health Service 1958–1979* (London: The Stationary Office, 1996), 620–27.

6. Joan Higgins, *The Business of Medicine: Private Healthcare In Britain* (Basingstoke: Macmillan, 1988), 185.

7. Connell, "Conversation with Philip Connell," 15.

8. Baggott, *Health and Health Care in Britain,* 161.

9. Ham, *Health Policy in Britain,* 46–47.

10. Ibid., 47.

11. Klein, *The Politics of the NHS,* 215.

12. Figures in Berridge, *Health and Society in Britain,* Table 4, 107–9.

13. Higgins, *The Business of Medicine,* 121.

14. Klein, *The Politics of the NHS,* 157–58.

15. Ibid., 154.

16. Contemporary Medical Archives Centre at the Wellcome Library for the History and Understanding of Medicine, London (hereafter CMAC), private papers of Dr Ann Dally, (hereafter PP/DAL) CMAC PP/DAL/E/4/12, Statement from Lyn Perry, Assistant Director of Release, with respect to Ann Dally, 27 January 1986.

17. Dally, *A Doctor's Story,* 85; Notices, *Lancet* (12 Dec 1981): 1358.

18. DHSS, *Guidelines of Good Clinical Practice in the Treatment of Drug Misuse* (London: DHSS, 1984) House of Commons, *Misuse of Drugs,* Evidence of AIDA, 27 February 1985, 108–24.

19. Dally, *A Doctor's Story,* 44, 57.

20. CMAC PP/DAL/E/17, Transcripts of the General Medical Council Professional Conduct Committee Hearing, 1986–1987, (hereafter GMC Hearing, 1986/7), 27 Jan 1987. Interview between author and Dr Ann Dally, 8 June 2005.

21. Dally, *A Doctor's Story,* 57–58.

22. Ibid., 62. See also Dally, "Personal view," 857.

23. CMAC PP/DAL/E/4/20, "Analysis of my addict practice," by Dally, prepared for her lawyers, January 1987.

24. CMAC PP/DAL/E/4/20, "Maintenance," by Dally, prepared for her lawyers, January 1987.

25. CMAC PP/DAL/E/4/22, Draft statement of Dr Ann Dally, 20 October 1986.

26. CMAC PP/DAL/E/4/17, GMC Hearing 1986/7, 26 January 1987.

27. Dally, *A Doctor's Story,* 80

28. CMAC PP/DAL/E/4/20, "Maintenance," by Dally, prepared for her lawyers, January 1987.

29. Ibid.

30. Dally, *A Doctor's Story,* 82.

31. Ibid., 79.

32. Aliases have been used where addicts' real names are mentioned. CMAC PP/DAL/E/4/11, Reply from "John" to Dally's letter of December 1985.

33. CMAC PP/DAL/E/4/11, Reply from "Mark" to Dally's letter of December 1985.

34. CMAC PP/DAL/E/4/11, Reply from "James" to Dally's letter of December 1985.

35. Dally, *A Doctor's Story,* 75, 78.

36. CMAC PP/DAL/E/4/20, "Analysis of my addict practice" by Dally, prepared for her lawyers, January 1987. CMAC PP/DAL/E/4/17, GMC Hearing 1986/7, 26 January 1987.

37. Higgins, *Business of Medicine,* 144.

38. CMAC PP/DAL/E/4/12, Statement of Annette Lingham, 20 November 1986. CMAC PP/DAL/E/4/9, Miscellaneous statements from patients, 1986. CMAC PP/DAL/E/4/20, "Frequency of my prescription" by Dally, prepared for her lawyers, 28 January 1987.

39. CMAC PP/DAL/E/2/4, GMC Hearing 1983, 5 July 1983.

40. Interview between author and Dally.

41. Dally, *A Doctor's Story,* 85.

42. Ann Dally, "Drug addicts in Piccadilly," letter to the *British Medical Journal,* 287 (22 October 1983): 1219.

43. Dally, *A Doctor's Story,* 85; Notices, *Lancet* (12 December 1981): 1358.

44. Dally, *A Doctor's Story,* 85.

45. CMAC PP/DAL/E/4/20, "Expansion on my skeleton document about the unpaid work I do and have done in relation to drug addiction," by Dally, prepared for her lawyers, 5 December 1986.

46. See CMAC PP/DAL/E/4/20, "List of witnesses, definite and possible," by Dally, prepared for her lawyers, 1986.

47. Dally, *A Doctor's Story,* 85

48. Lorraine Hewitt, "Drug clinics today," letter to the *Lancet* (30 April 1983): 990.

49. Anne Dally, 'Drug clinics today,' letter to the *Lancet* (28 May 1983): 1223

50. The members of AIDA in 1986 listed by Dally were: Dr Charles Cohen, status unknown; Dr Leighton Charles, private psychiatrist, stopped treating addicts in June 1986; Dr Patrick O'Connor, status unknown; Dr A.W. Beard, former NHS Consultant Psychiatrist at Middlesex Hospital, but then treating addicts privately; Dr Margaret McNair, private General Practitioner; Dr John Poncia, NHS consultant psychiatrist at various hospitals including Broadmoor, but also treated addicts privately; Dr Tessa Hare, NHS GP and Dr Badrawy, private practitioner, Harley Street.

See CMAC PP/DAL/E/4/20, List of AIDA members, 24 January 1987. Not included on this list, but a prominent member, was Dr Dale Beckett, a retired NHS consultant psychiatrist who also treated addicts privately. See CMAC PP/DAL/E/4/20, "List of witnesses, definite and possible," by Dally, prepared for her lawyers, 1986.

51. Dally, *A Doctor's Story*, 12.

52. CMAC PP/DAL/B/5/1/2, Letter from Ann Dally to Dr Dorothy Black, Senior Medical Officer at the DHSS, and representative of the DHSS to the Working Party on Drug Misuse, 26 March 1984.

53. Ibid.; Dally, *A Doctor's Story*, 130.

54. See CMAC PP/DAL/E/4/20, "List of witnesses, definite and possible," by Dally, prepared for her lawyers, 1986.

55. Dally, *A Doctor's Story*, 85.

56. Ann Dally, "Drug addiction and the independent practitioner," letter to the *Lancet* (23 January 1982): 228.

57. CMAC PP/DAL/E/4/20, "Expansion on my skeleton document about the unpaid work I do and have done in relation to drug addiction," by Dally, prepared for her lawyers, 5 December 1986; Dally, *A Doctor's Story*, 85–86.

58. Dally, *A Doctor's Story*, 100.

59. Spear, *Heroin Addiction Care and Control*, 287.

60. Ibid., 287.

61. CMAC PP/DAL/E/2/4, GMC Hearing 1983, 6 July 1983, 53.

62. Ann Dally, letter to the *Lancet*, "Drug clinics today" (28 May 1983): 1223–24.

63. CMAC PP/DAL/E/4/20, "Expansion on my skeleton document about the unpaid work I do and have done in relation to drug addiction," by Dally, prepared for her lawyers, 5 December 1986.

64. Ibid.

65. Dally, *A Doctor's Story*, 127.

66. CMAC PP/DAL/B/4/1/1/8, Association of Independent Doctors in Addiction comments on *Guidelines of Good Clinical Practice in the Treatment of Drug Misuse*, July 1985.

67. Social Services Committee, *Misuse of Drugs*, Evidence of AIDA, 27 February 1985, 108–24.

68. Ibid., 109, 110, 120–21.

69. Ibid., xxix, lvi.

70. Ibid., xxviii-xxx, vi

71. Ibid. Minutes of evidence, 6 February 1985, memorandum submitted by the Royal College of General Practitioners, 13–14; examination of witnesses, 15–21.

72. CMAC PP/DAL/E/4/20, "The drug clinic consultant group" by Dally, prepared for her lawyers, 18 October 1986.

73. CMAC PP/DAL/B/5/1/6, Dally's General Comments on the *Guidelines of Good Clinical Practice in the Treatment of Drug Misuse* sent to Dr Dorothy Black, DHSS, September 1984. CMAC PP/DAL/B/4/1/1/8, Association of Independent Doctors in Addiction comments on *Guidelines of Good Clinical Practice in the Treatment of Drug Misuse*, July 1985.

74. CMAC PP/DAL/B/4/1/1/8, Association of Independent Doctors in Addiction comments on *Guidelines of Good Clinical Practice in the Treatment of Drug Misuse*, July 1985.

75. "Rebellious GP who takes on rejected addicts," *General Practitioner* (12 August 1983): 21. Social Services Committee, *Misuse of Drugs*, 112–24.

76. CMAC PP/DAL/E/2/4, GMC Hearing 1983, written evidence of Dr A.W. Beard, 6 July 1983. CMAC PP/DAL/E/4/17, GMC Hearing 1986/7 evidence of Dr Dale Beckett, 27 January 1987, 3–13.

77. Spear, *Heroin Addiction Care and Control*, 214–18. Kohn, *Narcomania*, 100.

78. Spear, *Heroin Addiction Care and Control,* 214.

79. Editorial, *Lancet* (9 Jan 1982): 83.

80. Bewley and Ghodse, "Unacceptable face of private practice," 1877.

81. CMAC PP/DAL/E/4/17, GMC Hearing, 1986/7, 9 December 1986.

82. This was actually the second time Bewley attacked the treatment of addiction in private practice in an article in the *BMJ*; see also his 1980 article, Bewley, "Prescribing psychoactive drugs to addicts," 497–98.

83. A.B. Robertson, "Prescription of controlled drugs to addicts," letter to *British Medical Journal,* 287 (9 July 1983): 126.

84. Dale Beckett, "Prescription of controlled drugs to addicts," letter to *British Medical Journal,* 287 (9 July 1983): 127.

85. Dally, *A Doctor's Story,* 46–47.

86. Bewley, "Prescribing psychoactive drugs to addicts," 497. Bewley and Ghodse, "Unacceptable face of private practice," 1877. See also Editorial, *Lancet* (9 Jan 1982): 83.

87. Angela Burr, "The Piccadilly drug scene," *British Journal of Addiction,* 78 (1983): 5–19. Angela Burr, "Increased sale of opiates."

88. Burr, "Increased sale of opiates," 884.

89. Bewley and Ghodse, "Unacceptable face of private practice," 1877.

90. Editorial, "Drug dependence in Britain: a critical time," *Lancet* (27 August 1983): 493.

91. Bewley and Ghodse, "Unacceptable face of private practice," 1877.

92. Burr, "The Piccadilly drug scene," 8.

93. Stimson, "The war on heroin," 39–41.

94. Bewley and Ghodse, "Unacceptable face of private practice," 1877.

95. Dale Beckett, letter to *British Medical Journal,* 287 (9 July 1983): 27.

96. Spear, *Heroin Addiction Care and Control,* 288, 287.

97. Dally, *A Doctor's Story,* 115.

98. Bewley, "Conversation with Thomas Bewley," 890.

99. Connell, "Conversation with Philip Connell," 15.

100. Social Services Committee, *Misuse of Drugs* (6 March 1985) Evidence of Philip Connell, 125.

101. Spear, *Heroin Addiction Care and Control,* 283.

102. This can be seen, for example, in the reluctance of some psychiatrists to take on the treatment of addiction in the late 1960s. See Chapter 2.

103. Virginia Berridge, "Drug research in Britain: the relation between research and policy," in Virginia Berridge (ed.), *Drugs Research and Policy in Britain: A Review of the 1980s* (Aldershot: Avebury, 1990), 10.

104. Berridge, "AIDS and British drug policy," 141.

105. MacGregor et al., *Drug Services in England,* 45.

106. Margaret Stacey, *Regulating British Medicine: The General Medical Council* (Chichester: John Wiley & Sons, 1992), 15–17.

107. Ibid., 23.

108. Ibid., 56. This was also the view expressed in the GMC's Annual Report in 1987. See Russell G. Smith, *Medical Discipline: The Professional Conduct Jurisdiction of the General Medical Council, 1858–1990* (Oxford: Clarendon Press, 1994), 2.

109. Stacey, *Regulating British Medicine,* 56.

110. Lord Justice Scruton, 1930, quoted in GMC, *Professional Conduct and Discipline: Fitness to Prescribe, April 1985, Part I* [known as the 'Blue Book'] (GMC: London, 1985), 3.

111. Stacey, *Regulating British Medicine,* 57.

112. GMC, *Professional Conduct and Discipline: Fitness to Prescribe,* 12.

113. Stacey, *Regulating British Medicine,* 142.

114. Ibid., 142. GMC, *Professional Conduct and Discipline: Fitness to Prescribe,* 5.

115. GMC, *Professional Conduct and Discipline: Fitness to Prescribe*, 1.

116. Ministry of Health, *Report of the Departmental Committee on Morphine and Heroin Addiction*, 26.

117. Ministry of Health, *Report of the Interdepartmental Committee On Drug Addiction*, 12; Berridge, *Opium and the People*, 281; Spear, *Heroin Addiction Care and Control*, 45; Philip T. Bean, "Policing the medical profession: the use of tribunals," in Whynes and Bean, *Policing and Prescribing*, 62.

118. Ministry of Health, *Report of the Interdepartmental Committee On Drug Addiction*, 12. For more information on why Brain did not consider tribunals to be necessary, see Spear, *Heroin Addiction Care and Control*, 107–10.

119. Ministry of Health, *Report of the Second Interdepartmental Committee On Drug Addiction*, 11. For an account of the discussions that led to this recommendation, see Spear, *Heroin Addiction Care and Control*, 137–41.

120. Ministry of Health, *Report of the Second Interdepartmental Committee On Drug Addiction*, 11.

121. Smart, "Social policy and drug dependence," 174–75.

122. Lord Cohen's Presidential Address to the GMC in 1969 quoted in Ibid., 175.

123. *Misuse of Drugs Act, 1971*; Bean, "Policing the medical profession," 63–64.

124. GMC, *Professional Conduct and Discipline: Fitness to Prescribe*, Part III: Considerations and forms of professional misconduct that may lead to disciplinary proceedings; Spear, *Heroin Addiction Care and Control*, 62, 64, 268.

125. Social Services Committee, *Misuse of Drugs*, minutes of evidence from the GMC, 20 February 1985, 68–69.

126. ACMD, *Treatment and Rehabilitation*, 61.

127. Ibid., 61.

128. Social Services Committee, *Misuse of Drugs*, xxiii; CMAC PP/DAL/E/2/4, GMC Hearing 6 July 1983, 57.

129. Social Services Committee, *Misuse of Drugs*, xxiv, 70–71.

130. See figures quoted above for Home Office tribunals and Smith, *Medical Discipline*, 104, for a graph illustrating the upward trend in number of cases involving the prescription of drugs that came before the GMC.

131. Ashton, "Doctors at war, part one," 15.

132. CMAC PP/DAL/E/2/4, GMC Hearing 5 July 1983.

133. Ibid., 5 July 1983.

134. Ibid., 6 July 1983.

135. Ibid., 5 July 1983; Ibid., 6 July 1983.

136. Ibid., 6 July 1983.

137. Ibid., 6 July 1983.

138. CMAC PP/DAL/E/2/11, "Some thoughts on a lost case," by Dally, 18 July 1983. The assertion that the charge was changed to allow the prosecution to win the case was also reported by Michael O'Donnell in his column in the *British Medical Journal*. See Michael O'Donnell, "One man's burden," *British Medical Journal*, 287 (1 Oct 1983): 990.

139. CMAC PP/DAL/E/2/4, GMC Hearing 6 July 1983.

140. Ibid.

141. Diana Brahams, "Medicine and the law: no right of appeal against GMC finding of serious professional misconduct without suspension or erasure," *Lancet* (22 October 1983): 979.

142. Interview with Jean Robinson quoted in Stacey, *Regulating British Medicine*, 196.

143. O'Donnell, "One man's burden," 990.

144. Ibid.; Dally, *A Doctor's Story*, 122.

145. *Guardian*, 8 July 1983, 2.

146. O'Donnell, "One man's burden"; Editorial, "GMC Professional Conduct Committee: right of appeal," *Lancet* (22 Oct 1983): 951.

147. John Walton, "Verdict of the professional conduct committee," letter to the *British Medical Journal,* 287 (29 Oct 1983): 1300.

148. Mike Ashton, "Doctors at war—part two," *Druglink* (July/August 1986): 15.

149. Ibid., 14.

150. Dally believed there was a 'campaign' against her, led by what she termed the 'drug dependency mafia.' See Dally, *A Doctor's Story,* 139.

6—DISPUTED METHODS

1. A description of her treatment of 'Khalid' (not his real name) was given by Dally in her book, *A Doctor's Story,* 145–47, and at her second GMC hearing. See CMAC PP/DAL/E/4/17, GMC Hearing, 1986/7, 26 January 1987.

2. John Marks, "Opium, the religion of the people," *Lancet* (22 June 1985): 1439.

3. John Strang, "Abstinence or abundance—what goal?" *British Medical Journal,* 289 (8 September 1984): 604.

4. Armstrong, "The emancipation of biographical medicine," 5.

5. Berridge, "Morality and medical science," 79.

6. Smart, "DDUs in England and Wales: the results of a national survey," 138–39.

7. Strang, "Abstinence or abundance—what goal?" 604.

8. F.A. Jenner and P.V. Gill, "Helping heroin addicts kick the habit," letter to the *British Medical Journal,* 291 (3 August 1985): 345.

9. Social Services Committee, *Misuse of Drugs,* Evidence of Dr Connell, March 1985, 126.

10. CMAC PP/DAL/B/4/1/5, Minutes of the 1985 meeting of the Northern Drug Addiction Psychiatrists (DAPS) held at Liverpool Drug Dependence Clinic, 8 March 1985.

11. See Chapter 3.

12. J.S. Madden, "Editorial: The decline of long-term prescribing to opioid users in the United Kingdom," *British Journal of Addiction,* 82 (1987): 457–459, p. 457.

13. Burr, "The Piccadilly drug scene"; Burr, "Increased sale of opiates on the blackmarket in the Piccadilly area."

14. See, for example: Bewley, "Prescribing psychoactive drugs to addicts" and Gardner and Connell, "Necessary safeguards."

15. Jenner and Gill, "Helping heroin addicts kick the habit," 344.

16. ACMD, *Treatment and Rehabilitation,* 28.

17. Strang, "Abstinence or abundance—what goal?" 604.

18. CMAC PP/DAL/B/4/1/5, Minutes of the 1985 meeting of the Northern Drug Addiction Psychiatrists (DAPS) held at Liverpool Drug Dependence Clinic, 8 March 1985.

19. Hartnoll et al., "Evaluation of heroin maintenance in controlled trial," 883.

20. Strang, "Abstinence or abundance—what goal?" 604.

21. Connell was a consultant advisor to the DHSS on addiction, 1971–1986; Vice-President of the Royal College of Psychiatrists, 1979–1981, and a member of the GMC from 1979 until 1990. Bewley was a consultant advisor to the DHSS on addiction from 1972–1981 and for the WHO 1969–1978. He was also president of the Royal College of Psychiatrists from 1984 until 1987. Both men sat on the ACMD, and Connell was its chair from 1982 to 1988.

22. CMAC PP/DAL/E/4/18, Personal account of the case by Dally, 1986/7, 11 June 1987, p. 262; CMAC PP/DAL/E/4/20, 'The drug clinic consultant group,' by Dally, prepared for her lawyers, 18 October 1986; Dally, *A Doctor's Story,* 139.

23. Teaching hospitals had higher status than non-teaching hospitals, retaining a greater degree of autonomy from national structures through their own boards of governors. See Porter, *The Greatest Benefit to Mankind,* 653; Klein, *The Politics of the NHS,* 20–21.

24. Berridge discusses the greater role GPs played in the treatment of addiction in "AIDS and British drug policy," 146–47 and in Virginia Berridge, *AIDS in the UK: The Making of Policy, 1981–1994* (Oxford: Oxford University Press, 1996), 92.

25. CMAC PP/DAL/E/4/17 GMC Hearing, 1986/7, 29 January 1987.

26. Basson mentioned regional differences in the pattern of drug addiction and the impact that this had on local demands in J.V. Basson, "Attitudes to drug abuse," *British Medical Journal,* 292 (29 March 1986): 848.

27. Marks, "Opium, the religion of the people," 1440.

28. CMAC PP/DAL/B/4/1/5, Minutes of the 1986 meeting of the Northern Drug Addiction Psychiatrists (DAPS) held at the Royal Edinburgh Hospital, 7 March 1986.

29. Marks, "Opium, the religion of the people," 1440.

30. Bucknall, Robertson and Strachan, "Use of psychiatric drug treatment services by heroin users from general practice," 999.

31. Social Services Committee, *Misuse of Drugs,* Evidence of AIDA, 27 February 1985, 114.

32. Ibid., 119.

33. CMAC PP/DAL/B/4/2/8, Cindy Fazey, "The evaluation of Liverpool Drug Dependency Clinic," 29–30.

34. Dally, *A Doctor's Story,* 82.

35. CMAC PP/DAL/B/4/2/8, Fazey, "The evaluation of Liverpool Drug Dependency Clinic," 29–30

36. Ibid., 61

37. Social Services Committee, *Misuse of Drugs,* Evidence of AIDA, 27 February 1985, 114.

38. Alan Petersen and Deborah Lupton, *The New Public Health: Health and Self in the Age of Risk* (London: Sage Publications, 1996): 4–5.

39. Strang, "Abstinence or abundance," 604.

40. Bewley, "Advantages of special centres," *British Medical Journal* (20 May 1967): 498.

41. Peter A.L. Chapple, "Treatment in the community," *British Medical Journal* (20 May 1967): 500.

42. Lart, "HIV and English Drugs Policy," 60.

43. See Marinker, "'What is wrong' and 'how we know it,'" 74–77; Armstrong, "The emancipation of biographical medicine," 5–7.

44. Jefferys and Sachs, *Rethinking General Practice,* 50.

45. Porter, *The Greatest Benefit to Mankind,* 671.

46. Dally, *A Doctor's Story,* 61.

47. A few studies of patients attending DDUs do exist, such as Margaret Sheenan, Edna Oppenheimer and Colin Taylor, "Why drug users sought help from one London clinic," *British Journal of Addiction,* 81 (1986): 765–75, but as this was based on only 50 patients attending one clinic, it could not be called comprehensive.

48. Armstrong, "The emancipation of biographical medicine," 6–7.

49. Tudor-Hart, *A New Kind of Doctor,* 89.

50. Ibid., 99–107; Marikner, "'What is wrong' and 'how we know it,'" 84–87.

51. Glanz, "Views on treatment," 544.

52. Spear, *Heroin Addiction Care and Control,* 39–41.

53. Dally, *A Doctor's Story,* 147–49.

54. Ibid., 134, 149.

55. CMAC PP/DAL/E/4/22, Letter from the GMC to Ann Dally, 2 September 1986.

56. Dally, *A Doctor's Story*, 147.

57. CMAC PP/DAL/B/4/2/5, "Some problems in the treatment of heroin addiction," by Dally, May 1984.

58. Ibid.; CMAC PP/DAL/E/4/20, "The drug clinic consultant group," by Dally, prepared for her lawyers, 18 October 1986.

59. CMAC PP/DAL/B/4/2/5 "Some problems in the treatment of heroin addiction," by Dally, May 1984.

60. Ibid.; CMAC PP/DAL/E/4/20, "The drug clinic consultant group."

61. CMAC PP/DAL/E/4/20, "The drug clinic consultant group."

62. CMAC PP/DAL/E/4/20, "Politics and the GMC," by Dally, prepared for her lawyers, 15 October 1986.

63. CMAC PP/DAL/E/4/20, "The drug clinic consultant group."

64. CMAC PP/DAL/E/4/18, Personal account of the case by Dally, 1986/7, 2 September 1986.

65. Ibid., 20 November 1986.

66. The journalist was Nick Davies. He is still interested in drug issues. For references to his part in Dally's case, see Ibid., 24 October 1986; 22 November 1986. The private detective is named in Ibid., 7 December 1986. Ed Vulliamy also commented on the use of a private detective in the Dally case in an article in the *Guardian*, 26 January 1987, 17.

67. Dally discussed how the GMC was able to initiate and investigate cases using private detectives in a letter to the *British Medical Journal*. See Ann Dally, "Letter: Investigating the GMC," *British Medical Journal*, 298 (3 June 1989): 1518.

68. Stacey, *Regulating British Medicine*, 57, 62.

69. Ibid., 150.

70. While there are figures indicating what proportion of charges of serious professional misconduct were based on suspected irresponsible prescription, there are no corresponding figures indicating the origin of these charges. But, as these cases relied on detailed knowledge of prescription practices, it is likely many came from information passed on by the Home Office.

71. GMC Annual Report, 1985. Quoted in Spear, *Heroin Addiction Care and Control*, 289.

72. Dally, *A Doctor's Story*, 149–50; CMAC PP/DAL/ Box 7, Letter from Ann Dally to H.B. Spear, 4 March 1986; CMAC PP/DAL/ Box 7, Letter from H.B. Spear to Ann Dally, 11 March 1986.

73. A full transcript of the hearing can be found in CMAC, PP/DAL/E/4/17.

74. CMAC PP/DAL/E/4/17, GMC Hearing, 9 December 1986.

75. CMAC PP/DAL/E/4/17, GMC Hearing, 30 January 1987.

76. Ibid.

77. CMAC PP/DAL/E/4/17, GMC Hearing, 26 January 1987.

78. CMAC PP/DAL/E/4/17, GMC Hearing, 30 January 1987.

79. CMAC PP/DAL/E/4/17, GMC Hearing, 10 December 1986.

80. Ibid.

81. Ibid.

82. Ibid. See CMAC PP/DAL/E/4/12, Statement of Annette Lingham, 20 November 1986, for the prices of Dally's treatment sessions.

83. CMAC PP/DAL/E/4/17, GMC Hearing, 10 December 1986.

84. DHSS, *Guidelines of Good Clinical Practice in the Treatment of Drug Misuse*.

85. See Dally, *A Doctor's Story*, 127–32; and CMAC PP/DAL/B/5/1, DHSS Working Group On Drug Dependence, 1983.

86. DHSS, *Guidelines of Good Clinical Practice in the Treatment of Drug Misuse*.

87. Sarah Mars, "Peer pressure and imposed consensus: the making of the

1984 *Guidelines of Good Clinical Practice in the Treatment of Drug Misuse,"* in Virginia Berridge (ed.), *Making Health Policy: Networks in Research and Policy After 1945* (Amsterdam: Rodopi, 2005), 149, 175.

88. CMAC PP/DAL/E/4/17, GMC Hearing, 27 January 1987.

89. Ibid.

90. CMAC PP/DAL/E/4/17, GMC Hearing, 28 January 1987.

91. CMAC PP/DAL/E/4/17, GMC Hearing, 29 January 1987.

92. Ibid.

93. CMAC PP/DAL/E/4/17, GMC Hearing, 28 January 1987.

94. Ibid.; CMAC PP/DAL/E/4/17, GMC Hearing, 27 January 1987.

95. CMAC PP/DAL/E/4/17, GMC Hearing, 27 January 1987.

96. CMAC PP/DAL/E/4/17, GMC Hearing, 26 January 1987.

97. CMAC PP/DAL/E/4/17, GMC Hearing, 27 January 1987.

98. CMAC PP/DAL/E/4/17, GMC Hearing, 11 December 1986.

99. Ibid.

100. CMAC PP/DAL/E/4/20, "The drug clinic consultant group"; CMAC PP/DAL/E/4/18, Personal account of the case by Dally, 1986/7, 22 November 1986; CMAC PP/DAL/E/4/20, "Number of points Dally wishes to raise: Connell and Bewley as witnesses," 25 November 1986.

101. CMAC PP/DAL/E/4/17, GMC Hearing, 30 January 1987.

102. Ibid.

103. Stacey, *Regulating British Medicine,* 164.

104. Diana Brahams, "'Serious professional misconduct' in relation to private treatment of drug dependence," *Lancet* (7 February 1987): 340–41.

105. Ibid., 340–41.

106. Smith, *Medical Discipline,* 72.

107. Ibid., 71.

108. CMAC PP/DAL/E/4/18, Personal account of the case by Dally, 1986/7, 31 January 1987; Dally, *A Doctor's Story,* 216.

109. See particularly, *Lancet* (28 February 1987): 509–10 and *British Medical Journal,* 294 (28 February 1987): 573–74. Carmel Fitzsimons, *The Observer,* 25 January 1987, 6. Ed Vulliamy, *The Guardian,* 26 January 1987, 17.

110. CMAC PP/DAL/E/4/18, Personal account of the case by Dally, 1986/7, 13 November 1986, 7 December 1986, 8 December 1986; Dally, *A Doctor's Story,* 164–69; CMAC PP/DAL/E/4/1, Articles and newspaper cuttings, 1974–1987, Miranda Ingram, "Why women doctors are in the dock," *Cosmopolitan,* (August 1987): 8–10.

111. Clare Dyer, "Dr Ann Dally's continued brushes with the GMC," *British Medical Journal,* 295 (26 September 1987): 774.

112. Berridge, "AIDS and British drug policy: continuity or change?" 141.

7—THE IMPACT OF HIV/AIDS ON HEROIN ADDICTION TREATMENT, 1984–1994

1. J. Roy Robertson et al., "Epidemic of AIDS related virus (HTLV-III/LAV) infection among intravenous drug abusers," *British Medical Journal,* 292 (1986): 527–29.

2. Gerry Stimson, "AIDS and injecting drug use in the United Kingdom, 1987–1993: the policy response and the prevention of the epidemic," *Social Science and Medicine,* 41.5 (1995): 701.

3. Figures quoted in Ibid., 707.

4. ACMD, *AIDS and Drug Misuse: Part One* (London: HMSO, 1988): 1.

5. Interview with Dr Dorothy Black, DHSS, quoted in Berridge, *AIDS in the UK,* 222.

6. John Strang, "The roles of prescribing," in John Strang and Gerry Stimson (eds), *AIDS and Drug Misuse: The Challenge For Policy and Practice in the 1990s* (London and New York: Routledge, 1990), 144–46.

7. Gerry Stimson, "Revising policy and practice: new ideas about the drugs problem," in John Strang and Gerry Stimson (eds), *AIDS and Drug Misuse,* 128–29.

8. Paula A. Treichler, "AIDS, gender and biomedical discourse," in Elizabeth Fee and Daniel M. Fox (eds), *AIDS: The Burdens of History* (Berkeley, Los Angeles and London: University of California Press, 1988), 197; Gerald M. Oppenheimer, "In the eye of the storm: the epidemiological construction of AIDS," in Ibid., 270; Randy Shilts, *And The Band Played On: Politics, People and the AIDS Epidemic* (New York: St. Martin's Press, 1987), 53–112.

9. Berridge, *AIDS in the UK,* 15.

10. Ibid., 28; Treichler, "AIDS, gender and biomedical discourse," 198.

11. Treichler, "AIDS, gender and biomedical discourse," 198.

12. Berridge, *AIDS in the UK,* 45–46.

13. Treichler, "AIDS, gender and biomedical discourse," 192–95; Berridge, *AIDS in the UK,* 90–91.

14. Stimson, "AIDS and injecting drug use," 700.

15. Roy Robertson, "The Edinburgh epidemic: a case study," in Strang and Stimson, *AIDS and Drug Misuse,* 95–107.

16. Roy Robertson, *Heroin, AIDS and Society* (London: Hodder and Stoughton, 1987), 81.

17. Berridge, *AIDS in the UK,* 93.

18. Scottish Home and Health Department, *HIV Infection in Scotland: Report of the Scottish Committee on HIV Infection and Intravenous Drug Misuse,* (Edinburgh: Scottish Home and Health Department, 1986).

19. Stimson, "AIDS and injecting drug use in the UK," 702.

20. Gerry Stimson, et al., "Syringe exchange schemes for drug users in England and Scotland," *British Medical Journal,* 296 (18 June 1988): 1717–19.

21. A.R. Moss, "Editorial: AIDS and intravenous drug use: the real heterosexual epidemic," *British Medical Journal,* 294 (14 February 1987): 390.

22. ACMD, *AIDS and Drug Misuse: Part One,* 5.

23. Ibid., 82.

24. Ibid., 5; Berridge, *AIDS in the UK,* 221; Berridge, "AIDS and British drug policy," 144.

25. ACMD, *AIDS and Drug Misuse: Part One,* 1, 17, 75.

26. Ibid., 17.

27. Stimson, "Revising policy and practice," 125, 124.

28. *Drug Addiction: The Second Report of the Interdepartmental Committee,* 8.

29. Berridge also cites an observer who drew parallels between Brain and Runciman. See Berridge, "AIDS and British drug policy," 148.

30. Alan Glanz, "Editorial: Drug misuse and AIDS prevention: policy on the right track," *British Journal of Addiction,* 83 (1988): 1237.

31. Berridge, "AIDS and British drug policy," 148.

32. Ibid., 149; Berridge, *Opium and the People,* 75–109.

33. Ministry of Health, *Second Report of the Interdepartmental Committee on Heroin Addiction,* 8.

34. Alan Petersen and Deborah Lupton, *The New Public Health: Health and Self in the Age of Risk* (London: Sage, 1996), ix.

35. Figures taken from Berridge, *AIDS in the UK,* 338.

36. ACMD, *AIDS and Drug Misuse,* 41–42.

37. John Strang, "AIDS and drug misuse in the UK: achievements, failings and new harm reduction opportunities," *Heroin Addiction and the British System, Vol 1,* 200.

38. Janie Sheridan, "Needle exchange in Britain," in Strang and Gossop, *Heroin Addiction and the British System, Vol 2,* 150–51.

39. Glanz, "Editorial: Drug misuse and AIDS prevention," 1237.

40. White, *Slaying the Dragon,* 292.

41. Courtwright, *Dark Paradise,* 175.

42. Gerry Stimson, Martin Donoghoe, Kate Dolan and Lindsey Alldritt, "A volatile time for British drug policies: commentary on the editorial by Alan Glanz," *British Journal of Addiction,* 83 (1988): 1241.

43. Ernst Buning, "The role of harm reduction programmes in curbing the spread of HIV by drug injectors," in Strang and Stimson, *AIDS and Drug Misuse,* 154.

44. Sheridan, "Needle and syringe exchange," 148.

45. Berridge, *AIDS in the UK,* 142.

46. Interview between author, Virginia Berridge and Bill Nelles, March 2006.

47. Peter McDermott, "The great Mersey experiment: the birth of harm reduction," in *Heroin Addiction and the British System, Vol 1,* Strang and Gossop, 137–56.

48. Ibid., 142–45.

49. Gerry Stimson, "Minimising harm from drug use," in Strang and Gossop, *Heroin Addiction and Drug Policy: The British System,* 250.

50. Ministry of Health, *Departmental Committee on Morphine and Heroin Addiction,* 9–13.

51. McDermott, "The great Mersey experiment," 139.

52. Stimson, "Minimising harm from drug use," 251–52.

53. Alex Mold, "'The Welfare Branch of the Alternative Society'? The Work of Drug Voluntary Organisation Release, 1967–1978," *Twentieth Century British History,* 17:1 (2006): 50–73.

54. Modern Records Centre, University of Warwick, MSS.171/3/44/1, The Release Drug Hotline, draft press release, 1975.

55. ACMD, *AIDS and Drug Misuse: Part One,* 47–48.

56. John Strang and Gerry Stimson, "The impact of HIV: forcing the process of change," in Strang and Stimson (eds), *AIDS and Drug Misuse,* 11.

57. Jon E. Zibbell, "Can the lunatics actually take over the asylum? Reconfiguring subjectivity and neo-liberal governance in contemporary British drug treatment policy," *International Journal of Drug Policy,* 15 (2004): 57.

58. Virginia Berridge, "AIDS and the rise of the patient? Activist organisation and HIV/AIDS in the UK in the 1980s and 1990s," *Medizin Gesellschaft und Geshichte,* 21 (2002): 113.

59. Interview between author and Andria Efthimou Morduant, drug user activist, December 2005.

60. Berridge, "AIDS and the rise of the patient?" 109.

61. ACMD, *AIDS and Drug Misuse: Part One,* 47, 48.

62. Ibid., 47–48.

63. CMAC PP/DAL/E/4/18, Personal account of the case by Dally, 1986/7, 28 March 1987.

64. Ibid.; MacGregor, "Choices for policy and practice," 194.

65. *The Guardian,* 6 May 1987; *Today,* 6 May 1987; *Mail on Sunday,* 19 May 1987, p. 5; "AIDS prompts drug services review," *Druglink,* July/August 1987.

66. "Editorial—Management of drug addicts: hostility, humanity and pragmatism," *Lancet* (9 May 1987): 1068–69.

67. Royal College of Psychiatrists, *Drug Scenes: A Report on Drugs and Drug Dependence by the Royal College of Psychiatrists* (London: Royal College of Psychiatrists, 1987): 188–89.

68. Strang, "The roles of prescribing," 144–46.

69. Strang, "Abstinence or abundance—what goal?" 604.

70. Strang, "The roles of prescribing," 147–48.

71. Ibid., 149.

72. Stimson, "AIDS and injecting drug use in the UK," 704.

73. S. Gillam et al., "Evaluating the Drug Dependency Unit," *Public Health,* 106 (1992): 214, 211.

74. Steve Cranfield et al., "HIV and drugs services—the challenge of change," in Strang and Gossop, *Heroin Addiction and British Policy,* 322.

75. Ibid., 326.

76. Ibid., 323.

77. Strang, "The roles of prescribing," 146.

78. For a more thorough exploration of the impact of the CFI, see Alex Mold and Virginia Berridge, "Crisis and opportunity in drug Policy: changing the direction of British drug services in the 1980s," *Journal of Policy History,* 19:1 (2007): 29–48.

79. MacGregor et al., *Assessment of the CFI,* 45.

80. Stimson, "British drug policies in the 1980s," 477.

81. Jerome Jaffe in 1986 Okey Lecture to the Institute of Psychiatry, quoted in Berridge, "AIDS and drug policy," 143.

82. These are just some of the conditions associated with HIV and AIDS. For a more detailed account of these and how they affected drug users in particular, see R. Brettle, Michael Farrell and John Strang, "Clinical features of HIV infection and AIDS in drug takers," in Strang and Stimson, *AIDS and Drug Misuse,* 38–53 and M. Riccio and D. Hawkins, "Neuropsychiatric complications of HIV infection," in Ibid., 54–63.

83. Gerry Stimson, "Revising policy and practice: new ideas about the drugs problem," in Strang and Stimson, *AIDS and Drug Misuse,* 128–29.

84. Berridge, "AIDS and British drug policy," 147.

85. On the impact of AIDS on genitourinary medicine, see Berridge, *AIDS in the UK,* 173–74.

86. See Michael W. Adler, "Editorial: AIDS and intravenous drug abuse," *British Journal of Addiction,* 81 (1986): 307–10, and Moss, "Editorial: AIDS and intravenous drug use: the real heterosexual epidemic."

87. ACMD, *AIDS and Drug Misuse: Part One,* 81.

88. ACMD, *Treatment and Rehabilitation,* 87–88.

89. ACMD, *AIDS and Drug Misuse: Part One,* 1.

90. Ibid., 30.

91. Ibid., 49–50.

92. ACMD, *Treatment and Rehabilitation,* 56; DHSS, *Guidelines,* 17, 8.

93. Department of Health, *Drug Misuse and Dependence: Guidelines on Clinical Management* (London: HMSO, 1991): 18.

94. Ibid., 20.

95. Ibid., 22.

96. Berridge, "AIDS and British drug policy: continuity or change?" 152.

97. Stimson, "Revising policy and practice," 129.

98. MacGregor, "Choices for policy and practice," 197.

99. At a time when the reported cases of HIV are double what they were in the mid-1980s, some hesitation has to be expressed about referring to the present as the 'post' AIDS era, but at least in political terms, AIDS has largely disappeared from the drugs agenda. For the most recent figures on HIV prevalence, see Health Protection Agency, *A Complex Picture: HIV and Other Sexually Transmitted Infections in the United Kingdom, 2006* (London: Health Protection Agency, 2006).

8—TREATMENT WORKS?

1. Transcript of the Prime Minister's broadcast: 'Drugs,' 18 February 2000. Downloaded from http://www.pm.gov.uk/output/Page317.asp

2. Gerry Stimson, "'Blair declares war': the unhealthy state of British drug policy," *International Journal of Drug Policy,* 11 (2000): 260.

3. For more information on DTTOs, see Emily Finch and Mike Ashton, "Treatment to order: the new drug treatment and testing orders," in Strang and Gossop, *Heroin Addiction and the British System Vol 2,* 187–97.

4. Home Office, *Updated Drug Strategy* (London: The Stationary Office, 2002): 51.

5. Michael Gossop, *Drug Misuse Treatment and Reductions in Crime: Findings From the National Treatment Outcome Research Study (NTORS)* (London: NTA, 2005), 5.

6. See, for example, *The Guardian,* 21 November 2006; and Tom Carnwarth, "Doctors at war," *Druglink,* 22:1 (January/February 2007): 23.

7. Harry Shapiro, "A New Year Message," *Druglink,* 22 (January/February 2007): 1.

8. This figure includes funds spent on drug treatment by local authorities in addition to the pooled treatment budget. For figures and more information, see http://www.drugs.gov.uk

9. DrugScope Helpfinder Treatment Database, available at http://drugscope.soutron.com/helpfinder.asp; Susanne MacGregor, et al., *Drugs Services in England and the Impact of the Central Funding Initiative* (London: ISDD, 1991): 6.

10. NDTC Programme, 2006. Also available from http://www.exchange supplies. org/conferences/2006_NDTC/programme.html

11. See http://www.exchangesupplies.org/about/about.html

12. Department of Trade and Industry, *Social Enterprise: A Strategy for Success* (London: DTI, 2002), 7.

13. On the changing role of the voluntary sector around health in general and drugs in particular, see Mold and Berridge, *Voluntarism and Health.*

14. See http://www.exchangesupplies.org/conferences/2006_NDTC/delegates. html

15. NDTC Programme, 2006.

16. See http://www.schering-plough.com/

17. Participant observation by author, March 2006. For a list of the companies who had stands at the NDTC conference and links to their websites, see http://www.exchangesupplies.org/conferences/2006_NDTC/sponsors.html

18. Wayne Hall, "Editorial: avoiding potential misuses of addiction brain science," *Addiction,* 101 (2006): 1529.

19. See, for example, Jacky Law, *Big Pharma: How the World's Biggest Drug Companies Market Illness* (London: Constable and Robinson, 2006); John Abramson, *Overdosed America: The Broken Promise of American Medicine* (London: Harper Collins, 2004); Marcia Angell, *The Truth About Drug Companies: How They Deceive us and What to do About It* (New York: Random House 2004); and Ray Monyhian and Alan Cassels, *Selling Sickness: How the World's Biggest Pharmaceutical Companies Are Turning Us All Into Patients* (New York: Nation Books, 2005). For an overview of this literature, see Howard I. Kushner, "The other war on drugs: the pharmaceutical industry, evidence-based medicine and clinical practice," *Journal of Policy History,* 19.1 (2007): 49–70.

20. Royal College of General Practitioners, *Guidance for the use of Buprenorphine for the Treatment of Opioid Dependence in Primary Care* (RCGP: London, 2004). It is interesting to note that this guidance was produced with the help of an 'educational grant' from Schering Plough, the makers of Subutex (buprenorphine).

21. "Druglink Fact Sheet: Subutex and Methadone," *Druglink* (January/February 2006): 23.

22. See http://www.nice.org.uk/page.aspx?o=207023

23. See Alex Mold and Virginia Berridge, "'The rise of the user'? Voluntary organisations, the state and illegal drugs, since the 1960s," *Drugs: Education, Prevention and Policy* (forthcoming); and Mold and Berridge, *Voluntarism Health and Society Since the 1960s*.

24. See http://www.nta.nhs.uk/

25. Interview with Bill Nelles.

26. See, for example, the Declaration of the International Network of People who use Illegal Drugs made at the International Harm Reduction Association (IHRA) Conference in Vancouver, 2006. Available from http://www.correlation-net.org/pdf_news/int_user_network.pdf

27. For an overview of health consumerism, see Sara Hendersen and Alan Petersen (eds), *Consuming Health: The Commodification of Healthcare* (London and New York: Routledge, 2002).

28. On the internal market, see Charles Webster, *The National Health Service: A Political History* (Oxford: Oxford University Press, 2002), 187–207; and on the Patient's Charter, see Christine Hogg, *Patients, Power and Politics: From Patients to Citizens* (London: Sage, 1999), 42–48.

29. *NHS Plan*, 2000.

30. *Health and Social Care Act*, 2001.

31. Mold and Berridge, "'The rise of the user?'"

32. See Chapter 4.

33. Cmd 2846, *Tackling Drugs Together: A Strategy for England 1995–1998* (London: The Stationary Office, 1995).

34. Cmd 3945, *Tackling Drugs to Build a Better Britain* (London: The Stationary Office, 1998).

35. Stimson, "Blair declares war," 260.

36. See http://www.nta.nhs.uk/

37. Massing, *The Fix*, 191–207.

38. Keith Hellawell, *The Outsider* (London: Harper Collins, 2003), 296–320.

39. Ibid., 354–61.

40. Ibid., 371–74. See also "A career of controversy: Keith Hellawell," *BBC News Online*, 10 July 2002. See http://news.bbc.co.uk/1/low/uk/2120044.stm

41. Home Office, *Updated Drug Strategy*.

42. Karen Duke, "Out of crime and into treatment? The criminalization of contemporary drug policy since *Tackling Drugs Together*," *Drugs: Education, Prevention and Policy*, 13.5 (2006): 409.

43. Mike Hough, "Balancing public health and criminal justice interventions," *International Journal of Drug Policy*, 12 (2001): 429.

44. Gossop, *Drug Misuse and Reductions in Crime*, 3.

45. *Tackling Drugs to Build a Better Britain*, 1.

46. Gemma Kothari, John Marsden and John Strang, "Opportunities and obstacles for effective treatment of drug misusers in the criminal justice system in England and Wales," *British Journal of Criminology*, 42 (2002): 412.

47. Stimson, "Blair declares war," 259–60.

48. Gossop, *Drug Misuse and Reductions in Crime*, 4.

49. Duke, "Out of crime and into treatment?" 412.

50. Source: http://www.drugs.gov.uk/drug-interventions-programme/

51. Home Office, *Tackling Drugs, Changing Lives: Keeping Communities Safe From Drugs* (London: Home Office, 2004), 19.

52. *Drugs Act*, 2005.

53. *Tackling Drugs, Changing Lives*, 19.

54. Finch and Ashton, "Treatment to order," 189.

55. Kothari, Marsden and Strang, "Effective treatment of drug misusers," 415.

56. Carol Jenkins, "Thinking outside the docks," *Druglink*, 22.2 (March/April 2007): 10–11, 16.

57. Ministry of Health, *Second Report of the Interdepartmental Committee on Heroin Addiction*, 9.

58. Finch and Ashton, "Treatment to order," 190–91; Kothari, Marsden and Strang, "Effective treatment of drug misusers," 416.

59. Finch and Ashton, "Treatment to order," 190–91.

60. Gossop, *Drug Misuse Treatment and Reductions in Crime*, 6.

61. David Best and Angela Campbell, *Summary of the NTA's National Prescribing Audit* (London: National Treatment Agency, 2006), 3–4.

62. Susanne MacGregor, "'Tackling Drugs Together' and the establishment of the principle that 'treatment works,'" *Drugs: Education, Prevention and Policy*, 13.5 (2006): 402–7.

63. Gossop, *Drug Misuse Treatment and Reductions in Crime*, 5.

64. Home Office, *Tackling Drugs Changing Lives: Turning Strategy Into Reality* (London: Home Office, 2005), 4.

65. Gossop, *Drug Misuse and Reductions in Crime*, 4.

66. Ibid., 4.

67. Massing, *The Fix*, 111–12.

68. Information on PTB taken from http://www.drugs.gov.uk

69. Information taken from NTA's website, http://www.nta.nhs.uk/ (accessed 17 October 2006).

70. Ibid.

71. See *Updated Drug Strategy*; *Tackling Drugs to Build a Better Britain* and *Tackling Drugs Together*, 23.

72. Minutes of the Medical Working Group on Drug Misuse and Dependence, 1999. Cited in Sarah Mars, "Prescribing and Proscribing: The Public-Private Relationship in the Treatment of Heroin Addiction in England, 1970–99," PhD diss., University of London, 2005, 198.

73. John Polkinghorne, Michael Gossop and John Strang, "The Government Task Force and its review of drug treatment services: the promotion of an evidence-based approach," in John Strang and Michael Gossop (eds), *Heroin Addiction and the British System, Vol. 2*, 199.

74. Gossop, *Treatment Outcomes: What We Know and What We Need to Know*, 1–3.

75. White, *Slaying the Dragon*, 311–13.

76. Home Office, *Updated Drug Strategy*, 75–79.

77. Mars, "Prescribing and proscribing," 192.

78. Polkinghorne, Gossop and Strang, "The Government Task Force," 199.

79. M. Parker, "False dichotomies: EBM, clinical freedom and the art of medicine," *Medical Humanities*, 31 (2005): 23.

80. Berridge, *Health and Society in Britain Since 1939*, 83.

81. Baggott, *Health and Health Care in Britain*, 56.

82. Nick Black, "Evidence based policy: proceed with care," *British Medical Journal*, 323 (2001): 275.

83. Ibid., 276.

84. Gossop, *Drug Misuse Treatment and Reductions in Crime*, 3.

85. Polkinghorne, Gossop and Strang, "The Government Task Force," 202.

86. Duke, "Out of crime into treatment," 413.

87. MacGregor, "*Tackling Drugs Together*," 405.

88. Polkinghorne, Gossop and Strang, "The Government Task Force," 203.

89. Department of Health, *Statistics from the National Drug Treatment Monitoring System (NDTMS) 1 April 2003 – 31 March 2004* (London: Department of Health, 2005), 20.

90. Mars, "Prescribing and proscribing," 202.

91. *The Observer*, 9 December 2001.

92. *Updated Drug Strategy*, 56.

93. *The Guardian*, 19 February 2007.

94. See Ambros Uchtenhagen, *Prescription of Narcotics For Heroin Addicts* (Basel: Kartger, 1999); and Thomas V. Perneger et al., "Randomised trial of heroin maintenance programme for addicts who fail in conventional drug treatments," *British Medical Journal*, 317 (1998): 13–18.

95. *DrugScope Members Briefing* (December 2006): 3.

96. Nicky Metrebian et al, "Survey of doctors prescribing diamorphine (heroin) to opiate-dependent drug users in the UK," *Addiction*, 97 (2002): 1155–61. For more recent references to the number of heroin prescriptions issued, see also National Treatment Agency, *Injectable Heroin (And Injectable Methadone): Potential Roles in Drug Treatment* (London: NTA, 2003): 12; and British Medical Association, *Legalising Illicit Drugs: A Signposting Resource* (London: BMA, 2006): 13.

97. Best and Campbell, *Summary of the NTA's Prescribing Audit*, 6.

98. *DrugScope News*, 31 January 2001; *The Guardian*, 15 January 2001.

99. Deborah Zador, "Last call for injectable opiate maintenance: in pursuit of an evidence base for good clinical practice," in Strang and Gossop, *Heroin Addiction and the British System, Vol 2.*, 126.

100. National Treatment Agency, *Injectable Heroin (And Injectable Methadone)*, 3.

101. Ibid., 4.

102. NTA, *Injectable Heroin (and Injectable Methadone)*, 5.

103. NTA, *Injectable Heroin (and Injectable Methadone)*, 5; and Best and Campbell, *Summary of the NTA's National Prescribing Audit*, 4.

104. Press Release from the Healthcare Commission, "Drug treatment getting better but still too patchy, say watchdogs," 7 September 2006. Avaliable at: http://www.healthcarecommission.org.uk/newsandevents/pressreleases.cfm?cit_id=4402&FAArea1=customWidgets.content_view_1&usecache=false

105. Neil McKeganey, Zoe Morris, Joanne Neale and Michele Robertson, "What are drug users looking for when they contact drug services: abstinence or harm reduction?" *Drugs: Education, Prevention and Policy*, 11 (2004): 426.

106. David Best, Angela Campbell and Alison O'Grady, *The NTA's First Annual User Survey 2005* (London: NTA, 2006): 9.

107. McKeganey et al., "What are drug users looking for?" 433.

108. Brian Wells, "Narcotics Anonymous in Britain: the stepping up of a phenomenon," in Strang and Gossop (eds), *Heroin Addiction and the British System, Vol 2*, 168.

109. See *DrugScope News*, 21 June 2006. Available at: http://www.drugscope.org.uk/news_item.asp?a=1&intID=1332 For treatment outcome statistics by treatment modality, see Department of Health, *Statistics from NDTMS*, 20.

110. An audio file of the debate is available at http://www.exchangesupplies.org/conferences/2006_NDTC/speakers/debate.html#neil

111. Tom Carnwarth and Chris Ford, "Methadone challenged on its home turf: is there a worrying methadone backlash about?" *Drink and Drug News* (8 May 2006): 9.

112. Rowdy Yates, "Unpleasant and petulant," letter to *Drink and Drug News* (22 May 2006): 8.

113. David McCartney, "Polarisation problems," letter to *Drink and Drug News* (22 May 2006): 8–9.

114. *The Guardian*, 23 February 2004; *The Guardian*, 24 February; *The Independent*, 24 February 2004; *The Times*, 24 February 2004.

115. *The Independent,* 24 February 2004; *The Guardian,* 24 February 2004.

116. *The Guardian,* 24 February 2004.

117. Owen Dyer, "Seven doctors accused of over-prescribing heroin," *British Medical Journal,* 328 (28 February 2004): 483.

118. *The Guardian,* 23 February 2004.

119. *The Independent,* 24 February 2004.

120. *The Times,* 24 February 2004.

121. Nick Davies, "Doctors at top drugs clinic face charges," *The Guardian,* 16 February 2004.

122. Dyer, "Seven doctors accused of over-prescribing heroin," 483; Dally, *A Doctor's Story,* 263.

123. "The needle and the damage done," *Daily Telegraph,* 12 May 2004. Available at http://www.telegraph.co.uk/health/main.jhtml?xml=/health/2004/05/13/hstapelford13.xml&page=15

124. Ibid.

125. Davies, "Doctors at top drugs clinic face charges."

126. Dyer, "Seven doctors accused of over-prescribing heroin," 483.

127. For the GMC's judgement against Brewer, see http://www.gmc-uk.org/concerns/hearings_and_decisions/ftp/20061109_ftp_panel_brewer.asp

128. Carnwarth, "Doctors at war," 23.

129. See Ashton, "Doctors at war," parts one and two.

130. "Struck off clinic doctor defends his methods," *Guardian,* 21 November 2006. Article available at http://www.guardian.co.uk/medicine/story/0,,1953245,00.html

131. Home Office, *Changes to the Misuse of Drugs Legislation: Licensing of Controlled Drugs Prescribed in the Treatment of Addiction* (London: Home Office, 2000); and Home Office, *Changes to the Misuse of Drugs Legislation: Prescribed in the Treatment of Addiction* (London: Home Office, 2005).

132. Berry Beaumont et al., "Alternatives to licensing doctors," letter to *Druglink* (January/February 2001): 9.

133. Mark Gabbay, et al., "Editorial: Reducing deaths among drug misusers: tighter controls on drug prescribing are not the answer," *British Medical Journal,* 322 (31 March 2001): 749–50.

134. Mars, "Prescribing and proscribing," 203–6; 211.

135. Department of Health, *Drug Misuse and Dependence—Guidelines on Clinical Management* (London: HMSO, 1999): 9–12.

136. Ibid., 5.

137. Clare Gerada, "The GP and the drug misuser in the new NHS: a new 'British System,'" in Strang and Gossop (eds), *Heroin Addiction and the British System, Vol 2,* 72–73.

138. See http://www.smmgp.org.uk/ and http://www.rcgp.org.uk/substance_misuse/substance_misuse_home.aspx

139. Department of Health, *Statistics from NDTMS,* 19.

CONCLUSION

1. Office of Science and Technology, *Drugs Futures 2025: Executive Summary and Overview* (London: Department of Trade and Industry, 2005): 1.

2. Ibid., 20–21, 39.

3. Alan I. Leshner, "Addiction is a brain disease, and it matters," *Science,* 278 (1997): 45.

4. Kelly Morris, David Nutt and Leslie Iverson, *Foresight State of the Art Science Review: Pharmacology and Treatments* (London: Department of Trade and Industry, 2005).

5. Rita Z. Goldstein and Nora D. Volkow, "Drug addiction and its underlying neurobiological basis: neuroimaging evidence for the involvement of the frontal cortex," *American Journal of Psychiatry,* 159 (2002): 1642–52.

6. David Ball et al., *Foresight State of the Art Science Review: Genomics* (London: Department of Trade and Industry, 2005).

7. Alan I. Leshner, "Editorial: Science is revolutionizing our view of addiction—and what to do about it," *American Journal of Psychiatry,* 156.1 (1999): 1.

8. Howard I. Kushner, "Taking biology seriously: the next task for historians of addiction?" *Bulletin of the History of Medicine,* 80 (2006): 118.

9. David T. Courtwright, "Mr ATOD's wild ride: what do alcohol, tobacco and other drugs have in common?" *The Social History of Alcohol and Drugs,* 20 (2005): 105–24.

10. David T. Courtwright, "Addiction science, history and the ATOD paradigm: a reply to Hasso Spode, Ian Tyrrell, and James Mills," *The Social History of Alcohol and Drugs,* 20 (2005): 139.

11. Virginia Berridge and Tim Hickman, *Foresight State of the Art Science Review: History and the Future of Psychoactive Substances* (London: Department of Trade and Industry, 2005).

12. See for example, Berridge, *Opium and the People*; Mills, *Cannabis Britannica*; Courtwright, *Dark Paradise*; Acker, *Creating the American Junkie.*

13. ACMD, *Drug Misuse and the Environment* (London: Home Office, 1998): xi, xxiv-xxv.

14. Edwards, *Matters of Substance,* 270–71.

15. Leshner, "Science is revolutionizing our view about addiction," 1.

16. *BBC News Online,* "Birth control for methadone," 11 May 2006. See http://news.bbc.co.uk/go/pr/fr/-/hi/scotland/4763137.stm

17. Max Daly, "Turkey shoot," *Druglink,* 22:1 (2007): 3.

18. Leshner, "Science is revolutionizing our view about addiction," 1.

19. Leshner, "Addiction is a brain disease," 46.

20. Wayne Hall, "Editorial: Avoiding potential misuses of addiction brain science," *Addiction,* 101 (2006): 1529–32.

21. Robin Room, "Addiction concepts and international control," *The Social History of Alcohol and Drugs,* 20 (2006): 276–89.

22. House of Commons Science and Technology Committee, *Drug Classification: Making a Hash of It?* (London: The Stationary Office, 2006).

23. David Nutt, Leslie A. King, William Saulsbury and Colin Blakemore, "Development of a rational scale to assess the harms of drugs of potential misuse," *Lancet,* 369 (2007): 1047–53.

24. UNODC, *World Drug Report 2006: Executive Summary* (UNODC: Vienna, 2006).

25. Courtwright, "Mr ATOD's wild ride"; White, "The lessons of language," 40; and Virginia Berridge, "Science and policy: the case of British postwar smoking policy," in Stephen Lock, Lois Reynolds and E.M. Tansey (eds), *Ashes to Ashes: the History of Smoking and Health* (Amsterdam: Rodopi, 1998), 143–63.

26. Robin Room, *Foresight State of the Art Science Review: Social Policy and Psychoactive Substances* (London: Department of Trade and Industry, 2005).

27. Berridge, "Science and policy," 144–45; Hilton, *Smoking in British Popular Culture 1800–2000,* 62, 69, 125.

28. US Public Health Service, *The Health Consequences of Smoking: Nicotine Addiction, A Report of the Surgeon General* (Rockville, Md.: US Department of Health and Human Services, 1988).

29. Jim Orford, *Foresight State of the Art Science Review: Problem Gambling and Other Behavioural Addictions* (London: Department of Trade and Industry, 2005).

30. UNODC, *World Drug Report 2006*, 9; European Monitoring Centre for Drugs and Drug Addiction (EMCDDA), *The State of the Drugs Problem in Europe: Annual Report 2005* (Lisbon: EMCDDA, 2005).

31. UNODC, *World Drug Report 2006*; Diane Taylor, "The opium odyssey," *Druglink*, 21.6 (2006): 8.

32. UNODC, *World Drug Report 2006*.

33. Benedikt Fischer and Jurgen Rehm, "Illicit opioid use in the 21st century: witnessing a paradigm shift?" *Addiction*, 102 (2007): 499.

34. Ibid., 499.

Works Cited

ARCHIVAL SOURCES

Contemporary Medical Archives Centre (CMAC), Wellcome Library for the History and Understanding of Medicine, London

Private Papers of Dr Ann Dally (PP/DAL)

CMAC PP/DAL/B/4/1/1/8, DHSS Guidelines and reports.

CMAC PP/DAL/B/4/1/5, Minutes of Northern Drug Addiction Psychiatrists, 1987.

CMAC PP/DAL/B/4/2/5, "Some problems in the treatment of heroin addiction," by Ann Dally, 1984.

CMAC PP/DAL/B/4/2/8, "The evaluation of Liverpool Drug Dependency Clinic. The first two years 1985–1987," by Cindy S.J. Fazey, 1988.

CMAC PP/DAL/B/5/1/2, Correspondence regarding various aspects of DHSS working party and guidelines being prepared, 1983–1984.

CMAC PP/DAL/B/5/1, DHSS Working Group On Drug Dependence, 1983.

CMAC PP/DAL/B/5/1/6, *Guidelines of Good Clinical Practice in the Treatment of Drug Misuse,* 1984.

CMAC PP/DAL/E/2/4, Transcript of the 1983 GMC case.

CMAC PP/DAL/E/2/11, Dally's thoughts on the case and a description of the finances of the practice at Devonshire Place, 1983.

CMAC PP/DAL/E/4/1, Articles and newspaper cuttings, 1974–1986.

CMAC PP/DAL/E/4/9, Miscellaneous statements from patients, 1986.

CMAC PP/DAL/E/4/11, Response to questionnaire Dally gave to her addict-patients, 1982–1987.

CMAC PP/DAL/E/4/12, Statements and amended statements made by Dally and other witnesses.

CMAC PP/DAL/E/4/17, Transcripts of the 1986–1987 GMC case.

CMAC PP/DAL/E/4/20, Notes by Dally on the case and patients, 1986–1987.

CMAC PP/DAL/E/4/22, Correspondence between solicitors for the defence and the GMC, 1986–1988.

CMAC PP/DAL/ Box 7.

London Metropolitan Archive (LMA)

LMA H1/ST/A128/13, Minutes of the Meetings of the Board of Governors of St Thomas' Hospital, 1967–1968.

Modern Records Centre, University of Warwick (ModRC)

ModRC MSS.171/3/44/1, Controversy regarding the GPO's decision to disconnect the service, 1975.

The National Archives (TNA), London

Ministry of Health Papers (MH)

TNA MH 58/275, Medical Committee on Drug Addiction: Appointment, 1923–1926.

TNA MH 58/276, Medical Committee on Drug Addiction: Minutes of Meetings, 1924–1925.

TNA MH 58/277, Medical Committee on Drug Addiction: Evidence, 1924–1925.

TNA MH 58/564, Interdepartmental Committee on Drug Addiction: constitution and appointment, 1956–1960.

TNA MH 58/565, Interdepartmental Committee on Drug Addiction: joint evidence by Home Office, Ministry of Health and Department of Health for Scotland, 1958–1960.

TNA MH 58/566, Interdepartmental Committee on Drug Addiction: evidence from other organisations, 1958–1959.

TNA MH 58/567, Interdepartmental Committee on Drug Addiction: correspondence with chairman, 1958–1961.

TNA MH 58/568, Interdepartmental Committee on Drug Addiction: agendas and minutes of meetings, 1958–1959.

TNA MH 58/570, Interdepartmental Committee on Drug Addiction: interim report, 1959–1960.

TNA MH 58/571, Interdepartmental Committee on Drug Addiction: signed minutes of meetings, 1960–1961.

TNA MH 149/162, Advisory Committee on Drug Dependence: constitution, 1966–1970.

TNA MH 149/164, Interdepartmental Committee on Drug Addiction, 1964.

TNA MH 149/165, Interdepartmental Committee on Drug Addiction: minutes of meetings, 1964–1965.

TNA MH 149/166, Interdepartmental Committee on Drug Addiction: working papers, 1964–1965.

TNA MH 149/168, Interdepartmental Committee on Drug Addiction: presentation of final report, 1965.

TNA MH 149/169, Interdepartmental Committee on Drug Addiction: publication of report, 1965.

TNA MH 149/170, Interdepartmental Committee on Drug Addiction: action arising from report, 1965–1966.

TNA MH 149/171, Interdepartmental Committee on Drug Addiction: action arising from report, 1966.

TNA MH 149/172, Interdepartmental Committee on Drug Addiction: action arising from report, 1966.

TNA MH 150/94, Addiction Research Unit Maudsley Hospital: initial establishment and proposals for consolidation, 1967–1971.

TNA MH 150/369, Committee on Drug Dependence: treatment and supervision of heroin addiction: follow up action to circular H.M.(67)16: correspondence, papers and minutes of meetings, 1969–1970.

TNA MH 154/431, National Addiction and Research Centre: Chelsea Day Centre, 1967–1972.

TNA MH 160/709, London teaching hospitals, drug addiction facilities, implementation of the Brain Committee's recommendations, 1966–1967.

TNA MH 160/710, London teaching hospitals, drug addiction facilities, implementation of the Brain Committee's recommendations, 1967.

Medical Research Council Papers (FD)

TNA FD 7/878, Working Party on the Evaluation of Different Methods of Treatment of Drug Dependence: membership, correspondence and report, 1969–1970.

TNA FD 7/1583, Working Party on the Evaluation of Different Methods of Treatment of Drug Dependence: correspondence concerning setting up of the Working Party and details of membership, 1967–1968.

TNA FD 7/1584, Working Party on the Evaluation of Different Methods of Treatment of Drug Dependence: minutes and papers of meeting held on 13 May 1968.

TNA FD 7/1591, Working Party on the Evaluation of Different Methods of Treatment of Drug Dependence: minutes and papers of meeting held on 3 June 1970.

TNA FD 7/1599, Survey of research projects related to drug dependence: draft survey paper presented to Council, 1971–1972.

INTERVIEWS

Interview between author and Dr Ann Dally, 7 June 2005.
Interview between author and Professor Griffith Edwards, 20 October 2004.
Interview between author, Virginia Berridge and Bill Nelles, 10 March 2006.
Interview between author and Andria Efthimou Morduant (drug user activist), 13 December 2005.
Interview between author and David Turner, 25 February 2005.

NEWSPAPERS AND JOURNALS

Addiction, 1997–2007
British Journal of Addiction, 1960–1997
British Medical Journal, 1965–2007
The Daily Telegraph, 1960–2007
Drink and Drug News, 2006–2007
Druglink, 1986–2007
The Guardian, 1960–2007
The Hansard Journal of Parliamentary Debates: House of Commons, 1960–2007
The Hansard Journal of Parliamentary Debates: House of Lords, 1960–2007
The Independent, 1960–2007
The Lancet, 1960–2007
The Sunday Times, 1920–2007
The Times, 1916–2007

BOOKS, ARTICLES AND REPORTS

Abramson, John. *Overdosed America: The Broken Promise of American Medicine.* London: Harper Collins, 2004.

Acker, Caroline Jean. *Creating the American Junkie: Addiction Research in the Classic Era of Narcotic Control.* Baltimore: Johns Hopkins University Press, 2002.

Adler, Michael W. "Editorial: AIDS and intravenous drug abuse." *British Journal of Addiction,* 81 (1986): 307–10.

Advisory Committee on Drug Dependence. *The Rehabilitation of Drug Addicts.* London: HMSO, 1968.

Advisory Council on the Misuse of Drugs. *AIDS and Drug Misuse: Part One.* London: Home Office, 1988.

———. *Drug Misuse and the Environment.* London: Home Office, 1998.

———. *Treatment and Rehabilitation: Report of the Advisory Council on the Misuse of Drugs.* London: Home Office, 1982.

Angell, Marcia. *The Truth About Drug Companies: How They Deceive us and What to do About It.* New York: Random House, 2004.

Anon. *Phoenix House: The Featherstone Lodge Project Annual Report, 1970–71.*

Armstrong, David. "The emancipation of biographical medicine." *Social Science and Medicine,* 13A (1979): 1–8.

———. *The Political Anatomy of the Body.* Cambridge: Cambridge University Press, 1983.

Ashton, Mike. "Doctors at war, part one." *Druglink* (May/June 1986): 13–15.

———. "Doctors at war—part two." *Druglink* (July/August 1986): 13–15.

Ashton, Robert. *This Is Heroin.* London: Sanctuary House, 2002.

Baggott, Rob. *Health and Health Care in Britain.* Basingstoke: Macmillan, 2nd ed., 1998.

Ball, David, David Collier, Marcus Pembrey and Dai Stephens. *Foresight State of the Art Science Review: Genomics.* London: Department of Trade and Industry, 2005.

Ball, John C., Harold Graff and John J. Sheenan, "The heroin addicts' view of methadone maintenance." *British Journal of Addiction,* 69 (1974): 89–95.

Basson, J.V. "Attitudes to drug abuse," *British Medical Journal,* 292 (29 March 1986): 847–48.

Bean, Philip T. "Policing the medical profession: the use of tribunals," in David Whynes and Philip Bean (eds), *Policing and Prescribing: The British System of Drug Control,* 60–70. Basingstoke: Macmillan, 1991.

Beckett, H. Dale. "The Salter Unit—an experimental in-patient treatment centre for narcotic drug addiction in men." *British Journal of Addiction,* 63 (1968): 51–53.

———. "Society at work: maintaining heroin addicts." *New Society* (14 September 1967): 360–61.

Bennett, Douglas. "The drive towards the community," in German E. Berrios and Hugh Freeman (eds), *150 Years of British Psychiatry, 1841–1991,* 321–32. London: Royal College of Psychiatrists, 1991.

Bennett, Trevor. "The British experience with heroin regulation." *Law and Contemporary Problems,* 51 (1988): 299–314.

Berridge, Virginia. "AIDS and British drug policy: continuity or change?" in Virginia Berridge and Philip Strong (eds), *AIDS and Contemporary History.* 135–52. Cambridge: Cambridge University Press, 1993.

———. "AIDS and the rise of the patient? Activist organisation and HIV/AIDS in the UK in the 1980s and 1990s," *Medizin Gesellschaft und Geshichte,* 21 (2002): 109–23.

———. *AIDS in the UK: The Making of Policy, 1981–1994.* Oxford: Oxford University Press, 1996.

———. "The 'British System' and its history: myth and reality," in John Strang and Michael Gossop (eds), *Heroin Addiction and the British System, Volume One: Origins and Evolution,* 7–16. London and New York: Routledge, 2005.

———. "Drug research in Britain: the relation between research and policy," in Virginia Berridge (ed.), *Drugs Research and Policy in Britain: A Review of the 1980s*. Aldershot: Avebury, 1990.

———. *Health and Society in Britain Since 1939*. Cambridge: Cambridge University Press, 1999.

———. "Morality and medical science: concepts of narcotic addiction in Britain, 1820–1926." *Annals of Science*, 36 (1979): 67–85.

———. "Opium and the doctors: disease theory and policy," in R.M. Murray and T.H. Turner (eds), *Lectures on the History of Psychiatry: The Squibb Series*, 101–14. London: Royal College of Psychiatrists, 1990.

———. *Opium and the People: Opiate Use and Drug Control Policy in Nineteenth and Early Twentieth Century England*. London: Free Association Books, 1999.

———. "Science and policy: the case of British postwar smoking policy," in Stephen Lock, Lois Reynolds and E.M. Tansey (eds), *Ashes to Ashes: the History of Smoking and Health*, 143–63. Amsterdam: Rodopi, 1998.

———. "'Stamping out addiction': the work of the Rolleston Committee, 1924–1926," in Hugh Freeman and German E. Berrios (eds), *150 Years of British Psychiatry, Volume Two—The Aftermath*, 44–60. London: Athlone Press, 1996.

Berridge, Virginia and Tim Hickman. *Foresight State of the Art Science Review: History and the Future of Psychoactive Substances*. London: Department of Trade and Industry, 2005.

Berridge, Virginia and Sarah Mars. "Glossary: history of addictions." *Journal of Epidemiology and Community Health*, 58 (2004): 747–50.

Best, David and Angela Campbell. *Summary of the NTA's National Prescribing Audit*. London: National Treatment Agency, 2006.

Best, David, Angela Campbell and Alison O'Grady. *The NTA's First Annual User Survey 2005*. London: National Treatment Agency, 2006.

Bewley, Thomas H. "Advantages of special centres." *British Medical Journal* (20 May 1967): 498–99.

———. "Conversation with Thomas Bewley." *Addiction*, 90 (1995): 883–92.

———. "Drug dependence in the USA." *Bulletin on Narcotics*, 21 (1969): 13–20.

———. "Heroin and cocaine addiction." *The Lancet* (10 April 1965): 808–10.

———. "Prescribing psychoactive drugs to addicts." *British Medical Journal* (16 August 1980): 497–98.

Bewley, Thomas H. and A. Hamid Ghodse. "Unacceptable face of private practice." *British Medical Journal*, 286 (11 June 1983): 1876–77.

Bewley-Taylor, David R. *The United States and International Drug Control, 1909–1997*. London: Continuum, 1999.

Black, Nick. "Evidence based policy: proceed with care." *British Medical Journal*, 323 (4 August 2001): 275–79.

Blackman, Shane. *Chilling Out: The Cultural Politics of Substance Consumption, Youth and Drug Policy*. Maidenhead: Open University Press, 2004.

Block, Alan. "European drug traffic and traffickers between the wars: the policy of suppression and its consequences." *Journal of Social History*, 23 (1989): 315–37.

Brahams, Diana. "Medicine and the law: no right of appeal against GMC finding of serious professional misconduct without suspension or erasure." *The Lancet* (22 October 1983): 979–81.

Brahams, Diana. "'Serious professional misconduct' in relation to private treatment of drug dependence." *The Lancet* (7 February 1987): 340–41.

Bucknall, A.B.V., J.R. Robertson and K. Foster. "Medical facilities used by heroin users." *British Medical Journal*, 293 (8 November 1986): 1215–16.

Bucknall, A.B.V., J.R. Robertson and J.G. Strachan. "The use of psychiatric treatment services by heroin users from general practice." *British Medical Journal*, 292 (12 April 1986): 997–99.

Buning, Ernst. "The role of harm reduction programmes in curbing the spread of HIV by drug injectors," in John Strang and Gerry Stimson (eds), *AIDS and Drug Misuse: The Challenge For Policy and Practice in the 1990s*, 143–61. London and New York: Routledge, 1990.

Burr, Angela. "Increased sale of opiates on the blackmarket [sic.] in the Piccadilly area." *British Medical Journal*, 287 (24 September 1983): 883–85.

———. "The Piccadilly drug scene." *British Journal of Addiction*, 78 (1983): 5–19.

Campling, Penelope. "Therapeutic communities." *Advances in Psychiatric Treatment*, 7 (2001): 365–72.

Carnwarth, Tom. "Doctors at war." *Druglink*, 22:1 (January/February 2007): 23.

Carnwarth, Tom and Chris Ford, "Methadone challenged on its home turf: is there a worrying methadone backlash about?" *Drink and Drug News* (8 May 2006): 9.

Carnwarth, Tom and Ian Smith. *Heroin Century*. London and New York: Routledge, 2002.

Cassels, Alan. *Selling Sickness: How the World's Biggest Pharmaceutical Companies Are Turning Us All Into Patients*. New York: Nation Books, 2005.

Chapple, P.A.L. "Treatment in the community." *British Medical Journal* (20 May 1967): 500–501.

Cmd 2846. *Tackling Drugs Together: A Strategy for England 1995–1998*. London: The Stationary Office, 1995.

Cmd 3945. *Tackling Drugs to Build a Better Britain*. London: The Stationary Office, 1998.

Cocks, Harry G. and Matt Houlbrook (eds), *Palgrave Advances in the Modern History of Sexuality*. Palgrave: Basingstoke, 2005.

Cohen, Stanley. *Folk Devils and Moral Panics*. London: MacGibbon & Kee, 1972.

Connell, Philip H. "Conversation with Philip Connell." *British Journal of Addiction*, 85 (1990): 13–23.

———. "Document: treatment of drug dependent patients, 1968–1969," *British Journal of Addiction*, 86 (1991): 913–15.

———. "Drug dependence in Britain: A challenge to the practice of medicine," in H. Steinberg (ed.), *Scientific Basis of Drug Dependence*, 291–99. London: J&A Churchill, 1969.

———. "Importance of research." *British Medical Journal* (20 May 1967): 499–500.

———. "'I need heroin.' Thirty years of drug dependence and of the medical challenges at local, national, international and political levels. What next?" *British Journal of Addiction*, 81 (1986): 461–72.

Connell, Philip H. and Martin Mitcheson. "Necessary safeguards when prescribing opioid drugs to addicts: experience of drug dependence clinics in London." *British Medical Journal*, 288 (10 March 1984): 767–69.

Connell, Philip H. and John Strang. "The creation of the clinics: clinical demand and the formation of policy," in John Strang and Michael Gossop (eds), *Heroin Addiction and Drug Policy: The British System*, 167–77. Oxford: Oxford University Press, 1994.

Courtwright, David T. "Addiction science, history and the ATOD paradigm: a reply to Hasso Spode, Ian Tyrrell, and James Mills." *The Social History of Alcohol and Drugs*, 20 (2005): 138–40.

———. *Dark Paradise: A History of Opiate Addiction in America*. Cambridge, Mass.: Harvard University Press, 2001.

———. *Forces of Habit: Drugs and the Making of the Modern World*. Cambridge, Mass.: Harvard University Press, 2001.

———. "Mr ATOD's wild ride: what do alcohol, tobacco and other drugs have in common?" *The Social History of Alcohol and Drugs*, 20 (2005): 105–24.

Cranfield, Steve, Charlotte Feinmann, Ewan Ferlie and Cathy Walter. "HIV and drugs services—the challenge of change," in John Strang and Michael Gossop (eds), *Heroin Addiction and Drug Policy: The British System*, 322–30. Oxford: Oxford University Press, 1994.

Crossley, Nick. "R.D. Laing and the British anti-psychiatry movement: a socio-historical analysis." *Social Science and Medicine*, 47 (1998): 877–89.

Dally, Ann. *A Doctor's Story*. Basingstoke: Macmillan, 1990.

Dally, Ann. "Personal view." *British Medical Journal*, 283 (26 September 1981): 857.

Davenport-Hines, Richard. *The Pursuit of Oblivion: A Global History of Narcotics, 1500–2000*. London: Weinfield & Nicholson, 2001.

Deedes, William. *The Drugs Epidemic*. London: Tom Stacey, 1970.

DeGrandpre, Richard. *The Cult of Pharmacology: How America Became the World's Most Troubled Drug Culture*. Durham, N.C., Duke University Press, 2006.

Department of Health. *Drug Misuse and Dependence: Guidelines on Clinical Management*. London: HMSO, 1991.

———. *Drug Misuse and Dependence—Guidelines on Clinical Management*. London: HMSO, 1999.

———. *Statistics from the National Drug Treatment Monitoring System (NDTMS) 1 April 2003–31 March 2004*. London: Department of Health, 2005.

Department of Health and Social Security. *Guidelines of Good Clinical Practice in the Treatment of Drug Misuse*. London: DHSS, 1984.

Department of Trade and Industry. *Social Enterprise: A Strategy for Success*. London: Department of Trade and Industry, 2002.

Digby, Anne. *The Evolution of British General Practice, 1850–1948*. Oxford: Oxford University Press, 1999.

Dorn, Nick and Nigel South. "Introduction," in Nick Dorn and Nigel South (eds), *A Land Fit For Heroin? Drug Policies, Prevention and Practice*, 1–10. Basingstoke: Macmillan, 1987.

Downes, David. *Contrasts in Tolerance: Post War Penal Policy in the Netherlands and in England and Wales*. Oxford: Clarendon Press, 1988.

Duke, Karen. "Out of crime and into treatment? The criminalization of contemporary drug policy since *Tackling Drugs Together*." *Drugs: Education, Prevention and Policy*, 13.5 (2006): 409–15.

Dyer, Owen. "Seven doctors accused of over-prescribing heroin." *British Medical Journal*, 328 (28 February 2004): 483.

Edwards, Griffith. "British policies on opiate addiction: ten years working of the revised response, and options for the future." *British Journal of Psychiatry*, 134 (1979): 1–13.

———. *Matters of Substance: Drugs—And Why Everyone's A User*. London: Allen Lane, 2004.

———. "Relevance of American experience of narcotic addiction to the British scene." *British Medical Journal* (12 August 1967): 425–29.

European Monitoring Centre for Drugs and Drug Addiction. *The State of the Drugs Problem in Europe: Annual Report 2005*. Lisbon: EMCDDA, 2005.

Evans, David. "Tackling the 'hideous scourge': the creation of the venereal disease treatment centres in early twentieth-century Britain." *Social History of Medicine*, 5 (1992): 413–33.

Farrell Brodie, Janet and Marc Redfield. "Introduction," in Janet Farrell Brodie and Marc Redfield (eds), *High Anxieties: Cultural Studies in Addiction*, 1–15. Berkeley, Los Angeles & London: University of California Press, 2002.

Finch, Emily and Mike Ashton. "Treatment to order: the new drug treatment and testing orders," in John Strang and Michael Gossop (eds), *Heroin Addiction and the British System: Volume Two—Treatment and Policy Responses*, 187–97. London and New York: Routledge, 2005.

Fischer, Benedikt and Jurgen Rehm. "Illicit opioid use in the 21st century: witnessing a paradigm shift?" *Addiction*, 102 (2007): 499–501.

Foucault, Michel. *The Birth of the Clinic: An Archaeology of Medical Perception*. London: Tavistock Publications, 1973.

———. *The History of Sexuality, Volume One: An Introduction*. Middlesex: Penguin, 1990.

———. *Madness and Civilisation: A History of Insanity in the Age of Reason*. London and New York: Routledge, 2001.

Frankau, Isabella M. and Patricia M. Stanwell, "The treatment of drug addiction." *The Lancet* (24 December 1960): 1377–79.

Gabbay, Mark, Tom Carnwarth, Chris Ford and Deborah Zador. "Editorial: Reducing deaths among drug misusers: tighter controls on drug prescribing are not the answer." *British Medical Journal*, 322 (31 March 2001): 749–50.

Gardner, Ramon and Philip Connell. "One year's experience in a Drug-Dependence Clinic." *The Lancet* (29 August 1970): 455–58.

General Medical Council. *Professional Conduct and Discipline: Fitness to Prescribe, April 1985, Part I*. General Medical Council: London, 1985.

Gerada, Clare. "The GP and the drug misuser in the new NHS: a new 'British System,'" in John Strang and Michael Gossop (eds), *Heroin Addiction and the British System, Volume Two: Treatment and Policy Responses*, 72–80. London and New York: Routledge, 2005.

Gerhardt, Uta. "The dilemma of social pathology," in Dorothy Porter (ed.), *Social Medicine and Medical Sociology in the Twentieth Century*, 137–64. Amsterdam: Rodopi, 1997.

Gerritsen, J.W. *The Control of Fuddle and Flash: A Sociological History of the Regulation of Alcohol and Opiates*. Leiden: Brill, 2000.

Ghodse, A. Hamid. "Casualty departments and the monitoring of drug dependence." *British Medical Journal* (1977): 1381–82.

———. "Treatment of drug addiction in London." *Lancet* (19 March 1983): 636–38.

Gillam, S., F. Dubois-Arber, L. Strizacker, A. Croft and N. Das Gupta. "Evaluating the Drug Dependency Unit." *Public Health*, 106 (1992): 209–15.

Glanz, Alan. "Editorial: Drug misuse and AIDS prevention: policy on the right track." *British Journal of Addiction* 83 (1988): 1237–39.

Glanz, Alan. "The fall and rise of the general practitioner," in John Strang and Michael Gossop (eds), *Heroin Addiction and Drug Policy: The British System*, 151–66. Oxford: Oxford University Press, 1994.

———. "Findings of a national survey of the role of general practitioners in the treatment of opiate misuse: dealing with the opiate misuser." *British Medical Journal*, 293 (23 August 1986): 482–88.

———. "Findings of a national survey on the role of general practitioners in the treatment of opiate misuse: views on treatment." *British Medical Journal*, 293 (30 August 1986): 543–46.

Glanz, Alan and Colin Taylor. "Findings of a national survey of the role of general practitioners in the treatment of opiate misuse: extent of contact with opiate misusers." *British Medical Journal*, 293 (16 August 1986): 427–30.

Glatt, Max. "Conversation with Max Glatt." *British Journal of Addiction*, 78 (1983): 231–43.

Goldstein, Rita Z. and Nora D. Volkow. "Drug addiction and its underlying neurobiological basis: neuroimaging evidence for the involvement of the frontal cortex." *American Journal of Psychiatry*, 159 (2002): 1642–52.

Goodman, Jordan, Paul Lovejoy and Andrew Sherratt (eds). *Consuming Habits: Drugs in History and Anthropology*. London and New York: Routledge, 1995.

Gossop, Michael. *Drug Misuse Treatment and Reductions in Crime: Findings From the National Treatment Outcome Research Study (NTORS)*. London: National Treatment Agency, 2005.

Griffiths, Paul, Michael Gossop and John Strang. "Chasing the dragon: the development of heroin smoking in the United Kingdom," in John Strang and Michael Gossop (eds), *Heroin Addiction and Drug Policy: The British System,* 121–33. Oxford: Oxford University Press, 1994.

Hall, Wayne. "Editorial: avoiding potential misuses of addiction brain science." *Addiction,* 101 (2006): 1529–32.

Ham, Christopher J. *Health Policy in Britain: The Politics and Organisation of the National Health Service.* Basingstoke: Macmillan, 3rd ed., 1992.

———. "Power, patients and pluralism," in Keith Barnard and Kenneth Lee (eds), *Conflicts in the National Health Service,* 99–110. London: Croom Helm, 1977.

Harding, Geoffrey. *Opiate Addiction, Morality and Medicine: From Moral Illness to Pathological Disease.* Basingstoke: Macmillan, 1988.

Hartnoll, Richard. "The international context," in Susanne MacGregor (ed.), *Drugs in British Society: Responses to a Social Problem in the 1980s,* 36–51. London and New York: Routledge, 1989.

Hartnoll, Richard and Martin Mitcheson. "Conflicts in deciding treatment within drug dependency clinics," in D.J. West (ed.), *Problems of Drug Abuse in Britain: Papers Presented to the Cropwood Round Table Conference,* 74–78. Cambridge: Institute of Criminology, 1978.

Hartnoll, Richard, Martin Mitcheson, A. Battersby, Geoffrey Brown, Margaret Ellis, Philip Fleming and Nicholas Hendy. "Evaluation of heroin maintenance in controlled trial." *Archives of General Psychiatry,* 37 (1980): 877–84.

Hellawell, Keith. *The Outsider.* London: Harper Collins, 2003.

Hendersen, Sara and Alan Petersen (eds). *Consuming Health: The Commodification of Healthcare.* London and New York: Routledge, 2002.

Higgins, Joan. *The Business of Medicine: Private Healthcare in Britain.* Basingstoke: Macmillan, 1988.

Hilton, Matthew. *Smoking in British Popular Culture 1880–2000: Perfect Pleasures.* Manchester: Manchester University Press, 2000.

Home Office. *Changes to the Misuse of Drugs Legislation: Licensing of Controlled Drugs Prescribed in the Treatment of Addiction.* London: Home Office, 2000.

———. *Changes to the Misuse of Drugs Legislation: Prescribed in the Treatment of Addiction.* London: Home Office, 2005.

———. *Statistics of Drug Addicts Notified to the Home Office, United Kingdom, 1988.* London: HMSO, 1989.

———. *Tackling Drug Misuse: A Summary of the Government's Strategy.* London: HMSO, 1985.

———. *Updated Drug Strategy.* London: The Stationary Office, 2002.

Hough, Mike. "Balancing public health and criminal justice interventions." *International Journal of Drug Policy,* 12 (2001): 429–33.

House of Commons Home Affairs Committee. *First Report From the Home Affairs Committee, Session 1985–1986: Misuse of Hard Drugs.* London: HMSO, 1985–86.

House of Commons Science and Technology Committee. *Drug Classification: Making a Hash of It?* London: The Stationary Office, 2006.

House of Commons Social Services Committee. *Misuse of Drugs With Special Reference to the Treatment and Rehabilitation of Misusers of Hard Drugs, Session 1984–1985.* London: HMSO, 1984–1986.

Howells, John G. "The establishment of the Royal College of Psychiatrists," in German E. Berrios and Hugh Freeman (eds), *150 Years of British Psychiatry, 1841–1991,* 117–34. London: Gaskell, 1991.

Howie, J. "Research in general practice," in Irvine Loudon, John Horder and Charles Webster (eds), *General Practice Under the National Health Service 1948–1997,* 148–51. Oxford: Clarendon Press, 1998.

Jamieson, Anne, Alan Glanz and Susanne MacGregor. *Dealing With Drug Misuse: Crisis Intervention in the City*. London: Tavistock, 1984.

Janzen, Rod. *The Rise and Fall of Synanon: A California Utopia*. Baltimore and London: Johns Hopkins Press, 2001.

Jefferys, Margot and Hessie Sachs. *Rethinking General Practice: Dilemmas in Primary Medical Care*. London: Tavistock, 1983.

Jenkins, Carol. "Thinking outside the docks." *Druglink*, 22.2 (March/April 2007): 10–11, 16.

Jones, Kathryn. *Asylums and After: A Revised History of the Mental Health Services From the Early Eighteenth Century to the 1990s*. London: Athlone Press, 1993.

Judson, Horace F. *Heroin Addiction in Britain*. New York: Harcourt, Brace & Jovanovich, 1973.

Kaplan, John. *The Hardest Drug: Heroin and Public Policy*. Chicago: The University of Chicago Press, 1983.

Kennard, David. *An Introduction to Therapeutic Communities*. London: Jessica Kingsley, 1998.

Klein, Rudolf. *The Politics of the NHS*. Essex: Longman, 2nd edition, 1989.

Kohn, Marek. *Dope Girls: The Birth of the British Drug Underground*. London: Granta, 1992, this ed. 2001.

———. *Narcomania*. London: Faber and Faber, 1987.

Kothari, Gemma, John Marsden and John Strang. "Opportunities and obstacles for effective treatment of drug misusers in the criminal justice system in England and Wales." *British Journal of Criminology*, 42 (2002): 412–32.

Kushner, Howard I. "The other war on drugs: the pharmaceutical industry, evidence-based medicine and clinical practice." *Journal of Policy History*, 19.1 (2007): 49–70.

———. "Taking biology seriously: the next task for historians of addiction?" *Bulletin of the History of Medicine*, 80 (2006): 115–43.

Lart, Rachel. "Changing images of the addict and addiction." *International Journal of Drug Policy*, 1 (1992): 118–25.

———. "HIV and English Drug Policy." Ph.D diss., University of London, 1996.

Law, Jacky. *Big Pharma: How the World's Biggest Drug Companies Market Illness*. London: Constable and Robinson, 2006.

Lee, Julia. "Alcohol in Chinese poems: references to drunkenness, flushing and drinking." *Contemporary Drug Problems*, 13 (1986): 303–38.

Leech, Kenneth. "The junkies' doctors and the London drug scene in the 1960s: some remembered fragments," in David Whynes and Philip Bean (eds), *Policing and Prescribing: The British System of Drug Control*, 35–59. Basingstoke: Macmillan, 1991.

Leshner, Alan I. "Addiction is a brain disease, and it matters." *Science*, 278 (1997): 45–47.

———. "Editorial: Science is revolutionizing our view of addiction—and what to do about it." *American Journal of Psychiatry*, 156.1 (1999): 1–3.

Levine, Harry G. "The discovery of addiction: changing conceptions of habitual drunkenness in America." *Journal of Studies on Alcohol*, 39 (1978): 143–74.

Lewis, Roger. "Flexible hierarchies and dynamic disorder—the trading and distribution of illicit heroin in Britain and Europe, 1970–1990," in John Strang and Michael Gossop (eds), *Heroin Addiction and Drug Policy: The British System*, 42–65. Oxford: Oxford University Press, 1994.

Lindesmith, Alfred. *The Heroin Addict and the Law*. Bloomington & London: Indiana University Press, 1965.

Love, Jayne and Michael Gossop. "The process of referral and disposal within a London Drug Dependence Clinic." *British Journal of Addiction*, 80 (1985): 435–40.

MacGregor, Susanne. "Choices for policy and practice," in Susanne MacGregor (ed.), *Drugs in British Society: Responses to a Social Problem in the 1980s*, 170–200. London and New York: Routledge, 1989.

———. "The public debate in the 1980s," in Susanne MacGregor (ed.), *Drugs in British Society: Responses to a Social Problem in the 1980s*, 1–19. London and New York: Routledge, 1989.

———. "'*Tackling Drugs Together*' and the establishment of the principle that 'treatment works,'" *Drugs: Education, Prevention and Policy*, 13.5 (2006): 399–408.

MacGregor, Susanne and Betsy Ettorre, "From treatment to rehabilitation—aspects of the evolution of British policy on the care of drug takers," in Nick Dorn and Nigel South (eds), *A Land Fit For Heroin? Drug Policies, Prevention and Practice*, 125–45. Basingstoke: Macmillan, 1987.

MacGregor, Susanne, Betsy Ettorre, Ross Coomber, Adam Crosier and Harriet Lodge. *Drugs Services in England and the Impact of the Central Funding Initiative*. London: ISDD, 1991.

Madden, J.S. "Editorial: The decline of long-term prescribing to opioid users in the United Kingdom." *British Journal of Addiction*, 82 (1987): 457–59.

Marinker, Marshall. "'What is wrong' and 'how we know it': changing concepts of illness in General Practice," in Irvine Loudon, John Horder and Charles Webster (eds), *General Practice Under the National Health Service 1948–1997*, 65–91. Oxford: Clarendon Press, 1998.

Marks, John. "Opium, the religion of the people." *The Lancet* (22 June 1985): 1439–40.

Mars, Sarah. "Peer pressure and imposed consensus: the making of the 1984 *Guidelines of Good Clinical Practice in the Treatment of Drug Misuse*," in Virginia Berridge (ed.), *Making Health Policy: Networks in Research and Policy After 1945*, 149–82. Amsterdam: Rodopi, 2005.

———. "Prescribing and Proscribing: The Public-Private Relationship in the Treatment of Heroin Addiction in England, 1970–99." PhD diss., University of London, 2005.

Mason, Michael. *The Making of Victorian Sexuality*. Oxford: Oxford University Press, 1994.

Massing, Michael. *The Fix*. Berkley and Los Angeles: University of California Press, 1998, this ed. 2000.

McAllister, William B. *Drug Diplomacy in the Twentieth Century: An International History*. London and New York: Routledge, 2000.

McDermott, Peter. "The great Mersey experiment: the birth of harm reduction," in John Strang and Michael Gossop (eds), *Heroin Addiction and the British System, Volume One: Origins and Evolution*, 137–56. London and New York: Routledge, 2005.

McKeganey, Neil, Zoe Morris, Joanne Neale and Michele Robertson. "What are drug users looking for when they contact drug services: abstinence or harm reduction?" *Drugs: Education, Prevention and Policy*, 11 (2004): 423–35.

Metrebian, Nicky, Tom Carnwarth, Gerry V. Stimson and Thomas Storz. "Survey of doctors prescribing diamorphine (heroin) to opiate-dependent drug users in the UK." *Addiction*, 97 (2002): 1155–61.

Mills, James. *Cannabis Britannica: Empire, Trade and Prohibition*. Oxford: Oxford University Press, 2003.

Ministry of Health. *Departmental Committee on Morphine and Heroin Addiction*. London: HMSO, 1926.

———. *Drug Addiction: Report of the Interdepartmental Committee*. London: HMSO, 1961.

———. *Drug Addiction: The Second Report of the Interdepartmental Committee*. London: HMSO, 1965.

Mitcheson, Martin. "Drug clinics in the 1970s," in John Strang and Michael Gossop (eds), *Heroin Addiction and Drug Policy: The British System*, 178–91. Oxford: Oxford University Press, 1994.

Mold, Alex. "Illicit drugs and the rise of epidemiology during the 1960s." *Journal of Epidemiology and Community Health*, 61 (2007): 278–81.

————. "'The welfare branch of the alternative society'? The work of drug voluntary organisation Release, 1967–1978." *Twentieth Century British History,* 17:1 (2006): 50–73.

Mold, Alex and Virginia Berridge. "Crisis and opportunity in drug Policy: changing the direction of British drug services in the 1980s." *Journal of Policy History,* 19:1 (2007): 29–48.

————. "'The rise of the user'? Voluntary organisations, the state and illegal drugs, since the 1960s." *Drugs: Education, Prevention and Policy.* Forthcoming.

————. *Voluntarism, Health and Society Since the 1960s: Voluntary Action and Illegal Drugs.* Basingstoke: Palgrave, forthcoming.

Morgan, Myfanwy, Michael Calan and Nick Manning. *Sociological Approaches to Health and Medicine.* London: Croom Helm, 1985.

Morris, Kelly, David Nutt and Leslie Iverson. *Foresight State of the Art Science Review: Pharmacology and Treatments.* London: Department of Trade and Industry, 2005.

Mort, Frank. *Dangerous Sexualities: Medico-Moral Politics in Great Britain Since 1830.* London and New York: Routledge, 1987.

Moss, A.R. "Editorial: AIDS and intravenous drug use: the real heterosexual epidemic." *British Medical Journal,* 294 (14 February 1987): 390.

Musto, David. *The American Disease: Origins of Narcotic Control.* Oxford and New York: Oxford University Press, 3rd ed. 1999.

Musto, David F. and Pamela Korsmeyer. *The Quest For Drug Control: Politics and Federal Policy in the Period of Increasing Substance Use, 1963–1981.* New Haven: Yale University Press, 2002.

Nutt, David, Leslie A. King, William Saulsbury and Colin Blakemore. "Development of a rational scale to assess the harms of drugs of potential misuse." *The Lancet,* 369 (2007): 1047–53.

O'Donnell, Michael. "One man's burden," *British Medical Journal,* 287 (1 October 1983): 990.

Office of Science and Technology. *Drugs Futures 2025: Executive Summary and Overview.* London: Department of Trade and Industry, 2005.

Oppenheimer, Gerald M. "In the eye of the storm: the epidemiological construction of AIDS," in Elizabeth Fee and Daniel M. Fox, *AIDS: The Burdens of History,* 267–300. Berkeley, Los Angeles & London: University of California Press, 1988.

Orford, Jim. *Foresight State of the Art Science Review: Problem Gambling and Other Behavioural Addictions.* London: Department of Trade and Industry, 2005.

Owen, David. "Need for a scientific strategy to curb the epidemic of drug abuse in the United Kingdom, lecture to the Society of Clinical Psychiatrists Research Fund by Dr David Owen, MP, 15 October 1985." *The Lancet* (26 October 1985): 958.

Parker, M. "False dichotomies: EBM, clinical freedom and the art of medicine." *Medical Humanities,* 31 (2005): 23–30.

Parsons, Talcott. *The Social System.* Glencoe, Illinois: Free Press, 1951.

Parssinen, Terry. *Secret Passions, Secret Remedies: Narcotic Drugs in British Society 1820–1930.* Manchester: Manchester University Press, 1983.

Parssinen, Terry and Karen Kerner. "Development of the disease model of drug addiction in Britain, 1870–1926." *Medical History,* 24 (1980): 275–96.

Pearson, Geoffrey. "Social deprivation, unemployment and patterns of heroin use," in Nick Dorn and Nigel South (eds), *A Land Fit For Heroin? Drug Policies, Prevention and Practice,* 62–94. Basingstoke: Macmillan, 1987.

Pearson, Geoffrey and Gilman, Mark. "Local and regional variations in drug misuse: the British heroin epidemic of the 1980s," in John Strang and Michael

Gossop (eds), *Heroin Addiction and Drug Policy: The British System,* 102–20. Oxford: Oxford University Press, 1994.

Perkin, Harold. *The Rise of Professional Society: England Since 1880.* London and New York: Routledge, 1990.

Perneger, Thomas V., Francisco Giner, Miguel del Rio and Annie Mino. "Randomised trial of heroin maintenance programme for addicts who fail in conventional drug treatments." *British Medical Journal,* 317 (4 July 1998): 13–18.

Petersen Alan and Deborah Lupton. *The New Public Health: Health and Self in the Age of Risk.* London: Sage Publications, 1996.

Polkinghorne, John, Michael Gossop and John Strang. "The Government Task Force and its review of drug treatment services: the promotion of an evidence-based approach," in John Strang and Michael Gossop (eds), *Heroin Addiction and the British System, Volume Two: Treatment and Policy Responses,* 198–205. London and New York: Routledge, 2005.

Porter, Dorothy. *Health, Civilisation and the State: A History of Public Health From Ancient to Modern Times.* London and New York: Routledge, 1999.

Porter, Roy. "The drinking man's disease: the 'pre-history' of alcoholism in Georgian Britain." *British Journal of Addiction,* 80 (1985): 385–96.

———. *The Greatest Benefit to Mankind: A Medical History of Humanity From Antiquity to the Present.* London: Harper Collins, 1997.

———. *Madmen: A Social History of Madhouses, Mad-Doctors and Lunatics.* Stroud: Tempus, 2004.

———. "Two cheers for psychiatry! The social history of mental disorder in twentieth century Britain," in Hugh Freeman and German E. Berrios (eds), *150 Years of British Psychiatry Vol.2: The Aftermath,* 383–406. London: Athlone, 1996.

Porter, Roy and Mikas Teich. *Drugs and Narcotics in History.* Cambridge: Cambridge University Press, 1995.

Power, Robert. "Drug trends since 1968," in John Strang and Michael Gossop (eds), *Heroin Addiction and Drug Policy: The British System,* 27–41. Oxford: Oxford University Press, 1994.

Rawlings, Barbara and Rowdy Yates. "Introduction," in Barbara Rawlings and Rowdy Yates (eds), *Therapeutic Communities for the Treatment of Drug Users,* 9–25. London: Jessica Kingsley, 2001.

Robertson, J. Roy, A.B.V Bucknall, P.D. Welsby, J.J.K. Roberts, J.M. Inglis, J.F. Peutherer and R.P. Brettle. "Epidemic of AIDS related virus (HTLV-III/LAV) infection among intravenous drug abusers." *British Medical Journal,* 292 (22 February 1986): 527–29.

Robertson, Roy. "The Edinburgh epidemic: a case study," in John Strang and Gerry Stimson (eds), *AIDS and Drug Misuse: The Challenge For Policy and Practice in the 1990s,* 95–107. London and New York: Routledge, 1990.

———. *Heroin, AIDS and Society.* London: Hodder and Stoughton, 1987.

Room, Robin. "Addiction concepts and international control. *The Social History of Alcohol and Drugs,* 20 (2006): 276–89.

———. *Foresight State of the Art Science Review: Social Policy and Psychoactive Substances.* London: Department of Trade and Industry, 2005.

Rose, Nikolas. *Governing the Soul: The Shaping of the Private Self.* London: Free Association Books, 2nd ed., 1999.

———. *Inventing Our Selves: Psychology, Power and Personhood.* Cambridge: Cambridge University Press, 1996.

Rosenthal, Mitchell. "Therapeutic communities," in Ilana Belle Glass (ed.), *The International Handbook of Addiction Behaviour,* 258–63. London and New York: Routledge, 1991.

Royal College of General Practitioners. *Guidance for the use of Buprenorphine for the Treatment of Opioid Dependence in Primary Care.* RCGP: London, 2004.

Royal College of Psychiatrists. *Drug Scenes: A Report on Drugs and Drug Dependence by the Royal College of Psychiatrists.* London: Royal College of Psychiatrists, 1987.

Schur, Edwin M. *Narcotic Addiction in Britain and America: The Impact of Public Policy.* Bloomington & London: Indiana University Press, 4th ed., 1968.

Scottish Home and Health Department. *HIV Infection in Scotland: Report of the Scottish Committee on HIV Infection and Intravenous Drug Misuse.* Edinburgh: Scottish Home and Health Department, 1986.

Sheenan, Margaret, Edna Oppenheimer and Colin Taylor. "Why drug users sought help from one London clinic." *British Journal of Addiction,* 81 (1986): 765–75.

Sheridan, Janie. "Needle exchange in Britain," in John Strang and Michael Gossop (eds), *Heroin Addiction and the British System, Volume Two: Treatment and Policy Responses,* 145–55. London and New York: Routledge, 2005.

Shilts, Randy. *And The Band Played On: Politics, People and the AIDS Epidemic.* New York: St. Martins Press, 1987.

Shorter, Edward. *A History of Psychiatry From the Era of the Asylum to the Age of Prozac.* New York: John Wiley & Sons Inc., 1997.

Slater, Tony. "Treatment and Rehabilitation: report of the Advisory Council on the Misuse of Drugs, 1982. View from a therapeutic community: the spirit of the thing." *British Journal of Addiction,* 78 (1983): 118–19.

Smart, Carol. "Drug dependence units in England and Wales: the results of a national survey." *Drug and Alcohol Dependence,* 15 (1985): 131–44.

———. "Social policy and drug addiction: a critical study of policy development." *British Journal of Addiction,* 79 (1984): 31–49.

———. "Social policy and drug dependence: an historical case study." *Drug and Alcohol Dependence,* 16 (1985): 169–80.

Smith, David E. and George R. Gay (eds). *'It's So Good, Don't Even Try It Once': Heroin in Perspective.* Hemel Hempstead: Prentice Hall, 1972.

Smith, Russell G. *Medical Discipline: The Professional Conduct Jurisdiction of the General Medical Council, 1858–1990.* Oxford: Clarendon Press, 1994.

South, Nigel and Nicholas Dorn. *Helping Drug Users: Social Work, Advice Giving, Referral and Training Services of Three London Street Agencies.* Aldershot: Gower, 1985.

Spear, Henry B. "The early years of Britain's drug situation in practice, up to the 1960s," in John Strang and Michael Gossop (eds), *Heroin Addiction and the British System, Volume One: Origins and Evolution,* 17–42. London and New York: Routledge, 2005.

———. "The growth of heroin addiction in the United Kingdom." *British Journal of Addiction,* 64 (1969): 245–55.

———. *Heroin Addiction Care and Control: The British System 1916–84.* London: DrugScope, 2002.

Stacey, Margaret. "The health service consumer: a sociological misconception." *The Sociological Review Monograph: The Sociology of the National Health Service,* 22 (1978): 194–200.

———. *Regulating British Medicine: The General Medical Council.* Chichester: John Wiley & Sons, 1992.

Stedman Jones, Gareth. "Class expression versus social control? A critique of recent trends in the social history of leisure." *History Workshop Journal,* 4 (1977): 162–70.

Steinberg, H. "Chairman's Introduction," in H. Steinberg (ed.), *Scientific Basis of Drug Dependence,* 286–90. London: J & A Churchill, 1969.

Stimson, Gerry. "AIDS and injecting drug use in the United Kingdom, 1987–1993: the policy response and the prevention of the epidemic." *Social Science and Medicine,* 41.5 (1995): 699–716.

———. "'Blair declares war': the unhealthy state of British drug policy." *International Journal of Drug Policy,* 11 (2000): 259–64.

————. "British drug policies in the 1980s: a preliminary analysis and some suggestions for research." *British Journal of Addiction,* 82 (1987): 477–88.

————. "Minimising harm from drug use," in John Strang and Michael Gossop (eds), *Heroin Addiction and Drug Policy: The British System,* 248–58. Oxford: Oxford University Press, 1994.

————. "Revising policy and practice: new ideas about the drugs problem," in John Strang and Gerry Stimson (eds), *AIDS and Drug Misuse: The Challenge For Policy and Practice in the 1990s,* 121–31. London and New York: Routledge, 1990.

————. "Treatment or control? Dilemmas for staff in drug dependency clinics," in D.J. West (ed.) *Problems of Drug Abuse in Britain: Papers Presented to The Cropwood Round-Table Conference,* 52–73. Cambridge: Institute of Criminology, 1978.

————. "Treatment and Rehabilitation: report of the Advisory Council on the Misuse of Drugs, 1982. Views of a sociologist: drug problems as an everyday part of our society." *British Journal of Addiction,* 78 (1983): 120–22.

————. "The war on heroin: British policy and the international trade in illicit drugs," in Nick Dorn and Nigel South (eds), *A Land Fit For Heroin? Drug Policies, Prevention and Practice,* 35–61. Basingstoke: Macmillan, 1987.

Stimson, Gerry, Lindsey Alldritt, Kate Dolan and Martin Donoghoe. "Syringe exchange schemes for drug users in England and Scotland." *British Medical Journal,* 296 (18 June 1988): 1717–19.

Stimson, Gerry, Martin Donoghoe, Kate Dolan and Lindsey Alldritt. "A volatile time for British drug policies: commentary on the editorial by Alan Glanz." *British Journal of Addiction,* 83 (1988): 1241–42.

Stimson, Gerry and Rachel Lart. "The relationship between the State and local practice in the development of national policy on drugs between 1920 and 1990," in John Strang and Michael Gossop (eds), *Heroin Addiction and Drug Policy: The British System,* 331–41. Oxford: Oxford University Press, 1994.

Stimson, Gerry and Edna Oppenheimer. *Heroin Addiction: Treatment and Control in Britain.* London: Tavistock, 1982.

Strang, John. "Abstinence or abundance—what goal?" *British Medical Journal,* 289 (8 September 1984): 604.

————. "AIDS and drug misuse in the UK: achievements, failings and new harm reduction opportunities," in John Strang and Michael Gossop (eds), *Heroin Addiction and the British System, Volume One: Origins and Evolution,* 196–210. London and New York: Routledge, 2005.

————. "A model service: turning the generalist on to drugs," in Susanne MacGregor (ed.), *Drugs in British Society: Responses to a Social Problem in the 1980s,* 143–69. London and New York: Routledge, 1989.

————. "Personal View." *British Medical Journal,* 283 (1 August 1981): 376.

————. "The roles of prescribing," in John Strang and Gerry Stimson (eds), *AIDS and Drug Misuse: The Challenge For Policy and Practice in the 1990s,* 142–52. London and New York: Routledge, 1990.

Strang, John and Michael Gossop. "The 'British System': visionary anticipation or masterly inactivity?" in John Strang and Michael Gossop (eds), *Heroin Addiction and British Drug Policy: The British System,* 343–51. Oxford: Oxford University Press, 1994.

Strang, John, Sue Ruben, Michael Farrell and Michael Gossop. "Prescribing heroin and other injectable drugs," in John Strang and Michael Gossop (eds), *Heroin Addiction and Drug Policy: The British System,* 192–203. Oxford: Oxford University Press, 1994.

Strang, John and Janie Sheridan, "Heroin and methadone prescriptions from a London drug clinic over the first 15 years of operation (1968–1983): old records examined." *Substance Use and Misuse,* 41 (2006): 1227–38.

Strang John and Gerry Stimson. "The impact of HIV: forcing the process of change," in John Strang and Gerry Stimson, *AIDS and Drug Misuse: The*

Challenge For Policy and Practice in the 1990s, 3-15. London and New York: Routledge, 1990.

Szasz, Thomas. *Ceremonial Chemistry: The Ritual Persecution of Drugs, Addicts and Pushers*. London: Routledge & Kegan Paul, 1975.

Tantam, Digby. "The anti-psychiatry movement," in German E. Berrios and Hugh Freeman (eds), *150 Years of British Psychiatry, 1841–1991*, 333–47. London: Royal College of Psychiatrists, 1991.

Taylor, Diane. "The opium odyssey." *Druglink*, 21.6 (2006): 8–11.

Thom, Betsy. *Dealing With Drink: Alcohol and Social Policy From Treatment to Management*. London: Free Association Books, 1999.

Thom, Betsy and Virginia Berridge. "'Special units for common problems:' the birth of alcohol treatment units in England." *Social History of Medicine*, 8 (1995): 75–93.

Transform. *After the War on Drugs: Options for Control*. Transform: Bristol, 2006.

Trebach, Arnold. *The Heroin Solution*. New Haven & London: Yale University Press, 1982.

Treichler, Paula A. "AIDS, gender and biomedical discourse," in Elizabeth Fee and Daniel M. Fox (eds), *AIDS: The Burdens of History*, 190–266. Berkeley, Los Angeles and London: University of California Press, 1988.

Tudor-Hart, Julian. *A New Kind of Doctor: The General Practitioner's Part in the Health of the Community*. London: Merlin Press, 1988.

Turner, David. "The development of the voluntary sector: no further need for pioneers?" in John Strang and Michael Gossop (eds), *Heroin Addiction and Drug Policy: The British System*, 222–30. Oxford: Oxford University Press, 1994.

Uchtenhagen, Ambros. *Prescription of Narcotics For Heroin Addicts*. Basel: Kartger, 1999.

United Nations Office of Drug Control. *World Drug Report 2006: Executive Summary*. United Nations Office of Drug Control: Vienna, 2006.

United States Public Health Service. *The Health Consequences of Smoking: Nicotine Addiction, A Report of the Surgeon General*. Rockville, Md.: US Department of Health and Human Services, 1988.

Valverde, Mariana. *Diseases of the Will: Alcohol and the Dilemmas of Freedom*. Cambridge: Cambridge University Press, 1998.

———. "'Slavery from within': the invention of alcoholism and the question of free will." *Social History*, 22 (1997): 253–68.

Warner, Jessica. "'Resolv'd to drink no more': addiction as a pre-industrial construct." *Journal of Studies on Alcohol*, 55 (1994): 685–91.

Warren Holland, David. "The development concept houses in Great Britain and Southern Ireland, 1967–1976," in D.J. West (ed.), *Problems of Drug Abuse in Britain: Papers Presented to the Cropwood Round Table Conference*, 125–35. Cambridge: Institute of Criminology, 1978.

Webster, Charles. *The Health Services Since the War, Vol II: Government and Health Care, The National Health Service 1958–1979*. London: The Stationary Office, 1996.

———. *The National Health Service: A Political History*. Oxford: Oxford University Press, 2002.

———. "Psychiatry and the early National Health Service: the role of the Mental Health Standing Committee," in German E. Berrios and Hugh Freeman (eds), *150 Years of British Psychiatry, 1841–1991*, 103–16. London: Royal College of Psychiatrists, 1991.

Weisz, George. *Divide and Conquer: A Comparative History of Medical Specialisation*. Oxford: Oxford University Press, 2006.

Wells, Brian. "Narcotics Anonymous in Britain: the stepping up of a phenomenon," in John Strang and Michael Gossop (eds), *Heroin Addiction and the British System, Volume Two: Treatment and Policy Responses*, 167–74. London and New York: Routledge, 2005.

Welshman, John. *Municipal Medicine: Public Health in Twentieth-Century Britain*. Oxford & Bern: Peter Lang, 2000.

White, William L. "The lessons of language: historical perspectives on the rhetoric of addiction," in Sarah W. Tracy and Caroline Jean Acker (eds), *Altering American Consciousness: The History of Alcohol and Drug Use in the United States 1800–2000*, 33–60. Amherst & Boston, Mass.: University of Massachusetts Press, 2004.

———. *Slaying the Dragon: The History of Addiction Treatment and Recovery in America.* Bloomington, Illinois: Chestnut Health Systems, 1998.

Whynes, David K. "Drug problems, drug policies," in David K. Whynes and Philip T. Bean (eds), *Policing and Prescribing: The British System of Drug Control*, 1–14. Basingstoke: Macmillan, 1991.

Witton, John, Francis Keaney and John Strang. "Opiate addiction and the 'British System': looking back on the twentieth century and trying to see its shape in the future," in Janie Sheridan and John Strang (eds), *Drug Misuse and Community Pharmacy*, 5–16. London: Taylor & Francis, 2003.

Yates, Rowdy. "Treatment and Rehabilitation: report of the Advisory Council on the Misuse of Drugs, 1982. View from a street agency: money-shy." *British Journal of Addiction*, 78 (1983): 122–24.

Young, Jock. *The Drugtakers: The Sociological Meaning of Drug Taking.* London: Paladin, 1971.

Zador, Deborah. "Last call for injectable opiate maintenance: in pursuit of an evidence base for good clinical practice," in John Strang and Michael Gossop (eds), *Heroin Addiction and the British System, Volume Two: Treatment and Policy Responses*, 121–30. London and New York: Routledge, 2005.

Zibbell, Jon E. "Can the lunatics actually take over the asylum? Re-configuring subjectivity and neo-liberal governance in contemporary British drug treatment policy." *International Journal of Drug Policy*, 15 (2004): 56–65.

Index